D0599398

FUTURE MAN

FUTURE MAN

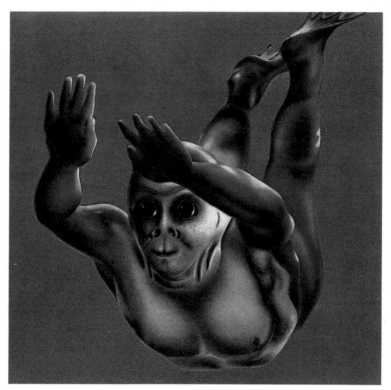

Brian Stableford

CROWN PUBLISHERS, INC.
New York

Published in the United States by
Crown Publishers, Inc
One Park Avenue,
New York, New York 10016

Published simultaneously in Canada by
General Publishing Company Limited

Library of Congress Cataloging in Publication Data
Stableford, Brian M.
Future man.
1. Genetic engineering – Social aspects. 2. Human
genetics – Social aspects. 3. Human biology – Social
aspects. I. Title.
QH442.S77 1984 573.2   84-4955
ISBN 0-517-55248-5   ISBN 0-517-55249-3 (pbk)

This book was created and produced by
Roxby Science Limited
Roxby and Lindsey Press
98 Clapham Common Northside
London SW4

Editor: **Emma Fisher**
Design: **Elizabeth Palmer**
Picture Research: **Jane Williams, Matthew Beardmore-Gray**
Typesetting: **Tradespools Limited**
Reproduction by: **David Bruce Graphics**

Manufactured in Spain

First edition

Contents

Introduction

The third revolution

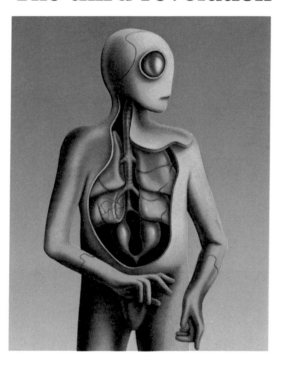

What a privileged generation we are. We are witnessing enormous revolutions in the human condition, and we *know* that these revolutions are taking place, and can watch with fascination.

One privilege is that of computerization. It was only a generation ago that computers were scientific curiosities, huge structures that could do amazing things, but were too unwieldy and expensive to play much of a role in ordinary life. And now they have shrunk and have moved into the office and the home and are absolutely essential to every phase of life. They even operate machines which have grown complex enough to mimic human activity sufficiently to be called 'robots'.

The result is that bookstores have been flooded with countless books on the new phenomenon telling you how computers work, how they are used, and what the computerized future holds in store for us.

A second revolution, equally dramatic and equally unexpected, is that of the human expansion into space. A mere generation ago, we were playing with crude German rockets that could penetrate to the thin upper atmosphere, but any thought of reaching the Moon with such things, let alone having human feet stand upon our satellite, was still left strictly to the science fiction writers.

And now not only have human feet tramped the soil of the Moon, but our machines have landed on the surface of Venus and Mars, and have skimmed by Mercury, Jupiter and Saturn, to take close-up pictures and make detailed studies of those planets. Telescopes in space have studied stars in new ways and made discoveries that could not have been made from Earth's surface.

The result? A veritable flood of books on every aspect of space exploration and predictions as to the kind of world we are going to have when present plans for construction of space stations and space settlements and power stations and all the rest come to fruition.

And yet there is a third revolution in progress, too; one that is greater still, or, at least, one that affects us more deeply. It affects us so deeply that most people maintain an uneasy silence about it and tend to look the other way, and few books are written about it.

It is the genetic revolution.

It was only in the 1860s that the laws of inheritance were worked out, and even so, the discovery remained unnoticed by biologists generally till 1900. In 1902, it was first shown that the chromosomes in the cell nucleus had something to do with inheritance and they were postulated to consist of 'genes', each one controlling a physical characteristic.

Chromosomes were found to consist of 'deoxyribonucleic acid' (DNA), but it was not till 1953 that scientists found out how DNA worked; how it was constructed and how this construction made it possible for the DNA to duplicate itself every time a cell divided.

In the 1960s, the 'genetic code' was worked out, and it was shown how the structure of the DNA was translated into the structure of molecules that controlled the chemistry of the cell.

In the 1970s, techniques were discovered by which DNA molecules could be snipped into pieces, in controlled fashion, and recombined in new ways; in which genes from one species could be transferred to the cells of another species and fitted into the chromosomes there; in which pieces of DNA molecules from one species could be combined with pieces from another species.

Such 'recombinant-DNA' experiments could produce genes in organisms that had never previously had them, or even genes that had never previously existed *anywhere*.

The result was that, for the first time in history, human beings had the beginnings of the power to redesign living things.

They had been doing this, in a way, since ancient times by breeding animals and plants and substituting artificial selection for the usual 'natural selection'. In that way they could in a very brief time (evolutionarily speaking) produce cattle that could swim in the milk they produced, sheep that were nearly all wool, chickens that did nothing but lay eggs, corn that had superlarge kernels – all from ancestral species that were skimpy and scrawny, with little to recommend them from the selfish human standpoint.

But that was done with total dependence on the natural genes. Now we can *adjust* the genes. We can decide on what we want and try to carve living things to suit, so to speak. Indeed, we can even ask ourselves, 'What kind of human beings might we like to be? What kind of abilities that we lack would it be good to have, and how do we go about getting them?'

And what kind of dangers would be involved? And what about morality?

This is something that should be discussed at book length, for it would not be wise to leap into this third revolution without looking first. People are not so ready to discuss this as they are ready to discuss computers and space. Here, however, is the necessary book.

Isaac Asimov

Chapter 1

Man: a new evolutionary phase

The human race is on the verge of the most profound revolution in its history. Even though it is always difficult to foresee the future, and therefore to know with certainty how this revolution will affect the lives of our children and our children's children, we can be sure that the next hundred years will give man an entirely new power over the natural and the human worlds. Our understanding of the fundamental processes of life is increasing so dramatically that we will soon be able to control and manipulate the biochemical system which living creatures use to reproduce themselves.

The new biotechnology, which is already coming into practical use, will carry us into a new phase of man's relationship with the environment, and a new phase of human evolution. In order to understand the importance of the coming revolution we must contrast this new evolutionary phase with the phases that have gone before. Once we have seen how different man's place in nature will be in future by comparison with the past, it will be easier to look in detail at the very many particular possibilities which arise from the revolution. It will then become clear how and why the sum of these possibilities will be nothing less than a complete transformation of the human world.

THE FIRST PHASE

The first phase of human evolution lasted for more than a million years. It was a phase in which 'human nature' was slowly shaped by natural selection, as *Homo erectus* evolved into *Homo sapiens*. The basic features of human physique emerged: our upright stance, our highly-developed brain, our clever hands and our keen eyesight evolved together, as a kind of 'package' of adaptations, fitting our ancestors for a particular and distinct way of life.

The fossil evidence is not sufficiently plentiful for us to be able to say exactly when the human package of characteristics first appeared, but it seems to have been assembled something over a million years ago, in the grasslands of North Africa. We can easily appreciate why this set of characteristics made our remote ancestors into a highly effective species. Upright stance permitted the growth of a large, heavy head containing a big brain and carrying eyes

capable of binocular vision. The arms and hands were freed of any supporting function, so that the hands could be adapted for gripping and manipulating objects. Eyes, hands and brain all became sophisticated together, every advantage acquired by one permitting and provoking the development of the others.

The process of natural selection, which governed this gradual sophistication of eye, hand and brain, is the process which governed the evolutionary history of life on Earth from the very beginning. The physical form of all organisms is determined by the genes, a set of chemically coded instructions carried in the nucleus of every cell in the body. New copies of the molecules carrying the genes are made whenever the cells divide to make more cells, which they do constantly, not only during growth and repair of the organism but also when the sex organs make egg and sperm cells. Sometimes this copying is not exact, and a new gene is produced. These changes – or mutations – can be encouraged by certain chemicals or by radiation, but often they are simply accidents.

Most mutations in eggs and sperm scramble the instructions carried by the genes in which they occur, making them useless; usually this leads to the production of a defective organism. Vary rarely, though, the mutation simply changes the instructions so that the gene still works, but differently. The organism carrying the new gene may be just as capable, or even more capable, or better adapted to its environment. As each generation gives rise to the next, defective organisms tend to be 'weeded out', because they are less efficient than their contemporaries and more likely to die before reproducing. Mutated genes which are not to the organism's advantage thus tend to be eliminated from the 'gene pool' of the species. On the other hand, mutated genes which make more capable or better adapted organisms tend to increase within the gene pool, because the organisms carrying them become more likely to reproduce themselves. Thus, over many generations and millions of years, the kinds of organisms which inhabit the Earth have become more numerous, more varied and more complicated.

All the great apes and their relatives, the monkeys and the prosimians (such as bush babies and lemurs), probably had a single common ancestor – a small, tree-living mammal which had become differentiated by mutation from other small mammal species. It may have resembled a small bush baby of today. This ancestor-species then gave rise, gradually, to dozens of variations on its own particular theme. These variations 'explored' many physical forms and many ways of life. A great number eventually disappeared because they could not find an 'ecological niche' – a particular way of life in which they were so expert that they could oust all other contenders. Some did find such a niche and

remained relatively unchanged until the present day. One chain of such variants – one chain among many – ultimately produced *Homo erectus*, the ancestor-species of modern man.

There are two ways in which a mutation or group of mutations can make an organism more capable. It can equip the organism with better 'tools of survival' that will help it to make better use of its environment and to stay alive longer; or it can help the organism to reproduce itself more efficiently. These two ways are not entirely independent of one another, but it makes some sense to distinguish between them if we are to understand how human beings appeared. When we hear the term 'natural selection' and related catch-phrases such as 'the survival of the fittest', we tend to think only of the first kind of evolutionary change, produced by the need to survive in a hostile world. The evolution of man, with his wonderful combination of eye, hand and brain, is too often seen simply as a matter of acquiring hunting skills and expertise in weaponry.

There is some sense in this. In order to reproduce, an organism must survive long enough to reach maturity and be parent to a new generation. It is not enough, though, simply to survive and reproduce. The successful organism is one which makes the most of its reproductive opportunities. There are different ways of trying to achieve this –

Many variations in the human form have evolved by natural selection as adaptations to different environments. Dark skin is common in very sunny countries as a protection against cancer-causing ultra-violet-rays; pale skin evolved as our ancestors began to colonize temperate zones.

Tightly curled hair insulates the brain from the heat of the sun. In a cold climate, a pronounced fold above the eyes helps protect the retina from the glaring light of a snowy landscape. Genetic engineers of the future will be able to adapt man far more radically.

different 'parental strategies'. Some organisms are geared to the mass-production of offspring, producing so many that, even if 99 out of 100 perish, there will still be enough to ensure a new generation. This strategy is almost universal among creatures such as insects and fish. The opposing strategy is to have only a few offspring, but to look after them, protecting them and caring for them as they grow. This alternative strategy is developed, to varying degrees, by almost all birds and mammals, and is developed to its highest degree in man.

Highly sophisticated parental care is associated with another feature of human nature which distinguishes hominid species from their nearest kin. The human infant is born at a much earlier stage of development than the young of any other species of great ape. The human infant thus *needs* parental care of a more complicated kind, for much longer, but it also *benefits* from that care much more remarkably: a human child's capacity for learning soon outstrips that of a baby chimpanzee.

The evolution of the eye-hand-brain complex in humans probably has at least as much to do with the development of parental care as it has to do with hunting efficiency and the use of weapons. Hands are as important in the handling of helpless human babies as in the handling of tools. Eyes and brains are vital to the process of learning by which children acquire the skills of their parents and are fitted to become parents in turn.

Throughout this first phase of human evolution,

all men followed a way of life which is usually known as 'hunting and gathering'. Some human societies still follow this way of life even today, though the spread of global civilization has just about put an end to it. Hunter-gatherers live in small nomadic or semi-nomadic groups which move over the land picking up what can be found in the way of edible vegetable matter, such as roots, fruit or nuts, and trapping or spearing whatever happens to be around in the way of game.

The key characteristic of the hunting and gathering way of life is that it accepts the environment as something given – something which is simply there – providing opportunities for exploitation and hazards to be avoided. As with other animal populations, the natural environment determines the set of 'selective pressures' which decide whether a particular genetic mutation will help the organism possessing it to succeed or not. In the first phase of human evolution, therefore, human nature was very largely the product of environmental pressures, acting on the raw material of genetic mutation.

Even in this first phase, however, man had an active part to play in making the many discoveries which provided the substance of what he could teach his children during the protracted period of parental care. Some of these discoveries were to do with methods of hunting, the making of tools and ways to avoid danger. Some had to do with ways to educate children and ways to handle relationships with

other people. Technical and social skills accumulated gradually, passed on from one generation to the next not by the genes but through the process of education, *via* spoken language. Thus, cultural evolution supplemented the evolution of the human gene pool, and paved the way for the second phase in man's relationship with his environment, and the second phase in human evolution.

THE SECOND PHASE

The second phase began when man began to free himself from his dependence on the generosity of nature. This happened when some groups abandoned the hunter-gatherer way of life and took up agriculture. Instead of relying upon the food-supplies produced naturally by the wilderness, they began to clear land of the plants that grew there in order to sow the seeds of their own food-plants. Instead of going out into the wilderness to catch wild animals, they began to breed animals in captivity and to build up their own livestock.

This fundamental shift in the relationship between some human groups and their environment had many vitally important consequences. Settling down allowed people to gather together into much larger groups than ever before: a tract of cultivated land can support many more people than a tract of wilderness. Because people stayed in one place instead of moving around, they were motivated to build sturdy and complicated permanent homes. They were able to amass elaborate possessions. They

Genetic engineering aims to take a dramatic short cut in the slow process of evolution, which produced the striking development from our remote tree-shrew ancestor to creatures like bush babies and apes and finally to man.

could own not only houses but furniture, containers, tools, clothes and ornaments in hitherto-unimagined abundance. The ability of human hands to make things had been important in the first phase of human evolution, but in this second phase that importance increased with a proliferation of new opportunities. The ingenuity of the brain had previously been important, too, but here again there was new scope for it to operate.

In the second phase it became possible to have kinds of property that just could not arise in the first phase. First-phase hunter-gatherers undoubtedly considered that certain tracts of wilderness were their territory, not to be invaded by outsiders, but they could not have made much sense out of the notion of *owning* land. A field ripe for cultivation, however, can easily be seen as property. Similarly, hunter-gatherers could not really think of themselves as *owning* the game they chased, but herdsmen necessarily have a strong sense of ownership in respect of their cattle or goats. Ownership of land and of livestock inevitably became a way of defining inequalities between men that could not have arisen in a hunter-gatherer society. Thus, the new relationship between man and his environment changed the relationships between men.

11

As well as a growth in material wealth, the second phase saw a dramatic growth in the wealth of knowledge – a growth so dramatic that the distribution of different kinds of knowledge became as important a factor in defining inequalities within society as the distribution of different kinds of property.

In the second phase of human evolution the force of natural selection was almost entirely set aside. *Cultural* evolution became all-important. The chances of a particular individual's surviving to reproductive age, or successfully rearing children, came to be determined not by the circumstances of his natural environment but by the circumstances of the social order and his position within it. His chances of falling victim to disease, starvation or violent death were also now more dependent on his social situation than on his physical constitution. The shaping of man by natural selection was decisively interrupted.

It might be argued that at that point in time 'human nature' was effectively frozen, but this is to take too narrow a view of what constitutes our nature. Our nature is not defined by our physical form, by the chemicals in our blood and the 'wiring' in our brains, although these are all parts of that nature. We are not *merely* the product of our genes, though our genes are certainly necessary to produce us. The kind of people we are depends largely on the kind of society we live in and how it treats us. Second-phase man, in becoming the architect of his own environment, also became the architect of his own nature, in a way that first-phase man never could.

All the plant and animal species in which second-phase man took an interest became subject to a new regime of genetic selection. Instead of new characteristics being selected according to the advantages they conferred upon the species, they were selected according to whether or not they made the species more useful to man.

The consequences of this artificial selection are easy to see in the world around us. The wheat which we grow today bears little resemblance to the wild wheat which used to grow half a million years ago, or even twenty thousand years ago. Our ancestors, when they entered the second phase, selected out those mutants which produced the most grain. Now modern wheats are phenomenal grain-producers. Domestic horses bear little resemblance to the wild stocks from which they originally came; we have bred special strains for riding, or for pulling ploughs and wagons. The power of artificial selection to create many variations on a theme can easily be seen in the vast range of domestic dogs and domestic fowl. This we have accomplished in the space of a few thousand years.

The consequences of artificial selection cannot be seen so readily in the genetic heritage of man himself. The physical differences between races are clearly a hangover from the days of first-phase

evolution – the products of natural selection. We have not bred special kinds of men by careful selection of mutants in the way that we have bred special kinds of sheep.

This does not mean, though, that we have let human nature alone. It is simply that we have usually attempted to shape human beings in a different way: their behaviour has interested us far more than their physiology, their minds rather than their bodies. Because the properties of the mind are much more a matter of learning than of genetic endowment, we have tried to 'select' them by cultural means. We have tried to control and mould patterns of behaviour through the instruments of custom, law, religion and political institutions.

Such genetic selection as has taken place in man during the second phase has mostly not been planned or deliberate. Sometimes physically distinct groups have been seen as a threat, and attempts have been made to exterminate them and to increase the numbers of the type of human being seen as desirable. But any other changes in the human gene pool which have come about as a result of civilization have been unintended consequences. We are not sure what changes there have been, but some people have argued that they are not ones we would have chosen. It has even been suggested that, by recklessly wasting the best of their young men in war, the societies of the past have not done much for the human gene pool, and that, by conserving the weak through the agency of modern medicine, present societies are not doing much for it either. Whether we agree or not, the main point at issue is that the effects of genetic selection on human evolution during its second phase are comparable neither with the previous effects of natural selection on man, nor with the contemporary effects of artificial selection upon animals and plants.

The sharp distinction between the way men control their own species and the way that they control others is one that breaks down as we enter the third phase in human evolution, when we obtain the power of genetic control over our own species along with greater power to manipulate others.

THE FINAL PHASE
During the second phase, most of our achievements in controlling the evolution of other species were accomplished haphazardly. Our ancestors had only a vague notion of what they were doing as they bred all the special strains of domestic plants and animals. The results they obtained provided the crucial test of their methods, but they knew nothing of the actual machinery of heredity. Only in the last

In the final phase of human evolution, man will be able to control the evolution of his own race through genetic engineering. Human growth will be monitored from its earliest stages and every physical characteristic determined by choice, not chance.

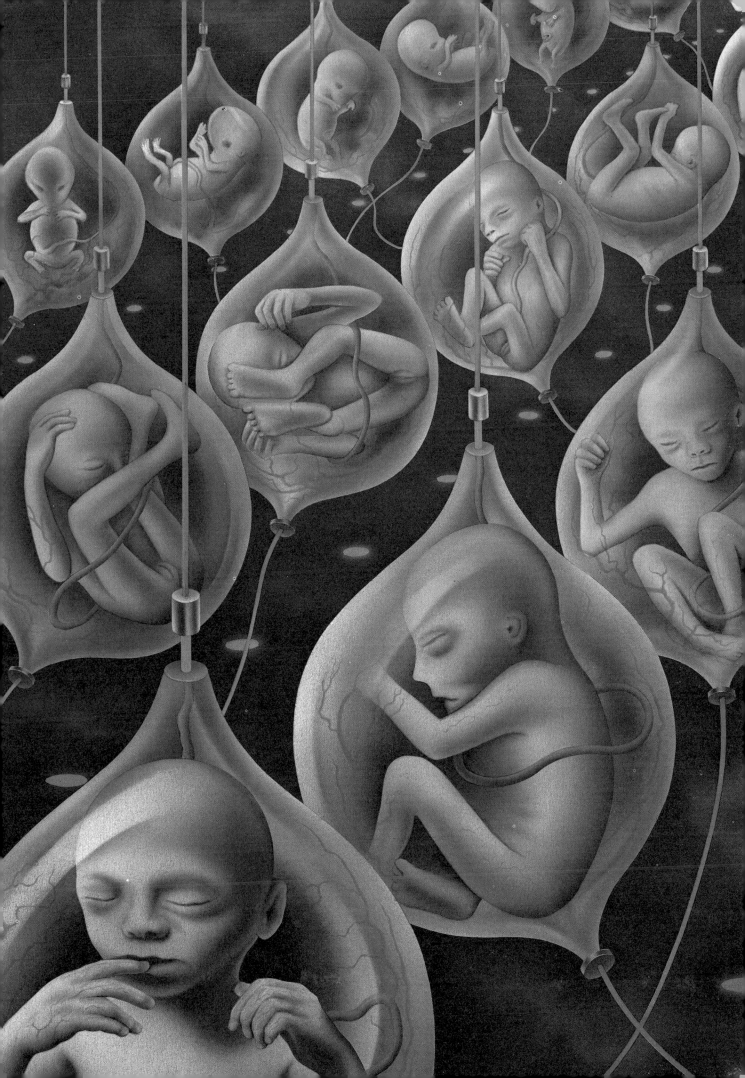

hundred years have we found out how the characteristics of parents are passed on to their children, and only in our own generation have we 'cracked the genetic code' and begun the vital business of figuring out how egg cells store and use the information that enables them to become whole complex organisms – and to make, in their turn, more egg cells.

We do not yet know in full detail how the 'natural technology' of heredity works, but we do know the basic features of the system. We know that DNA (deoxyribonucleic acid) is the hereditary material, and that the sequence of certain chemical structures (the 'bases'), which are strung along the very long, ribbon-like DNA molecule, constitutes a 'message' instructing cells how to build the proteins which are the functional components of living matter. Now that we are beginning to understand how DNA works, we are also acquiring techniques for tinkering with its working, which will enable us to become 'genetic engineers', and take control of the

living machinery of cells and organisms. The final phase of human evolution, therefore, is the phase in which we gradually acquire and put to use techniques which enable us to interfere *directly* with the process by which one generation of a species gives rise to the next.

In the first phase, nature provided both the mutations which allowed the possibility of evolutionary change, and the selective regime which sorted out the mutations. In the second phase, nature still provided the mutations, but men took a gradually more decisive role in providing the selective regime which sorted out mutations in hundreds of other species (but not their own). In the final phase, men will no longer be reliant on nature to provide the 'raw material' of random mutation. They will be able to make their own mutations and they will be able to choose what mutations to make. It will be possible, eventually, to make wholesale, planned alterations in living organisms. Men will become masters of evolution, and will be empowered

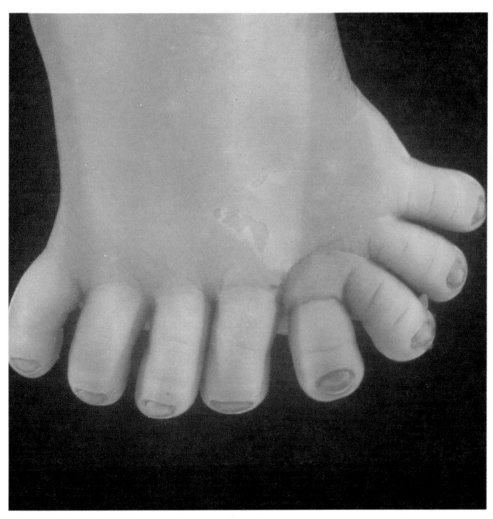

Most mutations scramble the instructions carried by the genes in which they occur; usually, as in the two examples above, this leads to the production of a defective organism. Very rarely, a random mutation gives an advantage. Such mutations have formed the raw material of evolution.

to control their own evolution as well as that of other species.

In the past it took many generations to bring about changes in form, and there were strict limitations on the kinds of changes that could be encouraged. In the future we may be able to transform any species, including our own, more or less as we please, adding or subtracting characteristics at will. This will not be easy, and we will acquire the power only gradually, but in a matter of centuries we can expect that flesh will become a medium in which our descendants can work as artists and craftsmen, moulding it at will to serve multifarious purposes. In time, we will obtain a power over the natural world which will be literally godlike.

This is a possibility that causes everyone some anxiety. It opens up an area of concern that is wholly new, facing us with a whole range of potential problems which were hardly imaginable fifty years ago. We can already feel the urgency of some of

these new problems as a result of the very limited technological innovations which allow human eggs to be fertilized, and to begin to develop, outside the womb. There are various ways in which scientists and doctors want to take advantage of this new ability, but each one inevitably raises a question. This is merely the beginning.

For thousands of years now, people have had to accept responsibility for passing on to their children some material wealth and some wealth of knowledge. We have grown used to the problems attached to these responsibilities, though we may still feel them to be uncomfortable. In future, the responsibilities will not only become heavier still, but will widen in scope. Future generations will have to decide not only what cultural heritage to pass on to their children, but what biological heritage. Even a refusal to intervene with the systems of human genetic inheritance would be an exercise of that responsibility: the choice will soon be there, and to refrain from using our opportunities is simply one way of exercising that choice.

Our purpose in this book is to explore in some detail the possibilities, short-term and long-term, which are likely to be opened up by new developments in biology. It will ask how we might use the new powers which scientific discovery is delivering into our hands. Many of the ideas contained in it will inevitably seem to some readers to be bizarre and extravagant; it is not easy to imagine that our world, to which we have become accustomed, will be so completely transformed in the future. Even if we can imagine it, we are bound to find the thought unsettling. Nevertheless, we can be sure that if the world has a future at all, that future will see vast changes. By the end of the twentieth century we will not have reached the end of scientific and technological progress; we will hardly have begun.

What would *Homo erectus*, wandering the plains of North Africa a million years ago, have thought of a vision which showed him the Egyptians toiling to build the Great Pyramid? What would he have thought of their cities, their planted fields and their religious ceremonies? What would one of those Egyptian peasants have made of a similar vision that showed him New York City, television and heart-transplants? Thanks to the efforts which *Homo erectus* and the ancient Egyptians made to improve their own situations, we now have powers of imagination that they had not. We can at least begin to imagine a future very different from the present, largely because we have realized how different the present is from the past. We have an ability to extrapolate logically from what we know now to see, albeit dimly, how we may be placed in the future. We must try to use this ability as best we can, because without the power of foresight the power of choice is useless, and we will soon have powers of choice which will give us dictatorship over the future evolution of all life on Earth.

Chapter 2

Foundations of the biological revolution

Our new power to affect and direct the evolutionary process is based on a detailed understanding of how individuals pass on their characteristics to their children. More than a hundred years have passed since an Austrian monk named Gregor Mendel first formulated some elementary 'laws of heredity' and thus founded the scientific discipline of genetics. For most of that hundred years, though, scientists could only study inheritance by looking at the characteristics of organisms and studying their patterns.

These early studies showed that a mature animal or plant has two sets of character determinants (genes), one set having come from its father and one from its mother. The two sets of genes give instructions covering the same bodily features, but sometimes the two instructions are different. For instance, a baby might receive a gene for blue eyes from his father and one for brown eyes from his mother. Some genes are either 'dominant' or 'recessive': since the gene for brown eyes is dominant, in this example his eyes will be brown.

When the baby grows up he passes on to his own offspring one complete set of genes made up of a mixed selection of his own two sets. In this case he could pass on to his children either the gene for blue eyes or the gene for brown eyes. The actual eye colour of his children will also depend on his wife's genes. If his wife has brown eyes, and like him carries one 'blue eyes' gene and one 'brown eyes' gene, the probability is that one in four of their children will have blue eyes, while the other three will have brown eyes.

Until recently, very little was known about how these sets of genes, or character determinants, worked. They were known to exist in the nuclei of cells: microscopic studies of sexual reproduction showed material from the nucleus of one cell – the sperm – migrating into the nucleus of another – the ovum – and fusing with it. But as long as we knew nothing about the actual chemistry of what was happening, our opportunities for interfering with the process were very limited. Careful selective breeding was the only way in which we could control the passage of characteristics through the generations.

In the last three decades, though, we have made very rapid progress in understanding the chemical mechanisms of heredity. Our knowledge of the way that characteristics are transmitted is not yet complete, but we do know a great deal about the fundamental nature of the process – enough to allow us to go into the nucleus of a cell (with the aid of chemicals or very delicate instruments) and interfere directly with the biochemistry of inheritance.

DISCOVERING THE UNIVERSAL CODE

Before scientists began to decipher the genetic code in the 1950s, they already knew that the core of the information transmitted from one generation to the next must comprise a set of blueprints for making proteins. Proteins – often called the building-blocks of life – play two vital roles in the body. First, they form the bulk of its structural materials. Second, they control all the chemical reactions which are vital to life. The hundreds of different enzymes in the body, each one controlling a specific chemical reaction, are all proteins. So are many of the hormones which regulate the activity of whole organs or systems. The development of the single cell of the fertilized ovum into the adult body, and the working of all the body's interlocking systems, depend on the right proteins being made at the right time.

The structure of the proteins themselves provides a clue to how the genes do their job. Proteins are chains of smaller chemical units called amino acids. Only about 20 amino acids are commonly used in building the proteins used by living organisms, but the number of possible combinations of these amino acids is unimaginably large. The eventual use of a protein molecule also depends on its shape; the chain can be folded or tangled so as to expose certain amino acids in a particular pattern. At its simplest, a blueprint for making proteins would have to specify which amino acids are needed, and what their order is in the chain.

For many years scientists were inclined to believe that the blueprints for proteins must themselves be protein molecules. The nuclei of cells certainly contained some proteinaceous material. There were, however, other chain-like molecules

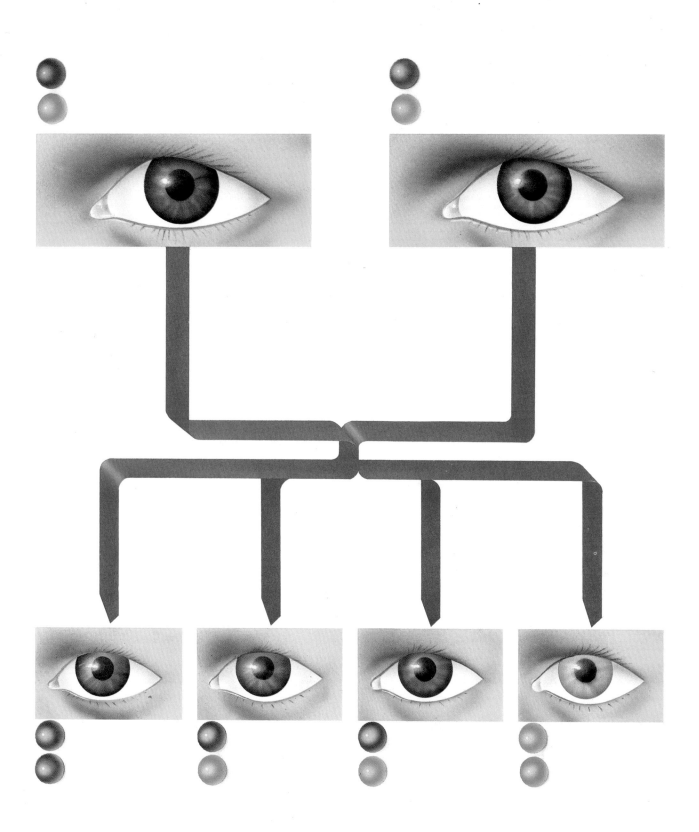

Our two sets of genes (one from each parent) may give different instructions. Some genes are 'dominant' and some are 'recessive'; where both are present the dominant gene will prevail. For example, the gene for brown eyes is dominant, but the gene for blue eyes is recessive. Where both are present, the eyes will be brown. In this example both parents possess the genes for brown eyes and for blue eyes. Both therefore have brown eyes.

Half of each parent's sex cells will pass on the 'brown eyes' gene, and half will pass on the 'blue eyes' gene. Four different combinations of the genes are possible. Only the child inheriting the 'blue eyes' gene from both parents can have blue eyes.

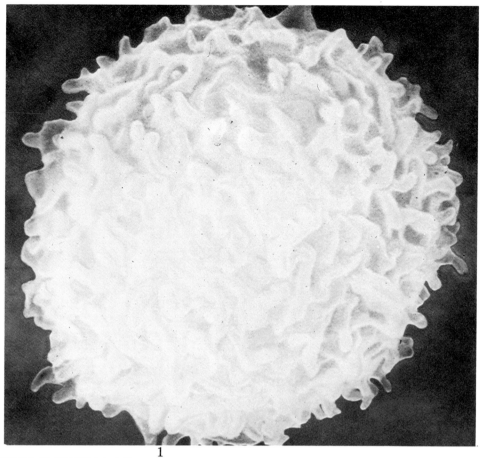

1

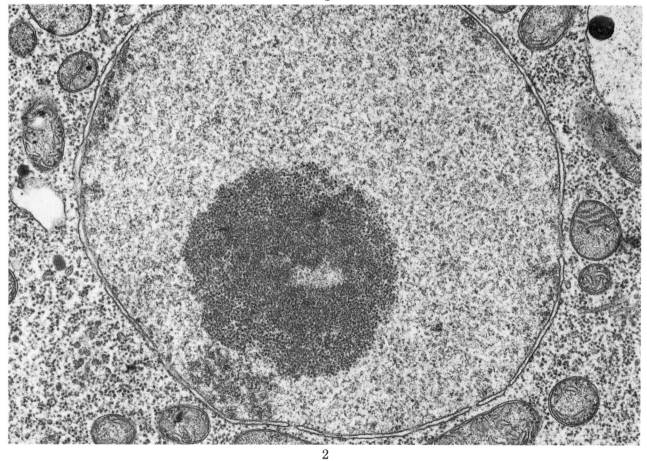

2

18

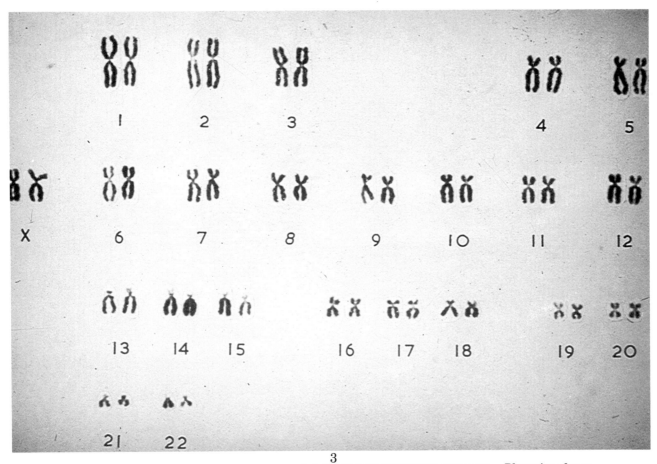

1 2 3 4 5

X 6 7 8 9 10 11 12

13 14 15 16 17 18 19 20

21 22

3

4

Blueprint of man

The entire genetic code of each human being is carried in every one of the 50,000,000,000,000 cells in the body (except the sex cells). Each cell is a complex structure whose activity is regulated by its central nucleus. (**1**) is a white blood cell; (**2**) is a section through the nucleus of a cell. The oblong bodies round the nucleus are mitochondria (chemical power sources), and the dark area is the nucleolus, connected with the manufacture of proteins. The instructions which the nucleus gives to the rest of the cell are carried on the chromosomes (**3**). Humans have 23 matching pairs of chromosomes in each cell – 46 in all. The DNA (**4**) of which the chromosomes are made contains all the information needed to grow the body from the fertilized egg and keep it functioning. Each chromosome consists of a very long, fine strand of DNA; when the cell is about to divide, each strand reproduces itself and coils into a compact mass, which can be seen under a microscope.

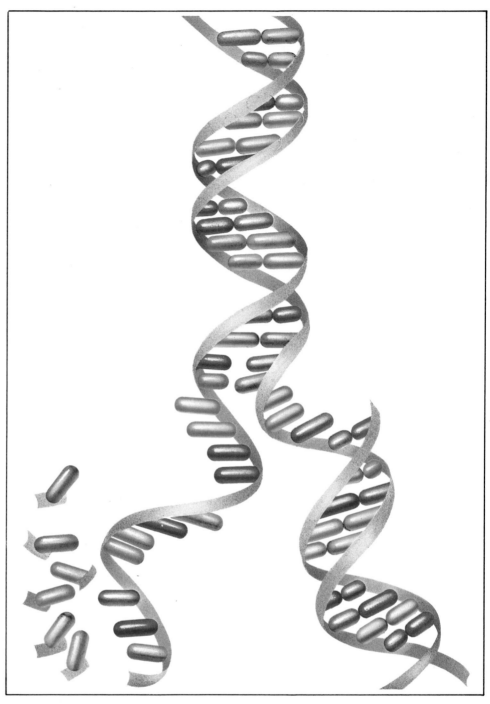

detected in the cell nuclei, called nucleic acids.
When it began to be suspected that the nucleic acids
were the molecules that actually carried the
hereditary information, the question of the
structure of the nucleic acid chain became vitally
important. There were good reasons to suppose that
it would be the key to understanding the
mechanisms of heredity.

There are two kinds of nucleic acid in the nucleus –
deoxyribonucleic acid, or DNA, and ribonucleic acid,
or RNA. We now know that DNA contains all the
necessary information for building all the proteins
used in the body, and RNA carries out the process of
manufacture. Both are constructed out of long
strings of four chemical units known as 'bases': in

DNA these are adenine, guanine, cytosine and
thymine (A, G, C and T for short); RNA uses A, G
and C, but uracil (U) replaces T. How can these few
components carry and pass on all the information
that goes to make up a living organism? In 1953
James Watson and Francis Crick took the first step
towards answering this question, by discovering the
structure of DNA.

Watson and Crick proposed a model in which the
bases are strung out along a chemical 'spine' formed
by sugars and phosphates. Two such strands make
up each molecule of DNA, and they are twisted
about one another in a 'double helix'. The two
strands are joined together by bonds linking the two
base sequences together: A can only bond with T,

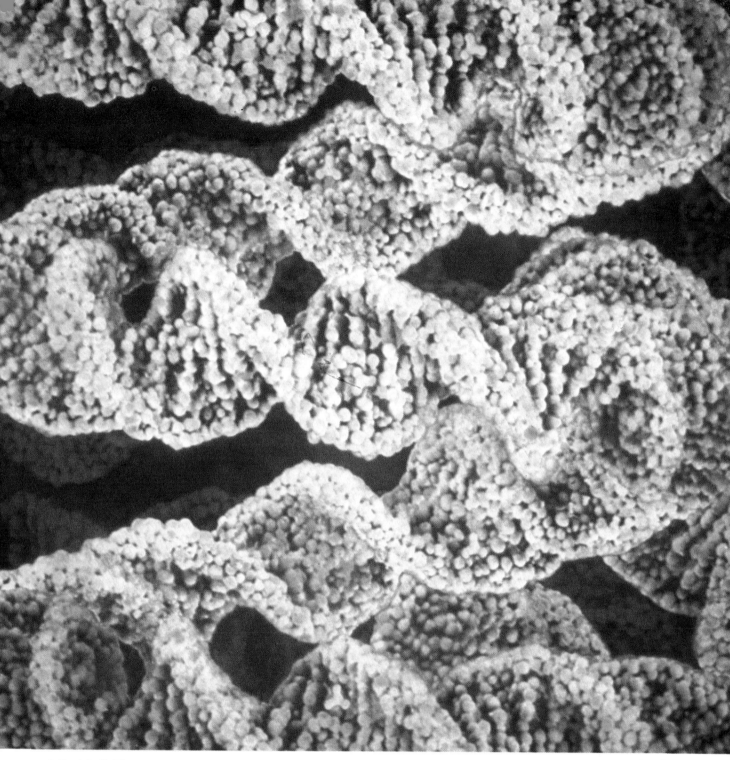

and C with G. Thus, the base sequences on the two strands are complementary. For instance, if one section of a strand has the base sequence AGCTGC, the corresponding section of the other strand must have the sequence TCGACG.

The importance of this structure can be seen in the way DNA reproduces itself when a cell is dividing. The two spiral strands, linked by the paired bases, split apart, and a new matching strand is built up beside each strand. Because A can only bond with T and C with G, the resulting double strands are identical with the old double strand. A full set of genetic information, exactly the same as in the old cell, is passed on to the two new cells. This accuracy is vital, as a mistake could cause physical

The major scientific advance in biology in the 20th century has been the discovery of the structure of DNA. It was found to be a double-helix, made up of four chemical bases supported on a spine of sugars and phosphates. Its spiral structure is shown above. The colours (opposite page) show how the bases always bond together in the same way – adenine pairing with thymine, guanine with cytosine. The importance of this specific pairing is that DNA can reproduce itself accurately.

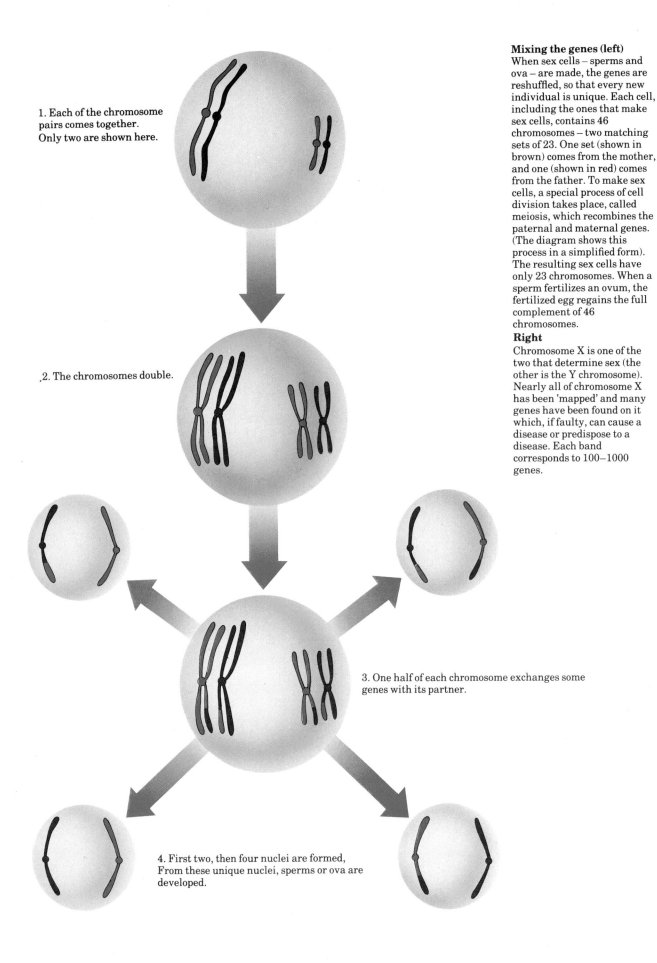

1. Each of the chromosome pairs comes together. Only two are shown here.

2. The chromosomes double.

3. One half of each chromosome exchanges some genes with its partner.

4. First two, then four nuclei are formed, From these unique nuclei, sperms or ova are developed.

Mixing the genes (left)
When sex cells – sperms and ova – are made, the genes are reshuffled, so that every new individual is unique. Each cell, including the ones that make sex cells, contains 46 chromosomes – two matching sets of 23. One set (shown in brown) comes from the mother, and one (shown in red) comes from the father. To make sex cells, a special process of cell division takes place, called meiosis, which recombines the paternal and maternal genes. (The diagram shows this process in a simplified form). The resulting sex cells have only 23 chromosomes. When a sperm fertilizes an ovum, the fertilized egg regains the full complement of 46 chromosomes.

Right
Chromosome X is one of the two that determine sex (the other is the Y chromosome). Nearly all of chromosome X has been 'mapped' and many genes have been found on it which, if faulty, can cause a disease or predispose to a disease. Each band corresponds to 100–1000 genes.

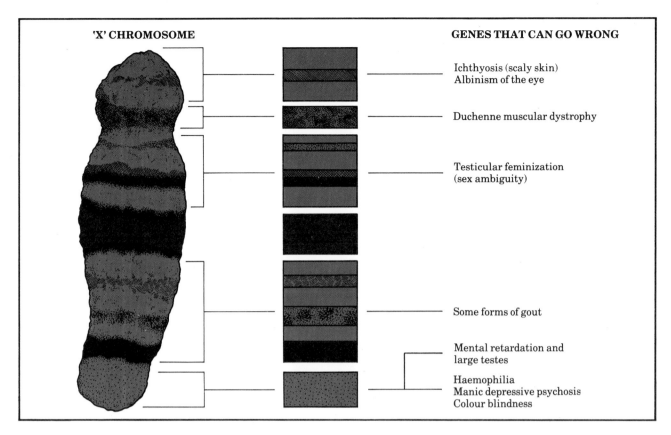

'X' CHROMOSOME

GENES THAT CAN GO WRONG

Ichthyosis (scaly skin)
Albinism of the eye

Duchenne muscular dystrophy

Testicular feminization
(sex ambiguity)

Some forms of gout

Mental retardation and
large testes

Haemophilia
Manic depressive psychosis
Colour blindness

deformities and malfunctions.

The only cells which are not given a full set of genetic information are the sex cells – sperms and ova. They are made by a special form of cell division (meiosis) which reshuffles the genetic information, and they only receive half the genetic information of the parent cell. But as in normal cell division, the process includes a stage where the DNA is copied, and here again accuracy is vital, since a mistake as small as one misplaced base in the sequence can lead to inherited disorders.

Watson and Crick showed how the structure of DNA, and the 'bonding' properties of its bases, allow it to reproduce itself accurately again and again. The bonding properties of the bases are also important in using the DNA to make a protein. In order to do this, RNA is needed. The two strands of the right section of DNA split apart, and an enzyme moves along one of the two strands, 'reading' the code, and makes a complementary strand of RNA. This 'messenger RNA' then migrates outside the nucleus to a site where proteins are being made. Here it acts as a template on which amino acids can be assembled and the protein molecule built up.

Before the discovery of how DNA and RNA work, the word gene simply meant a unit of heredity – the mechanism responsible for a single bodily characteristic such as blue eyes or red hair. With the new discovery, the implications of the word had to change. The word is now used more precisely, to mean a section of DNA containing the instructions for building a particular protein, or for regulating the behaviour of other genes. In coding for a

particular protein, a single gene may influence many physical characteristics, while every characteristic can be influenced by many genes. A gene may be made up of hundreds or thousands of bases. A molecule or strand of DNA may be very long, and contain many genes. Each long molecule of DNA is known as a chromosome.

Once the structure of DNA was known, scientists quickly worked out how the sequence of bases operates as a blueprint for building protein molecules. The sequence has to specify the order of the amino acids in the protein chain. A group of three bases (known as a codon) is used to specify a single amino acid. There are 64 possible triplet combinations of A, G, C and T, and 20 amino acids, so this gives room for a different codon for each amino acid, and some to spare. Often two or more codons seem to specify the same amino acid – for instance, AAA and AAG code for the amino acid lysine – and some codons indicate where to begin or end a chain.

The genetic code – which triplet codon corresponds to which amino acid – is universal in all forms of life, and must have been established at a very early stage in the evolution of life – possibly before the emergence of the simplest organism. Understanding the code, however, is a very different matter from being able to interpret each strand of DNA or identify each gene.

Bacterial genes have been studied in great detail. Bacteria make ideal experimental subjects, because their structure is simple: they have only one circular chromosome. In contrast, humans have 23

pairs of chromosomes so, when studying human genes, we have to find out first which chromosome the gene is on, then where it is on the chromosome. This 'mapping' of our genes is still at an early stage.

Locating human genes has so far been easiest on the X chromosome, one of the two that determine sex. A female has two X chromosomes, while a male has one X and one Y. Genes for sex-linked diseases which appear only in men are known to be on the X chromosome: if a female has a defective gene on one X chromosome, the other, healthy, X chromosome will still enable the relevant protein to be produced, but if a male has the defective X chromosome, the protein will not be produced and he will get the disease. (The Y chromosome, apart from specifying maleness, appears to be genetically inert.) Haemophilia, where a blood-clotting protein is

missing, is the best-known sex-linked disease, but there are many others. Most of the genes on the X chromosome have now been identified, though they may have other effects we do not yet know about.

Once a particular gene has been located, it can then be 'sequenced' – the order of its bases can be worked out. Less than 100 human genes have been sequenced, but an international library of genes (human and non-human) is gradually being built up. A complete set of human genes contains about six thousand million bases, and mapping and sequencing them all will take many years.

GENETIC ENGINEERING
In nature, organisms can only acquire new genes in certain limited ways. The re-ordering of genetic information during meiosis is one way: genetic

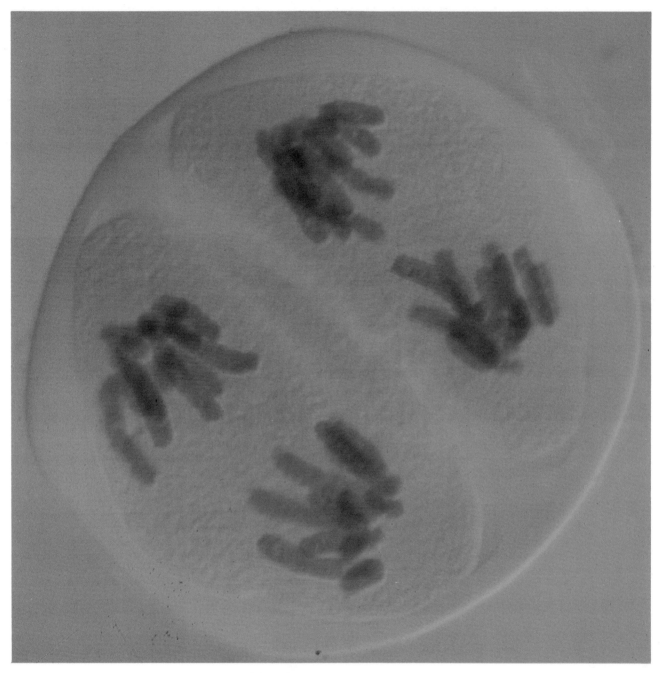

sub-units may come together that can only work in each other's presence. Another way is through rare chemical accidents: the DNA in any cell may be changed either in tiny details (alterations in a single base in the sequence) or in a rather more gross manner (bits of a chromosome may, for instance, be left out or duplicated, or change position, while it is reproducing itself). The vast majority of these changes (mutations) are unsuccessful, but due to the pressures of natural selection, the tiny percentage that do confer an advantage survive and are selected for.

The new science of genetic engineering aims to take a dramatic short cut in the slow process of evolution. In essence, it chops a gene out of the DNA of one organism and inserts it in the DNA of another, achieving something in a matter of days or

The formation of sex cells in the bluebell
In the first picture, the chromosomes have doubled and exchanged some genetic information. During this process they arrange themselves along a central axis in the cell. In the second picture, the chromosomes are being repackaged to form four separate cells.

months that would take natural selection millions of years. In theory, the recipient organism can thus be given the ability to make a protein it could not make before. Transforming bacteria in this way has already become a routine operation.

Isolating particular genes from DNA is not easy, but we now have techniques which, if patiently used, can do the job. DNA can be broken up simply by bombarding it with ultra-high-frequency sound waves, but this is a very hit-or-miss way of trying to isolate particular desirable sections. The method which is usually used now is to employ enzymes whose specific function is to break DNA chains, called 'restriction enzymes'.

There are hundreds of different DNA-breaking enzymes, each one of which operates at a particular base sequence. If a particular piece of DNA has been sequenced, so that we know the order of its bases, then by choosing the right restriction enymes we can slice up the DNA into a pre-planned collection of bits. Identifying the bits in order to get the desired one is laborious, but it can be done.

Transferring the isolated genes into the cells of the new host organism also tends to be a hit-or-miss business. We have invented some ingenious techniques to achieve this when dealing with bacteria, but with larger organisms it is much more difficult. This is partly because the cells of complex organisms have to specialize – in order to become, for instance, skin cells or muscle cells – so only a proportion of the genes contained in the cell are used: the rest are 'switched off'. When genetic engineering is performed on complex organisms, therefore, it is necessary not only to get the DNA into the host cell, but to make sure that it is 'switched on' once it is there, so that the gene is, in the technical terminology, 'expressed'.

One day it will be possible to think in terms of completely redesigning organisms. This would involve planning the make-up of the whole genetic blueprint and the radical transformation of egg cells by adding and subtracting genes, so that the mature individual ultimately grown from each egg cell would have a precisely-planned set of characteristics. We are a long way from achieving this ambition, but elementary experiments in this kind of genetic engineering have been carried out. The most widely-popularized of such experiments involved injecting the eggs of mice with genes coding for a growth hormone obtained from rats. By this means giant mice were produced.

At present, such techniques are extremely crude. There is no way of controlling how many copies of the new gene are inserted, or where they attach themselves to the chromosomes already in the nucleus. There is no way of controlling which kinds of specialized cells in the adult animal will manufacture the new protein and which kinds will not. Many eggs are ruined by the attempt to inject new genes into them (although egg cells are relatively large, and thus much easier to treat in this way than other kinds of cells), and there can be no guarantee that the organisms which develop from successfully transformed eggs will be able to pass on the inserted genes to their own offspring.

Despite these difficulties, we can use such methods even now in the attempt to create new strains of plants and animals. As long as we have enough egg cells to work with, we can tolerate a high failure rate. In time, as our techniques become more sophisticated, we can expect steady progress in this kind of operation. As far as getting egg cells to work with is concerned, we should not be troubled with any shortage of supply when we are working with plants or domestic animals, and we can capitalize on our successes, however few they are, by cloning. Once a fertilized egg cell has begun to develop it is usually not too difficult to separate the cells of the early embryo so that each one becomes an independent embryo in its own right. One egg

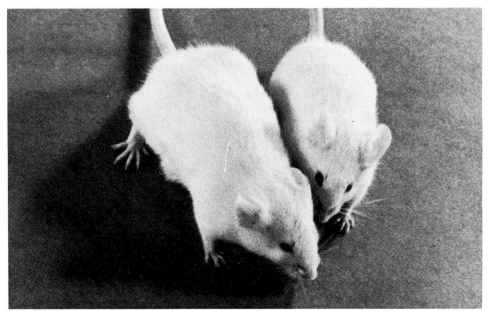

Genetically engineering complex animals is now possible. Present techniques are crude, but as they become more refined, the potential will increase. Scientists have transformed a mouse egg cell by adding the gene for growth hormone taken from a rat; the result was a 'giant' mouse (**left**). Three main techniques of genetic engineering are currently available. The second method (**b**) was the one used to produce the mice. At present, scientists using this method have no control of the 'expression' of the foreign gene – they do not know how to switch it on in the appropriate cells. Research is being concentrated on this problem and it may soon be solved.

How genetic engineering is done

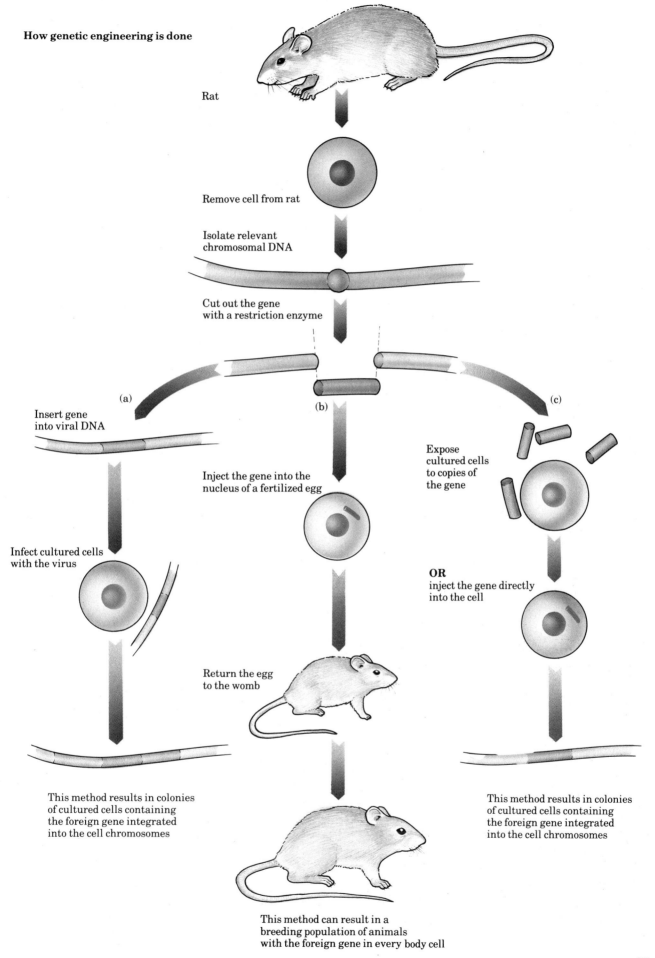

Rat

Remove cell from rat

Isolate relevant chromosomal DNA

Cut out the gene with a restriction enzyme

(a)

(b)

(c)

Insert gene into viral DNA

Inject the gene into the nucleus of a fertilized egg

Expose cultured cells to copies of the gene

Infect cultured cells with the virus

OR inject the gene directly into the cell

Return the egg to the womb

This method results in colonies of cultured cells containing the foreign gene integrated into the cell chromosomes

This method results in colonies of cultured cells containing the foreign gene integrated into the cell chromosomes

This method can result in a breeding population of animals with the foreign gene in every body cell

27

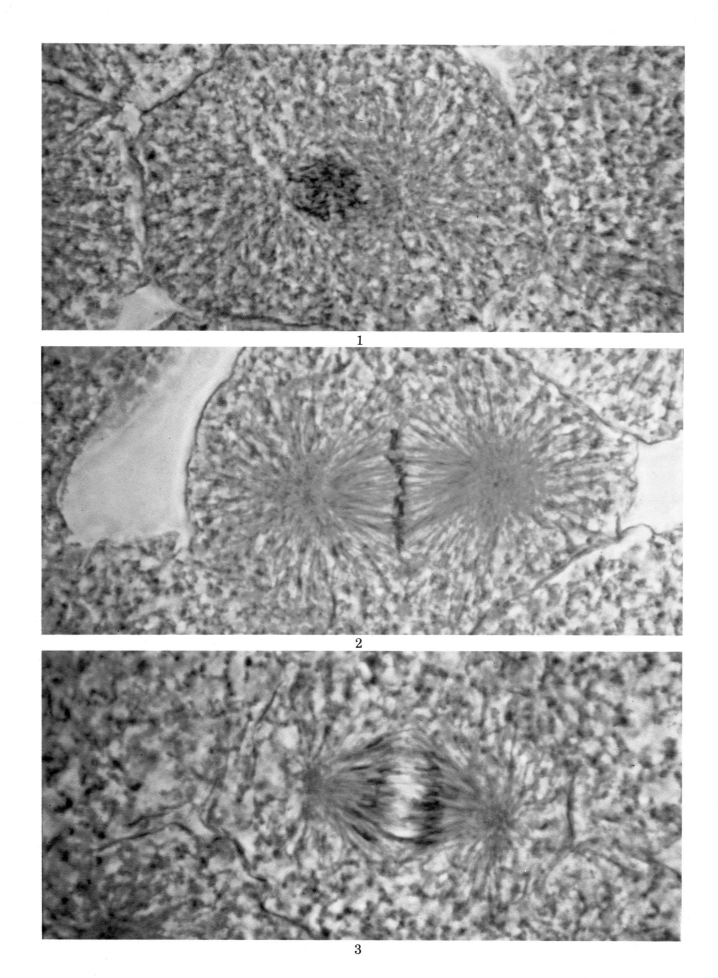

1

2

3

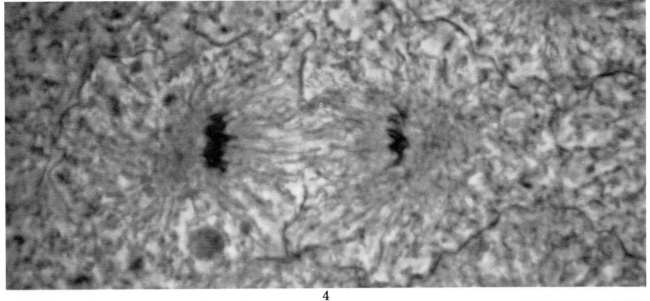

4

5

As an organism develops from a single fertilized egg to an adult, the cells must increase in number. In addition, all cells have a limited lifespan, and thus must be constantly replaced in the adult organism. Cells increase their number by dividing: all the components of the cell – including the DNA in the nucleus – are duplicated, by a process known as *mitosis*. Unlike *meiosis*, whose aim is to produce unique cells, the primary aim of mitosis is that both daughter cells are identical. Five stages of mitosis [in the white fish] are shown here. For clarity, the series of photographs shows only the division of the nucleus, not of the whole cell.

1. The chromosomes are in a condensed state, prior to cell division. All the DNA in the chromosomes has already duplicated.

2. The duplicated chromosomes line up in the centre of the nucleus. Also visible is the complex apparatus which draws apart the two complete sets of chromosomes.

3. Each complete set of chromosomes now migrates to different halves of the nucleus.

4. Shows the separation of the chromosomes and the beginnings of the separation of the nuclear wall.

5. Shows the separation of the two daughter nuclei.

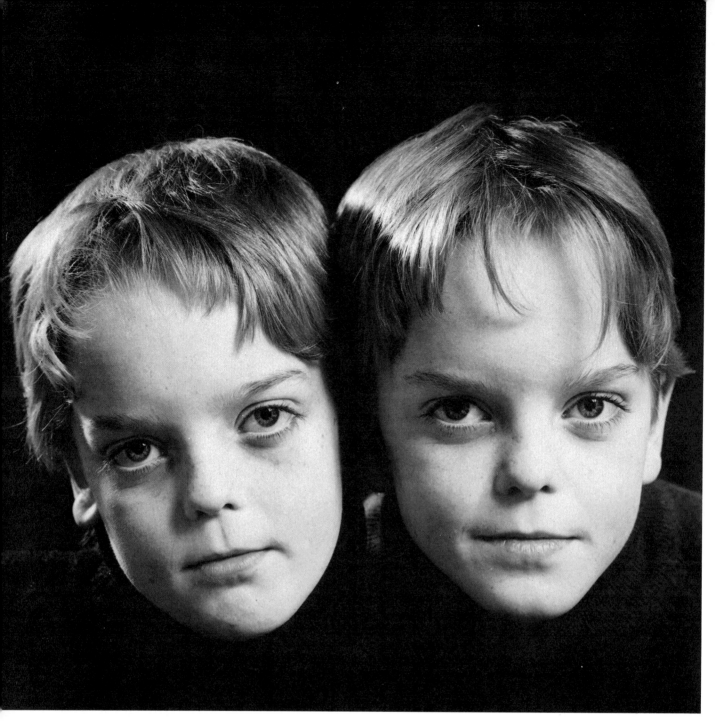

Identical twins result when a single fertilized egg splits and develops into two separate but identical organisms. Non-identical twins, by contrast, occur when two different sperm fertilize two different eggs.

can therefore be converted into two, four or eight if necessary, and we can repeat the process as many times as we like. Cloning occasionally happens accidentally in nature, producing two or more identical offspring.

At present we can only think of transplanting genes one or two at a time. It will probably be some time before we can go beyond the business of simple addition – the prospect of subtracting genes from the egg cells of complex organisms without destroying them is a daunting one. We should not, however, underestimate the possibilities opened up to us even by such simple transformations.

GENETIC PRE-SELECTION

It may take many years for us to learn how to transform egg cells and grow the kind of organisms we want, and still longer to apply this knowledge to humans. But the process of gene mapping which is going on all the time will soon greatly extend the possibilities of a kind of genetic pre-selection that is already being practised by humans. This is the prenatal diagnosis of inherited diseases, with abortion of foetuses found to be 'faulty'. There are a great many diseases which result from the fact that a particular gene is missing or damaged, or from some other genetic abnormality. In some countries abortion is routinely offered to women found to be carrying babies with Down's syndrome, or mongolism, which is caused by an extra chromosome. In Cyprus, 'therapeutic' abortion has reduced the incidence of thalassaemia (a form of anaemia, often fatal) by 85 per cent.

To examine the genes of the foetus, some foetal cells are needed. At present these are obtained by sampling the amniotic fluid in the womb – amniocentesis – and this cannot be done safely until about the eighteenth week of pregnancy. But a new method is now becoming available which gathers some foetal cells from the outer side of the placenta, by going through the cervix: the membrane surrounding the foetus need not be broken, and the test can now be done as early as the eighth week of pregnancy. The logical extension is to test the fertilized egg. Human eggs can now be fertilized outside the womb (*in vitro*, or 'in glass') and then implanted in it to grow to term, a process used at present to help childless couples. If we wanted to examine the egg's DNA, it could be cloned; one clone could be tested, while another – perhaps frozen in the meantime – could be implanted in the womb if the genes proved healthy.

Even with present tests, the characteristics which might be used as grounds for abortion are multiplying rapidly. As well as thalassaemia and sickle cell anaemia, genes have been found for Huntington's chorea – which causes major deterioration of mind and body in middle age – and phenylketonuria, or PKU, an enzyme deficiency which leads to brain damage. The symptoms of PKU can be controlled by the right diet, but no cure for Huntington's chorea is yet known. Genes may soon be precisely located which predispose to many diseases with an inherited component, such as schizophrenia, manic depressive psychosis, heart disease and diabetes.

Parents might not want to stop at selecting out children with a tendency towards inherited diseases. In some countries, where male babies are preferred, prenatal testing for sex has been offered commercially, with the abortion of female foetuses. This form of selection, involving the destruction of eggs or foetuses found undesirable, is seen by many people as morally wrong. But whatever doubts may be raised, many parents apparently find the abortions acceptable.

GENE THERAPY

It would be very convenient to be able to treat hereditary diseases by replacing defective genes with sound ones, or inserting missing genes, in the bodies of children or adults. This will probably be an intermediate step on the way to transforming the DNA in the egg itself.

One experiment of this kind was tried in 1980, but it failed. The man who carried out the experiment, an American named Martin Cline, was attempting to cure two people suffering from a kind of thalassaemia. In thalassaemia a few hundred bases are missing from the 70,000-base gene complex making haemoglobin. Haemoglobin is made in the bone marrow and carried in the red corpuscles of the blood. Its function is to absorb oxygen from the lungs, and patients with thalassaemia make defective haemoglobin which does not do this efficiently. Cline took bone marrow cells from his two patients – who had consented to the experiment – and tried to transform them in tissue-culture by adding DNA containing the required gene. He then returned the cells to the bone marrow of the patients, hoping that they would be able to make healthy red corpuscles of their own to relieve their dependence on blood transfusions and save them from the prospect of an early death.

Cline had already managed to transform mouse cells by this method, but before reimplanting the transformed cells he had killed off, by irradiation, the bulk of the marrow tissue still in the long bones of the limbs. He dared not do this to his human patients, and thus the chances of the transformed tissue being substituted in their bodies for the original defective tissue were much reduced. Neither patient showed any improvement, and Cline, who had bypassed recommendations made by ethics committees in America in order to carry out his experiments in Italy and Israel, was severely criticized.

The main difficulty which prevents our being able to 'cure' people suffering from genetic deficiency diseases – and which prevents us from transplanting new genes into the cells of mature individuals for any other reason – is the difficulty we have in getting new DNA into cells in such a way that it can function. We can be sure that if we inject lots of DNA into a tissue, some of the cells will absorb it, and may well begin to make the protein for which it codes. Unfortunately, the proportion of cells which will actually be transformed will be very tiny – perhaps of the order of one in ten thousand (this is known as 'the rate of transformation'). The chances are, therefore, that if we squirt DNA into a living tissue it is unlikely that enough cells will be transformed to make much difference to its overall functioning.

If in the next few years we can find techniques of introducing DNA into cells more efficiently, so that we can raise the rate of transformation considerably, the way will be open for us to attempt to cure thalassaemics by transforming their bone marrow tissue *in situ*, and there are many other

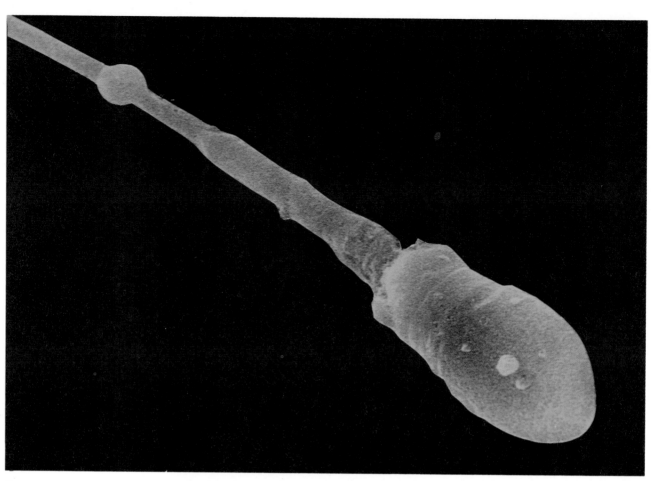

1

2

The human sex cells

The DNA carrying half the blueprint for a new human being is contained in the head of the sperm (1). The thicker part of the tail, behind the head, provides the energy for swimming, and the long tail lashes to give forward motion. In the ovum (2), the nucleus contains the DNA – the other half of the blueprint – and a large proportion of the cell consists of food for the developing embryo.

Ova are much bigger than sperms, which can be seen here trying to penetrate the ovum to fertilize it. Once a single sperm has penetrated the outer membrane, changes take place which make the ovum hostile to other sperms. The fertilized cell divides into two, then four, then eight and so on. The two-cell human egg here (3) is shown 48 hours after fertilization. Further rapid division takes place (4), and the cells begin to differentiate to perform their varied roles in the developing embryo.

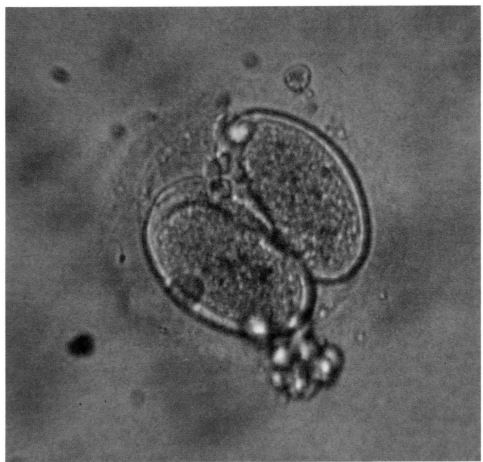

3

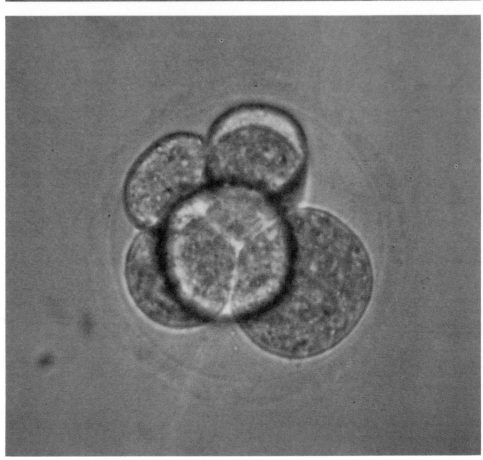

4

genetic deficiency diseases that could be helped. Scientists have already had great success in transforming the DNA of bacteria, and experimental successes in treating the cells of higher organisms have been claimed. Experiments on humans similar to Cline's may soon be tried again. Gene therapy may not be so far away.

ENGINEERING BACTERIA

Transforming bacterial cells is easier than transforming the cells of complex organisms for two reasons. One is that it is relatively easy to get new DNA into a bacterial cell and make it function. Bacteria do not have cell membranes separating various areas of the cell from one another – thus, they do not have an isolated nucleus. Also, in addition to their circular chromosome, they often have tiny rings of DNA called 'plasmids' which work independently of the main chromosome. If the would-be genetic engineer, using restriction enzymes, can put the gene he wants to transplant into a plasmid ring – or, perhaps, make an artificial plasmid ring of his own – there is a good chance that if he simply introduces such plasmids into the environment of a bacterial culture some of the cells will take them up spontaneously.

The other reason why transforming bacteria is a much more practical proposition than transforming cells in animal or plant tissues is that transformed cells can readily be selected out from untransformed ones. Because of this ease of selection, the fact that rates of transformation are low becomes irrelevant. Genetic engineers place the gene which they want to transplant into a plasmid containing a gene which can make bacteria resistant to a particular antibiotic. If they can find plasmids already containing such genes that is an advantage, but if not they simply have to transplant two genes into the plasmid instead of one. They then introduce their plasmids into a culture of bacteria which are not resistant to the relevant antibiotic. After some lapse of time they introduce the antibiotic into the culture, killing off all the untransformed cells, to leave a pure culture of transformed bacteria which can be made to multiply rapidly simply by feeding in nutrients.

It seems probable that attempts to use this kind of selection process on the tissues of complex animals are bound to be too destructive: for instance, in Cline's experiment, the final step he could not take was to try to kill off all the untransformed marrow cells that were still in the bones of his patients.

The techniques developed for engineering bacteria have many extremely useful applications. Locating and identifying human genes is done by transplanting sections of human DNA into bacteria so that they are reproduced in vast numbers and can then be studied further. Bacterial engineering can also be used to create 'bacterial factories' for the production of certain desirable proteins by transplanting into the bacteria the gene for making the required protein.

Because proteins are such complicated molecules, it is very expensive and time-consuming to synthesize them in the laboratory, and at present we can only synthesize the smaller protein molecules. Nevertheless, there are a great many functional proteins needed in medicine: for instance, insulin for the treatment of diabetics, human growth hormone for the treatment of dwarfism and interferon for possible uses in the treatment of cancers and virus diseases. Previously, we have only been able to extract such compounds from living animal tissue, and the techniques of extraction are complicated and extremely expensive. Transplanting genes from human cells into bacteria, to make the bacteria produce large quantities of the required protein quickly and cheaply, can revolutionize the medical supplies business. Many such useful proteins are already being made and big corporations have begun to exploit them.

Setting up manufacturing processes of this kind can be very laborious. Locating and isolating the genes in which we are interested is difficult because we are still a long way from obtaining a complete map of the genes on all the human chromosomes. Nevertheless, we can expect that as the years go by more and more useful proteins will be made in this way. Some of the probable applications of this kind of process will be described in greater detail in subsequent chapters.

Much experimental work – using bacteria as well as more complex cells as subjects – is now directed to the possibility of increasing rates of transformation by using viruses instead of plasmids as 'vectors' to take the required DNA into the cell. The advantage of viruses is that they actively invade cells instead of waiting passively to be picked up by them. Viruses are used routinely with bacteria when copying mammalian genes for further study: a bit of DNA is introduced into the viral DNA using enzymes, the virus infects bacterial cells, and it then multiplies, reproducing the desired bit of DNA each time.

Viruses have been used to put new DNA into mammalian cells, but this research is at an early stage, and is mainly restricted to cells in tissue cultures. Once we understand more about how viruses affect cells and how they then ensure that their own genes become active within the cells, it may be possible to obtain the higher rates of transformation needed to secure a new breakthrough in genetic engineering.

UNSOLVED PROBLEMS

As well as the practical difficulties mentioned above, there are other unsolved problems in genetic theory which must be cleared up before biological engineering can really fulfil its potential. There are still some significant gaps in our knowledge of how the hereditary system works.

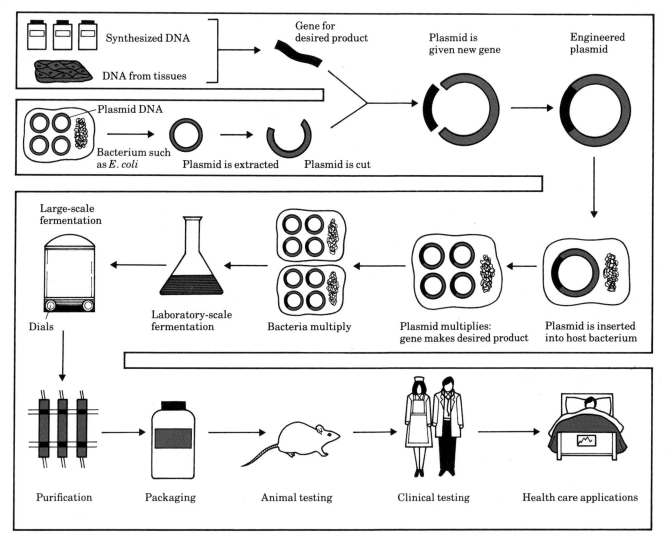

Synthesized DNA

DNA from tissues

Gene for desired product

Plasmid is given new gene

Engineered plasmid

Plasmid DNA

Bacterium such as _E. coli_

Plasmid is extracted

Plasmid is cut

Large-scale fermentation

Dials

Laboratory-scale fermentation

Bacteria multiply

Plasmid multiplies: gene makes desired product

Plasmid is inserted into host bacterium

Purification

Packaging

Animal testing

Clinical testing

Health care applications

We now understand how DNA functions as a blueprint for making proteins. We also know how the cellular factory reads this blueprint and assembles proteins to its specifications. One thing we do not know, though, is how the genes encode instructions for building the structure of a whole organism.

Somehow, a single undifferentiated egg cell must be provided with instructions which tell it how to make hundreds of different kinds of specialized cells, how to put these different kinds of cells together in highly specific patterns to make complicated organs within an entire functioning body, and what kind of body that will be. We presume that the DNA carries this information but we do not know how it determines the process of tissue specialization in growing embryos. There is no way of knowing how long it will take to solve this problem, but the logical place to start is with an investigation of the process by which some genes in specialized cells are 'switched off'. Research along these lines is already being carried out.

The other major gap in our knowledge of heredity is that we have very little idea how genes might influence behaviour. Even in lower animals some behavioural patterns are transmitted from

Creating biological factories
Techniques of genetic engineering are now being widely used in industry. This diagram shows their use in the manufacture of pharmaceuticals.

A new gene is introduced into the plasmid rings of a bacterium such as _E. coli_, which then multiplies rapidly. The desired product is extracted, purified and tested before being used for medicinal purposes.

generation to generation by learning, but it also appears that many of the things animals do are programmed into them by some means. A great deal of human behaviour seems to be learned, but this implies that there must be a good deal of genetic pre-programming to make us such clever learners. Chimpanzees can learn quite a lot if reared by human beings but it is clear that they do not have the same capacity for learning as human children, and that special capacity for learning must be part of our genetic endowment.

It is very difficult to figure out just how much influence genes do have on patterns of human behaviour, and the debate about the relative power of nature and nurture has been raging for over a century now. One of the reasons why it is difficult to settle the question is that we have no idea how a tendency to behave in a particular way can be transmitted through the chemical mechanisms of heredity. The simple reflexes that primitive animals have are presumably 'wired in' to their nervous systems in some way, so that their behaviour is a reflection of structure, but when we try to figure out how more complicated patterns of behaviour might be determined it becomes very difficult to imagine appropriate wiring. We have invented a word to describe inherited behaviour patterns – we call them 'instincts' – but having a name is only the first step on the long road to understanding.

Again, it is impossible to guess how far we are from a solution to this problem. Intensive research into the physiology and chemistry of the brain seems to be the best way to tackle it, but the brain is the most complicated organ in the body, and it is very difficult to connect up the chemical and electrical events in an animal's brain with specific items of its behaviour. The human brain, of course, presents problems of an even greater magnitude.

When we consider the progress in genetic science that has taken place over the last 100 years, and in particular the very rapid progress of the last 30 years, it is difficult to believe that these unsolved problems will delay genetic engineers for very long. It would not be surprising if we were to solve the problem of how genes determine structure by the end of this century; it would be very surprising if we had not discovered how they determine behaviour before the end of the next. If these estimates are correct – and they certainly do not seem reckless – then our children and our grandchildren will be the ones creating the new world that will arise out of the application of these discoveries.

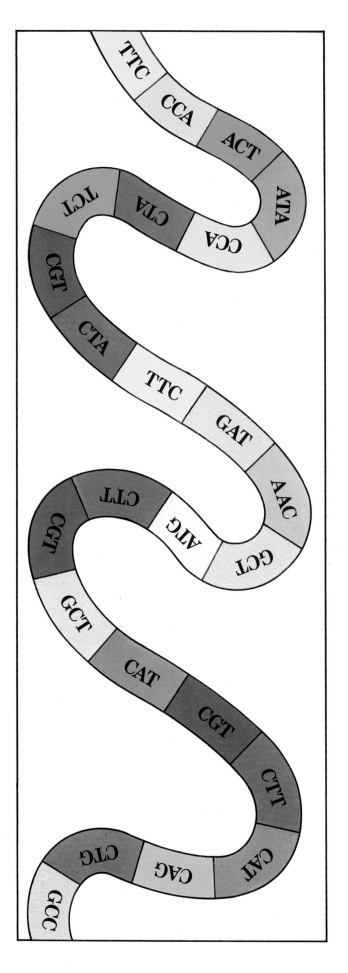

The order of the four chemical bases of DNA contains all the information needed for making the world's diverse living creatures. A sequence of three bases signals one of the 20 amino acids which are used in making a chain-like protein molecule. A gene is a section of DNA that codes for a particular protein.
Shown here are the first 72 bases of the gene for human growth hormone, coding for the first 24 amino acids of its chain. When supplies of this hormone are needed, the information in the DNA is translated into new copies of the molecule.

36

Chapter 3

Mastering our environment

Genetic engineering will eventually enable us to turn the working of all living things on Earth – the entire biosphere – to the particular advantage of our own species. The first steps towards this control were taken when men abandoned hunting and gathering and began to exploit some species of plants and animals in a systematic way. But it is bacteria and other very simple organisms which will become the main agents through which we will gradually extend our command over the biosphere. Micro-organisms – including bacteria, yeasts and moulds – are the most versatile of all the 'living machines' which will be placed at our disposal by genetic engineering.

We have seen that cultures of bacteria can be transformed into factories to make useful proteins, including enzymes, vitamins, insecticides and medicines. But there are many other ingenious ways

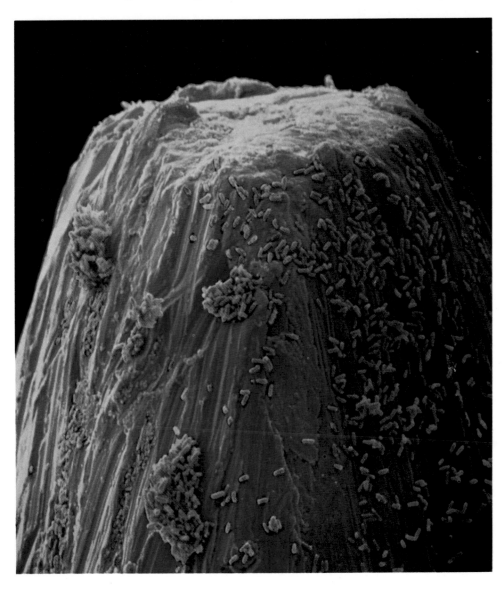

The minute size of bacteria can be seen in this photograph, where hundreds of them are clustered on a single pinhead. Invisible micro-organisms are all around us: fortunately for us, only a few species cause disease. The vast majority of them are beneficial and play an essential part in many biological processes. Due to their simplicity and growth rate, bacteria were the ideal subjects for early genetic engineers.

in which we already use micro-organisms, not only in food production and energy production, but also in mining and pollution control. Until recently these uses depended on the properties of existing micro-organisms evolved through natural selection. Genetic engineering gives us the power to tailor micro-organisms precisely for the jobs we have in mind.

Whether some of these processes can be economic or not depends partly on the price of the raw material used to feed the micro-organisms. Genetic engineering can help to make such projects economically viable, by increasing the productiveness of the micro-organisms or by adapting them to live on material that is cheap and plentiful. It will also enable us to use micro-organisms for a kind of ecological streamlining: to convert energy-rich materials which we cannot use directly – such as industrial wastes – into things we *can* use.

For thousands of years we have been using plants and animals to do a similar job for us: converting energy we cannot use directly into food and other things we need. Over this time we have artificially selected hundreds of species in order to make them produce more abundantly. When genetic engineers attain the ability to transform plants and animals, many opportunities will open up for improving their efficiency still more. This will mean an extension of present-day factory farming

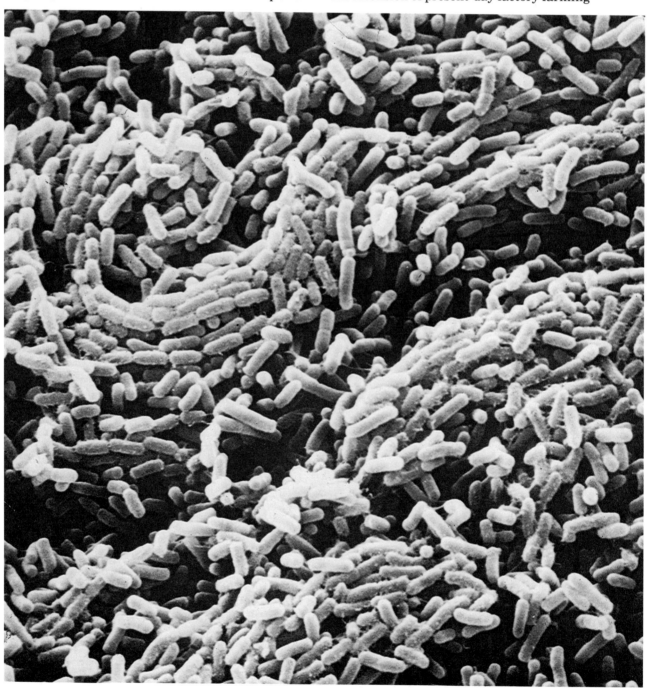

techniques: familiar cows, chickens and pigs may be replaced by redesigned substitutes.

With a really comprehensive knowledge of how biochemical processes are organized and controlled, we could go a stage further. We should not need to deal with living organisms at all. We may one day be able to produce food substances – and other materials – directly, without requiring plants, animals or micro-organisms to do it for us. When this happens, our relationship with our environment will again be changed profoundly. While we would still be able to control the evolution of any living species, we would no longer have a pressing need to exploit them in order to supply ourselves with the fundamental necessities of life. We would be able to

These rod shaped bacteria are called *Escherichia coli* and are commonly found in the human gut where they produce vitamin K for us. *E. coli* is the organism of choice for genetic experiments and as a result more is known about the organization and expression of its genes than about those of any other organism.

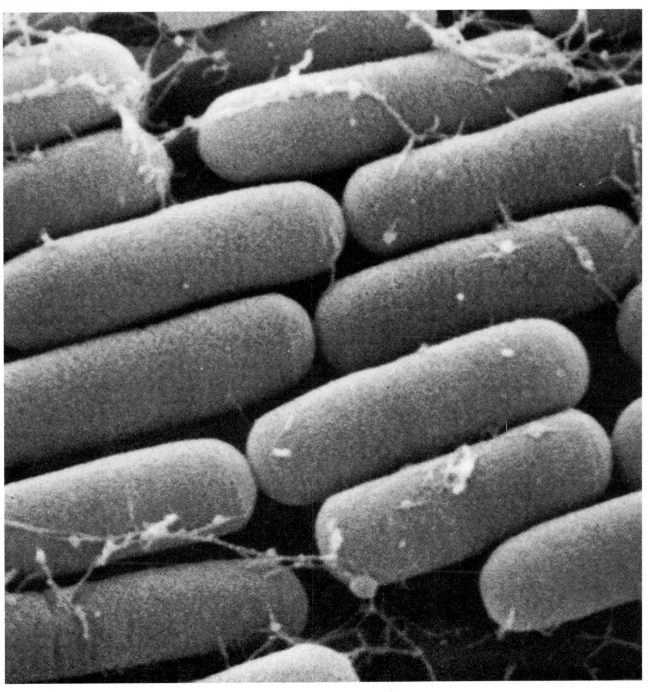

respect the natural diversity of species produced by evolution in all its three phases.

BIOLOGICAL FACTORIES

Our new 'living tools' will be the microscopic single-celled organisms. Such organisms are everywhere in the environment – around us and inside us – and they are constantly at work transforming and reprocessing organic molecules. When we talk about plant or animal waste 'rotting', what we mean is that it is slowly being ingested by bacteria or fungi (yeasts and moulds). These break down complicated molecules for their own use, and in so doing return carbon and nitrogen to a form in which other creatures can make use of them. Because they help to recycle the materials of the organic world, micro-organisms are vital to the survival of all the other species on Earth.

The fermentation caused by these microbes has been exploited for thousands of years in making beer, wine, cheese, bread and other fermented foods. Many of the substances that micro-organisms make naturally are also useful, and since the beginning of the century we have been developing techniques to grow them on an industrial scale and harvest their products.

Vessels for growing micro-organisms are usually called 'fermenters'. Not so very long ago, a fermenter was simply a vat full of bacterial soup which was stirred by men with long sticks. Nowadays, micro-organisms are grown in gigantic fermentation towers, inside which the culture is mechanically stirred and aerated. Conditions are closely monitored so that essential nutrients can be fed in as required, and the organisms or their products extracted. The process is continuous: a perfect biological production line.

Some of the products – such as enzymes, vitamins, acids and amino acids – can then be used in other industries. For instance, an enzyme which can break down proteins is added to washing powder to 'digest stains'. One group of micro-organisms makes a product of great importance to medicine: the antibiotics, which are poisonous to other micro-organisms but harmless to man. In their natural state, these poisons help the organisms to survive by killing off the competition. They are therefore

Some bacteria can be cultivated, harvested, dried and then eaten directly as single-cell protein. An example is the organism shown here (**right**). The final dried product, Pruteen (**left**) was developed at ICI and is now being sold as cattle food. This kind of product will soon join soya protein on the supermarket shelves.

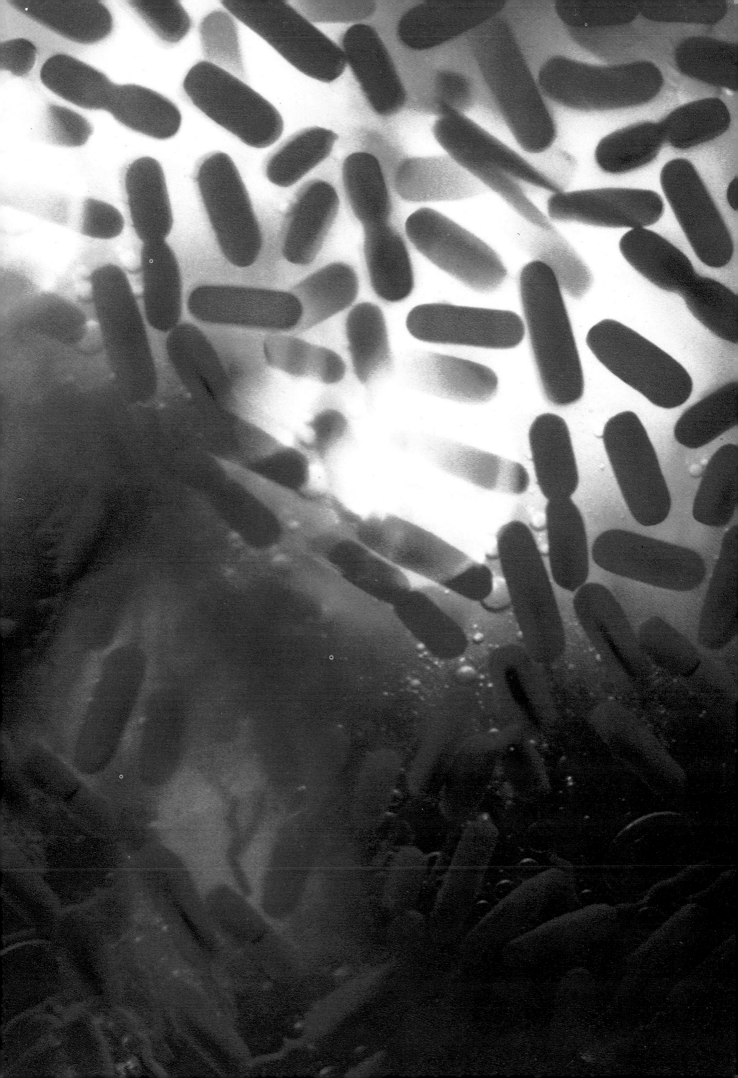

extremely useful in treating bacterial infections. Thousands of naturally occurring antibiotics have been discovered. Only a few are useful to us, such as penicillin obtained from the mould *Penicillium*, discovered by Alexander Fleming in the 1920s; but new ones are still being found, and we have also created many synthetic antibiotics as our knowledge of their structure has increased.

Because of the energy crisis caused by the rising price of oil, the alcohol made by yeasts and the gases produced by bacteria have begun to seem attractive as fuels. In Brazil, ethyl alcohol is produced by yeast fermentation from sugar cane and cassava, and used as a substitute for petrol. In India, China and Pakistan, methane gas for generating energy is widely produced from animal dung – a cheap and adaptable technology.

Micro-organisms themselves consist mainly of protein and can be eaten as food, if their taste is acceptable. Micro-organisms have been grown industrially as food for humans or animals since the First World War. They have not usually been very economical to produce, but there has recently been a resurgence of interest in microbial foods, now known as single-cell protein, or SCP. For instance, ICI have built a fermentation tower which grows bacteria on methyl alcohol to make an SCP product called Pruteen. This is sold as animal feed, as are most SCP products, though humans can, and do, eat them.

Micro-biological industries are facing the prospect of a boom because of the possibilities opened up by the use of genetically engineered bacteria. The techniques of gene-splicing described in the previous chapter will enable us to transform bacteria into biological factories producing any protein we want. Some proteins are structurally too complicated for us to synthesize, but once we have identified the gene which codes for a particular protein and successfully transplanted it into bacteria, the bacteria will make that protein, and we can grow them in fermenters to produce it quite cheaply in any quantity we desire.

This has its most immediate application in medicine. There are many diseases caused by the failure of the human body to make enough of a particular protein. Diabetics, for instance, fail to make enough insulin. Luckily for them, the insulin produced by sheep and other animals is similar enough to human insulin to function well when injected into people. But although it controls the major symptoms of diabetes, it does not prevent some of its effects, such as deterioration of the kidneys and the retina. The gene coding for human insulin, which is quite a short one, has now been synthesized in the laboratory and inserted into bacteria. The human insulin made by bacteria will be preferred to animal insulin if the bacteria can be made productive enough.

Human growth hormone and interferon are two other important proteins which can now be made by bacteria that have been given the appropriate human gene. A lack of human growth hormone causes dwarfism. Until recently it could only be obtained from human tissue, and was so expensive that its use had to be severely rationed. Now it can be produced cheaply enough to treat anybody who needs it. Interferon is a compound made in minute quantities by human cells. It appears to help cells resist invasion by viruses, and there is a possibility that it may help to combat virus diseases and in the treatment of some cancers. With the new techniques, it can now be made cheaply enough for clinical trials and for treating patients if its usefulness is established. Previously it could only be extracted from human blood, and was so expensive to make and purify that research into it was severely restricted. Many other human proteins are now being made, or will soon be made, by engineered bacteria in fermenters, with dramatic implications for medical research and the treatment of deficiency diseases.

As well as human or animal proteins, we can make bacteria which will produce plant proteins by transferring the appropriate plant gene. Products could include medicines, pesticides, oils and flavourings that are at present extracted from the plants themselves. The genes we insert into micro-organisms do not necessarily have to come from a human, a plant or an animal. We can now make artificial genes in the laboratory which encode instructions for making a molecule unknown in nature, and introduce them into a micro-organism to manufacture the substance in quantity. As our expertise increases, we may be able to discover new useful proteins which natural selection has not yet managed to invent.

Economic factors will inevitably govern the choices we make in attempting to transform bacteria to make particular substances. Genetic engineering can make micro-organisms thousands of times more productive. Before we learnt how to splice genes, the productiveness of some industrial bacteria was increased greatly by crude methods of genetic manipulation, stimulating mutations with radiation and chemicals. As a result, the *Penicillium* mould which we use today to make penicillin is 10,000 times more productive than Fleming's original culture. Improving the efficiency of micro-organisms hundreds or thousands of times over so as to make them commercially viable is likely to be an important area of research for genetic engineers, if less newsworthy than creating new organisms.

The multiplicity of possible uses for engineered micro-organisms enables us to see the techniques of genetic engineering for what they are: tools for making more tools – the biological equivalent of the lathe. They will allow us to make living instruments, and the number of things the living instruments will eventually be able to do is very great indeed. If we look back over the last 200 years, to consider how rapidly our mechanical technology

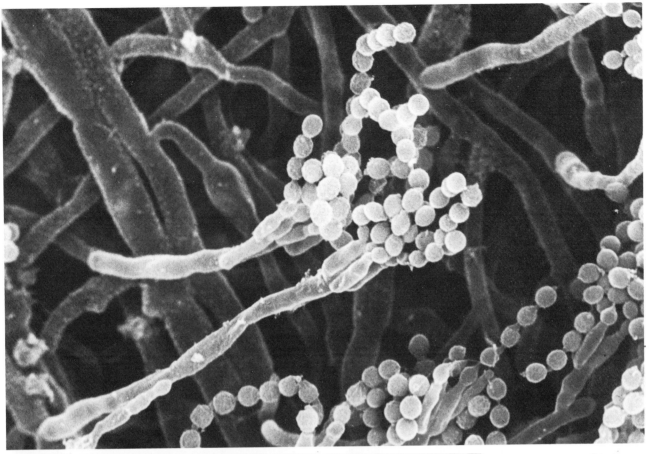

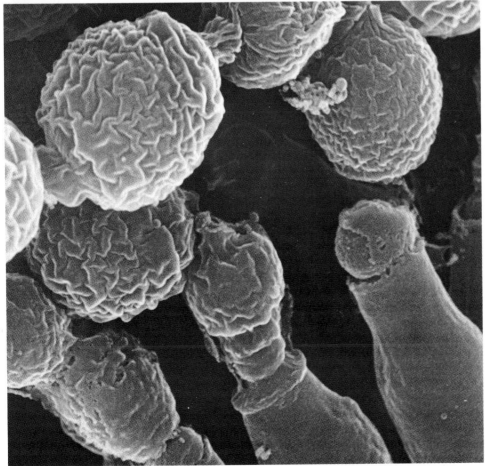

The best known antibiotic, penicillin, is used against a range of diseases – meningitis, pneumonia, syphilis and other infections. It is a toxic compound produced by various species of the penicillin fungus, which attacks other micro-organisms by interfering with their cell wall formation. It is harmless to human cells. These pictures show the species *Penicillium chrysogenum*, magnified under an electron microscope 2,000 times (**top**) and 20,000 times (**left**).

Plants are vital to life on Earth. They convert sunlight into stored energy by photosynthesis (**opposite page**), and during this process they absorb carbon dioxide and give off the oxygen that other organisms need to breathe. Tropical rainforest (**this page**) is a vast, self-renewing and highly efficient system for converting solar energy into stored proteins.

has proliferated, from the steam engine to the microcomputer, we might be better able to imagine what we might do in the next 200 years with the wholly new technology of biological systems.

ECOLOGICAL STREAMLINING

In 24 hours of continuous operation, some bacteria inside a fermenter can reproduce themselves 50 times over. Some micro-organisms can reproduce themselves in only 20 minutes. In contrast, moulds and algae take nearly six hours to double their weight; fast-growing plants take six days; a young cow takes about six weeks. Their fast rate of reproduction makes the micro-organisms the most efficient producers in nature.

Bacteria in a fermenter, however, still have to be fed. They can do without sunlight as an external supply of raw energy because they are exploiting foodstuffs which already have energy locked up in them. Plants need sunshine in order to make proteins from atmospheric carbon dioxide and water: the process known as photosynthesis. Whether the bacteria are digesting methyl alcohol, waste-paper pulp or petroleum, they are capitalizing on work which has already been done at some time in the past by plants. At present, the cost of the raw materials needed to feed micro-organisms means that such processes are often not particularly attractive economically.

This problem offers an obvious invitation to genetic engineers. As well as attending to what the

bacteria make, they can look at what the bacteria consume. It would be helpful if bacteria could be adapted to feed on plant wastes from other industries. Some existing organisms can already grow on waste: *Penicillium* mould can be grown on molasses left over from the crystallization of sugar. Genetic engineering may enable us to adapt other useful micro-organisms to live on the most economical substrates.

We might even look beyond plant wastes to other kinds of organic materials such as those synthesized by man. Waste plastics have energy locked up within them which might be released by the right enzymes. As the manufacture of goods continues to expand, waste products will become more abundant and more troublesome. Eventually it will be economical and convenient to reprocess our waste into food for micro-organisms.

One breakthrough which genetic engineers might make in the near future would open up a particularly abundant resource for the feeding of micro-organisms, at least for a while. This would be the creation of bacteria equipped to deal efficiently with cellulose, the major structural component of plant cell walls. Some bacteria already have the capacity to convert cellulose into useful proteins (this includes the bacteria which live inside the stomachs of cows and sheep – nature's fermenters), but naturally occurring bacteria are generally not highly competent at breaking down cellulose, and one can see why this is logically necessary. Plants

44

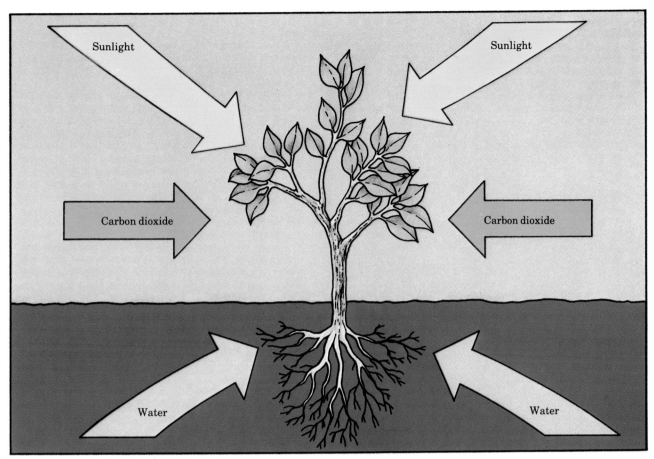

are in the business of preserving themselves while they are alive, and natural selection has obviously had to make certain that they build themselves mainly out of substances that are not very vulnerable to attack. The sheer quantity of cellulose in the world has encouraged the evolution of many species which depend on it as a food supply, but they can only do so with some difficulty – as evidenced by the fact that cows and sheep need bacteria to help them out, and even then take a long time about digesting the grass they eat.

If genetic engineers do manage to produce such bacteria, they must be very careful with them. It would be very convenient to have industrial fermenters into which we could feed grass-cuttings and out of which we could take anything we pleased (foodstuffs, fuels or medicines) without waste – but if the bacteria inside those fermenters ever got out, there could be an ecocatastrophe of spectacular dimensions. This kind of possibility is one of the reasons why people contemplate the future of biological engineering with some trepidation, and why the strains of bacteria that are produced by genetic engineers are produced with built-in vulnerabilities which ensure that they can only live within the strictly controlled conditions of a fermenter.

There are already some biotechnologies which are not confined within fermenters. We already use micro-organisms in sewage processing, to attack the pests that destroy our crops, and to help in mining. If genetic engineers are to improve these technologies, then their products will have to be designed for use in the greater world. Many people still insist that genetically engineered organisms must not be released into the environment lest there be unforeseen consequences. But the possible rewards attached to their use are so great that such opportunities cannot be permanently shelved.

One area in which they might be extremely useful is that of pollution control. In recent times, the industrialized nations have experienced various new pollution problems. The extensive burning of coal releases pollutants into the atmosphere, notably sulphur dioxide, which eventually results in toxic 'acid rain'. The use of lead compounds as 'anti-knock' agents in petrol also results in atmospheric pollution, and certain other heavy metals, including mercury, have become serious environmental pollutants.

Even more dangerous are some of the products of our organic chemical industries: chlorinated hydrocarbons such as the insecticide DDT or the fire-fighting agent PBB have caused acute problems. When PBB was accidentally mixed with animal feed in the American state of Michigan it caused considerable damage to cattle, rendered some tracts of land unusable, and may even have affected humans through polluted beef. These new pollutants are problematic because they are 'non-biodegradable'. This means that there are no natural organisms which have the capability of

Algae are micro-organisms that can be grown cheaply using the sun's energy rather than a costly energy source provided by man. They are already cultivated industrially in similar ways to bacteria, to be used as a food source like Pruteen, or for the production of useful chemicals. Genetic engineering can increase their yield or indeed modify them to produce a variety of compounds.

breaking them down. Thus, something like DDT will accumulate in the tissues of the insects that eat the fruit on which it is sprayed, and in the tissues of the birds that eat the insects. The substance simply builds up within the tissues, because there is no natural mechanism for destroying it or excreting it. This is why indiscriminate use of DDT had to be curtailed, and why most chlorinated hydrocarbons are used very circumspectly.

There are bacteria which can metabolize sulphur and which might in principle be used to make sulphurous coal safer to burn. Genetic engineers might be able to breed special ones better equipped for the job. To produce micro-organisms with new genes adapting them to take up and render harmless heavy metals such as lead and mercury would be much more difficult, but worth attempting. It would be just as difficult to give micro-organisms genes that would equip them to break down chlorinated hydrocarbons, but this too is conceivable.

Specialized micro-organisms for fighting pollution would probably be released in a controlled fashion to help in particular emergencies. The bacteria would probably have some built-in vulnerability – perhaps a metabolic defect which would allow them to live and thrive only when supplied with a particular nutrient. They could be condemned to death by withdrawing the supportive nutrient once the immediate task had been accomplished. Nevertheless, such engineered organisms probably would, in the end, adapt by mutation to the business of living free, and this

could cause problems. A friendly bug that would soak up environmental lead pollution might not seem so friendly if it were chewing holes in your pipes.

Engineered micro-organisms which would help us in mining would also have to be let loose in the environment, and again the benefits might have to be measured against the possible costs. Bacteria and other micro-organisms are already used quite widely in mining, but their assistance is at present mostly indirect. They usually set off a chain of chemical reactions which converts the metal compound into soluble salts which can be washed or 'leached' out of the ore with water.

Rather than simply improving leaching techniques, genetic engineers might be able to produce tailor-made organisms which would take up metals directly from their environment. Some micro-organisms, such as algae, which vary in form from very simple one-celled types to more complex organisms such as seaweeds, often have the ability to take up particular elements from their environment. A certain kind of seaweed which selectively takes up iodine has been used as a source of iodine for more than a century. There is no reason in principle why other algae should not be engineered to do similar things. Given time, genetic engineers might design algae which could pick up all kinds of different metals from the sea-water in which they live. The concentrations of heavy metals dissolved in sea-water are very small, but because there is such a vast amount of sea, its resources are huge. Every cubic mile of sea-water contains gold – literally – by the ton. We cannot exploit such a resource mechanically, but we might make organisms to do it for us.

Such genetically engineered micro-organisms would present ecological dangers unless they were carefully controlled. A bacterium which could extract copper from its environment, for instance, might not be a good thing to have around electrical cables. There is another kind of micro-organism which might be engineered, which could only be used at large in the environment, but whose side-effects might be ecologically very beneficial: an alga which we could grow in the sea and harvest as a food.

Algae are micro-organisms which carry out photosynthesis. It would make sense to try to exploit this ability, instead of using plants to convert the sun's energy into stored energy and then feeding the plants to bacteria in fermenters. Most algae live in water, and many of them can be found in the plankton that inhabit the surface layer of the sea. The algae in the plankton support a prolific and complicated life system, providing food for many other micro-organisms and for the larvae of many different sea-creatures. We already exploit plankton indirectly by eating the fish which stand at the top of the food-chains whose first link is the planktonic algae. But when we think that the surface of the sea covers two-thirds of the Earth, and think of all the sunlight that falls upon it every day, we are encouraged to wonder whether we might make more use of this resource.

We might in time be able to engineer new species of algae, which would mop up more of the sun's energy, turning the surface of the sea into a gigantic field that could be harvested by ships equipped with a mechanical version of a whale's filter-feeding apparatus. Such a scheme was suggested as long ago as 1923 by J.B.S. Haldane, the first biologist to write a speculative essay about the possibilities of genetic engineering. Indeed, he said then that we would probably have such an alga by now. It is a project which still seems plausible, and one which might conceivably get off the ground within the next generation.

The raw materials that such an alga would depend on are the most basic of all. It would need sunlight and water (both of which are present in relative abundance at the surface of the sea), certain trace elements (also available in sea-water) and carbon dioxide from the atmosphere. In soaking up carbon dioxide such an alga might well help to solve another problem. When we burn fossil fuels such as coal, carbon dioxide is added to the atmosphere, and it is feared that this could eventually affect the world's climate by means of the 'greenhouse effect', melting the polar ice-caps and causing a devastating rise in sea-level. If we greatly increased the amount of algae in the ocean, there would be a significant drop in the amount of carbon dioxide in the atmosphere. By such means as this we might hope eventually not only to secure food supplies for a large world population, but also to take control of one of the most fundamental aspects of the balance of nature.

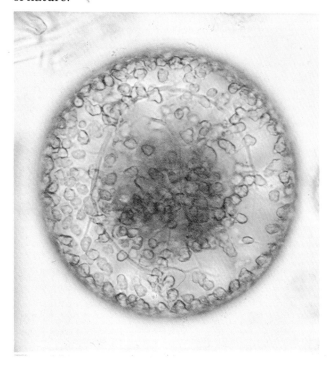

Algae will be one of the most useful tools of future genetic engineers. These microscopic organisms (above) convert sunlight into energy and could become the crops of the future, cultivated on vast expanses of ocean in a similar way to the wheat fields of North America. Such a source of food could alleviate food problems of future generations.

THE NEW AGRICULTURAL REVOLUTION

Modern agriculture is highly efficient, but its efficiency is expensively bought, because it relies upon elaborate technological support. The core of contemporary agricultural endeavour is the cultivation of five cereals: wheat, rice, maize, barley and sorghum. This is supplemented by the cultivation of various other useful plants such as vegetables, fruit trees, coffee, sugar, rubber, cotton and tobacco. All of these tend to be grown in monocultures – tracts of land, often very large, given over to the sowing of a single species of plant.

The bits of plants that we eat are mainly the storage proteins that the plants lay down around their seeds for the purpose of feeding the developing plants of the next generation. Cereal crops generally give high yields of highly nutritious storage proteins but, in order to accomplish this, they drain the soil of essential nutrients, particularly nitrates. The corn fields of ancient Egypt were refertilized each year by silt from the flooding of the Nile. The farmers of medieval Europe fertilized their fields by crop rotation, allowing fields to lie fallow (uncultivated) for some of the time, and growing leguminous plants – lentils or peas – at other times. Leguminous plants can fix atmospheric nitrogen, and hence enrich the soil rather than deplete it, especially if they are ploughed back as 'green manure'. Modern farmers fertilize the soil with industrially produced nitrates, so that they can grow cereals year after year on the same land.

This heavy use of artificial fertilizers makes modern agriculture dependent on energy-expensive manufacturing processes. Planting and harvesting such vast fields as those found in Kansas or the Ukraine also requires expensive machinery. Further expensive effort has to be invested in keeping the fields free from other invading species (weeds) which would 'steal' nutrients from the crop, and in keeping the valuable storage proteins themselves free from the depredations of pests. Monoculture farming is not only convenient for us – it is convenient too for the specialist parasites and hungry insects which are ever ready to compete with us for our food.

Apart from the sheer cost of maintaining this kind of system, it works well only in the Earth's temperate zones. A large proportion of the world's population is concentrated in the tropics, but it is very difficult to produce cereal crops there by monoculture farming. The irregularity of the rainfall makes irrigation and drainage problematic, and the tropical heat hastens the decay of organic matter, which means that nutrients are quickly lost from the soil. Some kinds of crops can be grown efficiently in the tropics, because they are well

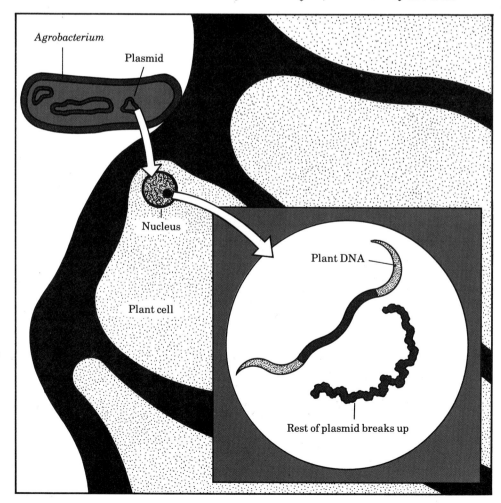

The bacterium *Agrobacterium tumefaciens* is a natural genetic engineer. By inserting some of its own genes into a plant's DNA, it turns the plant into a food factory. The genes to be transferred are on a plasmid, which the bacterium introduces into the nucleus of a plant cell. The affected cells become cancerous and start producing molecules known as opines, which the bacterium can break down into carbon, nitrogen and other substances it needs. Genetic engineers may be able to use *Agrobacterium* as a 'vector' for putting other genes into plants, such as genes giving resistance to disease or insects.

Agrobacterium

Plasmid

Nucleus

Plant cell

Plant DNA

Rest of plasmid breaks up

50

These tiny Rhizobium bacteria live in the root hair of leguminous plants and allow them to fix atmospheric nitrogen. This ability could be extended to other plants either by engineering other kinds of bacteria or by adding nitrogen-fixing genes to the plant's own DNA.

adapted to this kind of climatic regime, but they tend to be plants which can hardly form the solid basis of a staple diet: tea, coffee, rubber, tobacco or sugar.

We have already had one revolution in world agriculture: the recent so-called 'green revolution', brought about by the application of rigorous scientific method and determined effort to the production of high-yield hybrids. These specially bred hybrids were obtained by careful crossing of strains to accumulate desirable features. The 'green revolution' did boost the total world output of food, but mostly in the temperate zones. Third World nations did not benefit greatly, except insofar as the rich nations had a bigger surplus, some of which might reach them as aid. Even though some hybrids were adapted for growth in the tropics, most Third World farmers could not afford the supportive technology needed to use them.

For this reason, one of the most obvious challenges facing genetic engineers is to initiate a new agricultural revolution, which will not only increase the total world output of all crops, but will also allow the wider cultivation of staple crops in the tropics without requiring heavy initial capital investment. This is a very wide field of operation, and there are thousands of particular projects within it, but there is one which currently stands out above all others, and which is the focus of much research. This is the possibility of helping cereal crops to grow without the intensive use of artificial fertilizer, by providing them with some kind of biological system – inside or outside their roots – for fixing atmospheric nitrogen.

The fact that leguminous plants such as lentils and soybeans can fix atmospheric nitrogen is due to the presence in their roots of bacteria of the genus *Rhizobium*, which do the job for them, much as the

bacteria which live in the stomach of a cow perform the vital task of breaking down cellulose for the cow. There are various lines of approach which genetic engineers might take to the problem of allowing cereal crops to benefit from a similar arrangement. The simplest way would be to transplant the nitrogen-fixing genes from *Rhizobium* to another kind of bacterium, which already infests the roots of cereal crops but performs no useful function there. Unfortunately, this is actually not so very simple. It requires 17 genes to provide the whole biochemical apparatus for nitrogen fixation, and that is a very big package to transplant. Also, the nitrogen-fixing enzyme is easily de-activated by oxygen, so a gene for producing a protein which can mop up oxygen would have to be transplanted too – perhaps into another species of root bacterium.

Once we have better techniques for transforming plant cells, we can try to transplant nitrogen-fixing capability directly into the plants themselves. It is difficult to know when these techniques will be developed, but it is worth noting that it should be easier to transform plant gene-complexes than animal ones. For one thing, it is much easier to regenerate whole plants from cells grown in tissue-culture; and for another, there seem to be more promising vectors available for use with plants than there are for use with animals. In particular, there is a bacterium called *Agrobacterium tumefaciens* which has the interesting ability to insert its own plasmids into the gene complex of a plant, initiating a tumour. This bacterium could prove very useful as an agent of transformation. Unfortunately, *A. tumefaciens* will not infect cereal crops – but this is simply one more project for the genetic engineer to tackle.

Cereal crops which are given nitrogen-fixing capability, by whatever means, will probably yield less than cereal crops fed with artificial fertilizers. If they became hosts to nitrogen-fixing bacteria, they will have to provide sufficient nutrients to allow the bacteria to flourish; if they are given the ability to fix nitrogen themselves, they will have to use up some of their own energy in doing the job. The lower yields would have to be set against the greater convenience and lower cost of using them.

Apart from the nitrogen-fixing bacteria, there is another useful class of micro-organisms which associates with some of the plants we cultivate. These are thread-like soil fungi called mycorrhizae, which attach themselves to the roots of various kinds of plants. From their host plant they get nutrients which they cannot make themselves (because fungi cannot photosynthesize), but in return they act as an extension of the plant's root system, allowing the plant to take up water more effectively and also making available some kinds of soil compounds that the plant needs, including phosphates. Many trees can hardly grow at all unless they enter into a relationship with mycorrhizae, and these fungi are already of some importance in forestry.

There is scope for genetic engineers to operate here in supplying new mycorrhizae to crop plants that may benefit from them. Mycorrhizae can enable some plants to flourish in areas where the soil would otherwise be too poor in phosphates. The enhancement of the plant's capacity for gathering water may be crucial to the successful exploitation of dry areas, and this research might also provide a starting point for the job of reclaiming derelict land and bringing life to the world's deserts. Again, in the longer term such projects will probably be tackled by direct engineering of the plants themselves.

Other micro-organisms which help the plants on which they grow are ones which protect their hosts from other infections. *Pseudomonas* bacteria, which attach themselves to the root hairs of sugar beet, protect their territory by extracting iron from the soil, so that other micro-organisms are denied that essential trace element and hence cannot flourish. Bacteria such as *Bacillus popilliae* produce 'natural insecticides'. Some plants produce their own natural insecticides without the aid of bacteria, and great interest is being shown by genetic engineers in the genes which produce those compounds.

These is nothing new about the idea of using 'biological methods' to control pests. As long ago as 1762 the Indian Mynah bird was imported into Mauritius in order to control the red locust. Such strategies became common after 1888, when vedalia beetles imported from Australia saved the Californian citrus fruit industry from devastation by a fungal parasite. Recently there have been several successes with an ingenious method: very large numbers of a pest species have been reared in captivity, sterilized with radiation, and then released to mate with the wild individuals, whose fertility is thereby very much reduced. Another

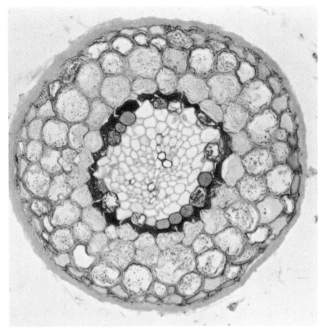

(**Above**) Many familiar trees and plants rely on small fungi such as mycorrhizae (one is seen here in cross-section) which supply them with water and phosphates in return for nutrients. Improved techniques of genetic engineering may provide an alternative to this symbiotic relationship by giving the plants the ability to extract these substances themselves.

(**Right**) This sheep-goat chimera was produced by combining one 8-cell sheep embryo with three 8-cell goat embryos. Its body contains a mixture of sheep and goat cells. It has a mixture of hairy and woolly areas in its coat, and goat-like horns twisted like sheep horns.

technique involves the use of synthetic pheromones (sex hormones) to attract pests into traps. Mass-production of an insect pheromone is something that might easily by done by plasmid engineering, once the pheromone-producing gene can be identified and transplanted. Genetic engineers might work, too, with bacteria capable of causing disease in pestilential insects.

Giving our crops genes for creating their own insecticides is one project which we will work on as soon as we are able to engineer plants directly, but there are numerous other projects which will quickly recommend themselves to the manipulators. Storage proteins, especially those laid down by cereal plants, are highly nutritious, and supply almost everything that human beings need to sustain themselves. 'Almost everything' is, however, not quite enough. Our nutritional requirements are quite complicated, and we generally need to eat bits of several different kinds of plant in order to have a 'balanced diet'. Partly this is because we have to take in small quantities of compounds which the body cannot synthesize – vitamins – but there is also the problem that to build human proteins we need amino acids in slightly different proportions from those contained in cereal proteins. One of the reasons that 'man does not live by bread alone' is that bread is rather short of the amino acid lysine.

Genetic engineering offers us the opportunity of altering the genes which code for plant storage proteins so as to make them more 'complete' as human foods. We might still prefer to eat lots of different things, but it would be convenient to have available a kind of genetically engineered 'manna' that could supply all our needs if it became necessary. A whole-diet crop might be very welcome to the subsistence farmers of the Third World.

As well as making our crop plants grow more nutritious food more abundantly, we will want to make them grow in places where they could not grow before, and we will want to make them so tough that they will never wither from disease or fall prey to our insect competitors. If we can transplant genes from one plant to another, ultimately achieving the power to design plants more or less at will, then all these ends can be attained.

ENGINEERING ANIMALS
Animal husbandry stands to benefit more than agriculture from the new advances in biotechnology. Breeding animals has always been more difficult than plant breeding. Most domestic animals take more than a year to grow to maturity, and the modern methods of hybridization which have produced the 'green revolution' in agriculture are more difficult to apply. Recent advances in techniques of interfering directly with the hereditary process have enabled us to improve the methods of selecting out the best domestic animals from each generation as breeding stock. By means of artificial insemination, a good bull can impregnate many more cows without actually moving away from his home base. The use of *in vitro* fertilization allows eggs to be selected as well as sperms, so that embryos derived from the eggs of one exceptional mother can now be implanted in the wombs of 'surrogate mothers'. Separation of the cells of early embryos allows the creation of genetically identical clones, so that the progeny of the best breeding crosses can be made even more numerous.

These new breeding techniques have helped us to improve our domestic stocks. But there is a strong incentive for us to look for ways of improving yields even further, because raising livestock has a kind of built-in inefficiency. Animals must be fed on plant

53

material, and only a percentage of the plant protein is eventually made available as animal protein. It is true that animals eat plant material that we could not eat ourselves, but that material still has to be grown on land that might, in principle, be used to grow crops, with a much higher yield of protein per acre than we get from cattle or sheep.

The variety of products we derive from animals helps to offset this disadvantage. We get leather from cows and wool from sheep. Some animal foods are highly nutritious and convenient, as well as highly palatable: eggs and milk are cardinal examples. Nevertheless, any gain in the efficiency with which a cow converts grass into milk, beef and leather is vitally important to the economic considerations which surround the decision as to whether we ought to grow wheat or raise cattle.

The obvious project in this area which recommends itself immediately for the consideration of genetic engineers is to improve the efficiency of digestion in cattle and sheep. Because these ruminants have their own 'built-in fermenters', where bacteria do the essential work of breaking down cellulose, it seems probable that genetic engineers might be able to improve this process by transforming the bacteria rather than the host animals – a much more practical project in terms of today's techniques.

The digestive process of ruminants is slow, and requires a good deal of co-operative work on the part of the host animals, such as chewing the cud. It is also rather energy wasteful – some of the breakdown products generated by the bacteria are gases which the host animal simply belches away. If these bacteria could be transformed so as to perform more efficiently, this could make a considerable difference to the rate at which beef cattle put on weight and dairy cattle produce milk. There is no reason in principle why cows and sheep should not be equipped to eat all kinds of organic material – plant wastes or even waste plastics – simply by transplanting into their gut bacteria the genes to produce the right enzymes.

A more straightforward approach to efficiency in meat production is to induce each animal to get fatter – to create more meat per animal. In the last 12 years or so this has been achieved by the addition to animal feed of synthetic growth hormones, such as anabolic steroids. This is a primitive form of biological engineering, using the body's own 'chemical messengers' to instruct the living machine to operate in a more convenient way. Plant growth hormones are similarly used to increase the size of fruits and to control their ripening.

Many people object to present-day factory farming techniques, designed to get the optimum yield from animals at the lowest possible cost. With genetic engineering we could design animals to be even more productive, and dispense with those parts of the body for which we have no use.

54

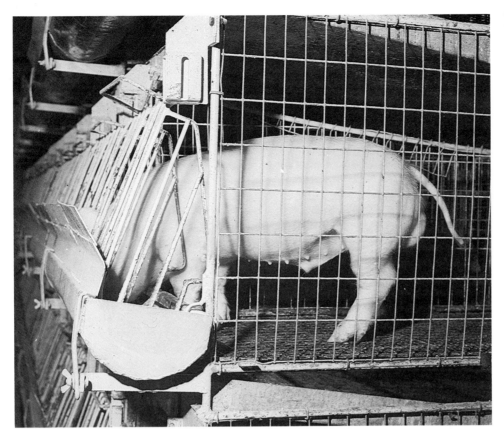

This pig farm in Belgium resembles a factory production line rather than the natural environment. The pigs are kept in small cages and given high concentrate feeds in order to increase their weight rapidly.

The natural rate at which animals grow is controlled by two hormone systems; one makes the animal put on weight, and the other inhibits growth. The balance between the two is controlled by the hind brain, and the synthetic growth hormones upset the balance to our advantage. The same effect can be gained by cancelling out the growth-inhibiting hormones. Genetically engineered bacteria have recently been used to make a substance which 'immunized' sheep against their own growth-inhibiting hormones, in much the same way that people can be immunized against virus diseases. The sheep grew larger than normal, again creating more meat.

Forcing an animal to put on weight very quickly has disadvantages as well as advantages. The strain of carrying around the extra weight may prove too much for young grazing animals. The intensive use of these methods is therefore associated with the trend towards factory farming, in which animals are kept virtually immobile in a confined space. Their food is pumped in at one end and their wastes are pumped away at the other. We are already familiar with such methods as they are applied to battery hens and to pigs, and they have recently been applied also to turkeys and even fish. In the future, all meat animals are likely to be kept in this fashion in order to maximize their efficiency.

The high productivity of factory farms could be increased even further by using genetic engineering to modify the structure of the animals. The project of making meat animals more productive by biological engineering offers much more scope than a similar attempt in plants. This is because when we eat animals, we are eating and digesting the actual structures of the animal's body. The bodily structures of plants are usually made out of indigestible material – cellulose – which passes straight through the gut (though it aids digestion by functioning as 'roughage'). It is only their storage proteins which we use as nourishment. There is a limit, therefore, to the ways in which plants can be modified to make them more productive.

To speak of animals 'putting on weight' in a general way is to some extent to blur the issue, because not all bits of an animal's body are equally palatable or useful. In principle, we would also like to control the particular tissues where weight is put on. Of course, most bits of an animal's body have some use – you only have to pull the teeth out of a pig's head and cut off its trotters before you grind it up to make sausagemeat – but for preference we want muscle rather than bone, hair or skin.

Genetic engineering could one day be used to make meat animals produce more muscle and less of the structures we do not need. If we can figure out how the growth of embryos is controlled, we might be able to engineer the forms of adult animals even without techniques of gene transplantation. It may very soon be possible to exercise much more power over the bodies of our domestic animals than we can at present by means of growth hormones, and the animals that would fit in perfectly with the demands of factory farming might not look much like the farm animals of yesteryear.

A hen which is being bred only for its meat has

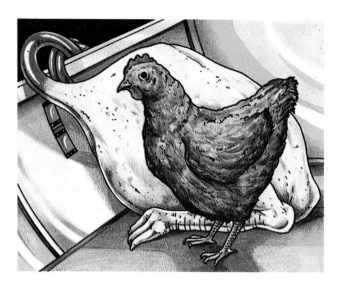

no need of feathers and no need of wings, and we might decide to stop such structures ever forming. We might leave its eyes and its beak so that it could remain active enough to pick up its own food, fed to it along a chute, but it might even become more convenient simply to pump the food directly into its throat, and dispense with most of the head too. A chicken bred to be eaten would not need sexual organs, so perhaps they too could be instructed not to develop. The perfect pig designed for the ultimate factory farm might well be instructed to develop without feet, without teeth, without eyes, and perhaps without anything much in the way of a brain. It would be, in effect, not a pig but a pork-making biological machine.

The rights of our domestic animals have not received much consideration in the past, but today there are pressure groups which have taken up their cause. As biotechnology gradually transforms animal husbandry, the fervour of their pleas is bound to increase. At present, the majority view – even if people do not think about it much – is that the benefits to humans of having cheap eggs and meat outweighs the cost to chickens and pigs of being reared in factory farms. In deciding whether to put the new techniques into practice, animal welfare will have to be taken into account as well as efficiency, but there is nothing described here which is not simply a logical extension of trends which have been well established for many years.

FURTHER HORIZONS
Most of the projects described have been ones on which work has already begun, or ones where a start might plausibly be made within the next generation. Many of them will surely be attempted, and perhaps brought to fruition, within the lifetime of people who are reading this book. There are, however, further horizons which warrant some consideration: things which we may one day achieve when we have a truly mature biotechnology to command.

The projects which we have considered so far all

involve tinkering with the genetic heritage of living organisms in order to enhance their usefulness to us. In some cases, at least, such tinkering raises moral questions about the propriety of ruthless exploitation of other species. Once we have a really comprehensive knowledge of how biochemical processes are organized and controlled, we should not need to deal with living organisms at all. We should be able to perfect a biological technology which produces food independently of plants, animals or micro-organisms.

56

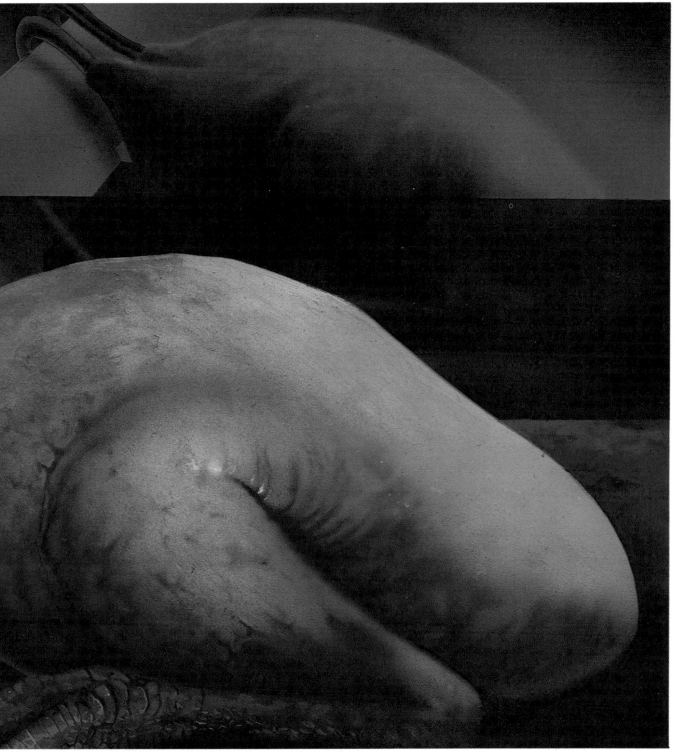

It has long been known that some tissues can be taken out of living organisms and grown in nutrient solutions. Such tissue-cultures are frequently used in laboratory experiments but have not been exploited as a means of producing food. For one thing, it is uneconomic to feed a tissue-culture by comparison with what it costs to rear animals; and for another, the cells in a tissue-culture will not continue to divide indefinitely – eventually they 'age' and die just like living organisms. For a while, scientists were optimistic about the prospect of

Whether they are being used to produce eggs or meat, the battery chickens of the future will look very different from the familiar birds of today. In battery conditions heads, wings and tails are not necessary, and with genetic engineering techniques we could design chickens without them. Nutrients would be pumped in and wastes pumped out through tubes connected to the body. Such redesigned chickens would form a perfect biological production line.

developing large-scale tissue-cultures that would produce beef and pork, but the idea is not so often mentioned nowadays. A sophisticated biotechnology would certainly give us the means to control the development and multiplication of specialized cells *in vitro*, and would therefore allow us to grow meat in tissue-culture.

Perhaps we could start such cultures from tissues extracted surgically from living animals, but even this might not be necessary. Once we understand the processes that govern the way that single, undifferentiated egg cells develop into complex structures of specialized cells, then we should be able to custom-design eggs to grow into any kind of structure we desire. Instead of requiring eggs to grow into complete organisms capable of independent life, we can make them develop into structures which are only marginally alive, and which certainly could not be regarded as conscious beings. We could produce pure muscle-tissue (steak without any trace of gristle or fat), or we could duplicate exactly the patterns and combinations of tissue that we find in the cuts of meat we are used to. If we wanted to, we could grow 'neck chops' of lamb on an infinite production line, with red meat and fat attached to an ever-elongating spine of bone. As long as all essential nutrients were supplied in a surrounding soup, we might be able to slice off chops at either end at the rate of several a minute, 24 hours a day.

There is no reason why, when we have the available biotechnology, the factory farms of the future should contain any animals at all. How long it will take to achieve this aim we can only guess, but it is entirely conceivable that the scientific knowledge we will need to allow us to go in for the tissue-culture production of meat on a grand scale will be gained within the next few decades. Domestic animals specially bred – and genetically engineered – as producers of meat could be displaced in the developed countries within the next century, if all goes well. That really would pave the way for animal liberation, and it is *only* by developing a sophisticated biotechnology that we will ever be in a position to liberate the animals we habitually exploit.

Plant species, too, might eventually become unnecessary, if we can design our own artificial photosynthetic systems. What we require of plants is that they should use their green leaves to intercept and trap sunlight, and then put some of the energy they trap into the production of things we can use. One day, we will be able to make our own artificial 'leaves' to trap solar energy, and these leaves will use *all* the energy they trap to make things for us to use: things to eat, materials for making clothes, materials for building and for making machines.

In the distant future we will not have to plant our fields and sow them with seeds. We might simply lay out something that would look like a great green shag-pile carpet, or make shallow lakes full of a translucent green solution. These devices would absorb and exploit the radiant energy falling upon them by day more efficiently than ever a field of wheat did, and would churn out products around their edges, according to our needs and whims. We would probably have similar systems installed on the roofs of our houses, and perhaps on the walls too. Perhaps, if our biological designers become clever enough, we can make such systems build and furnish our houses for us, so that even the machines we live in will become quasi-living systems.

It will probably take a long time to get such a technology off the ground, and it will undoubtedly take centuries to explore and develop its potentialities. There may be scope here to keep biotechnologists occupied for millennia. Artificial photosynthesis will be the real foundation stone of the future transformation of the world. It will bring Earth's energy input directly under our control, and it will allow us to exploit that energy as cleverly and as comprehensively as our ingenuity will allow.

It would be possible, given time, to banish all other life from the surface of the Earth, so that there would only be humans and their biotechnology left. We probably would not want to do this, though. We would probably wish to conserve as many as we can of the species which nature has produced. At present, natural species are becoming extinct with every year that passes, and the situation may well get worse before it gets better. The reason why this is happening is that there is at present a conflict of interest between our desire to conserve the natural environment and our need to feed the growing human population. That conflict can only be resolved by the development of a biotechnology so sophisticated that feeding ourselves and conserving land for other species become easy and compatible. Then, if we wish it, the whole Earth can become an Ark where every species known to man can be given a home – those which currently exist alongside mankind, and those which will be created in the future *by* mankind.

Chapter 4

The war against disease

A hundred years ago, everyone was involved in a perpetual lottery with the agents of death: catching and surviving diseases was largely a matter of luck and the strength of one's own constitution. There were many losers in the lottery, of all ages. Nowadays, the odds have swung so far in our favour that we tend to feel that we have a right to good health, and if it comes to the point where a doctor tells us that nothing can be done we feel betrayed.

This rapid progress of medical science has come about largely as a result of the advancement of organic chemistry. The more we have understood about the structure and properties of complex carbon compounds, the more insight we have gained into the kinds of chemical processes that go on in living tissue. As we have developed techniques for synthesizing new organic molecules, we have armed ourselves with a vast array of compounds that have the potential to be biologically active. Most of these compounds are useless or poisonous, but those we have found useful have given us considerable power over the health of human beings.

The most important steps in this pattern of progress are well known. The discovery of anaesthetics permitted the birth of modern surgery. Anaesthetics were followed by gentle pain-relieving drugs such as aspirin (analgesics), then by sleeping-pills, tranquillizers and anti-depressants – all of them relatively simple organic compounds newly synthesized by man. The most crucial breakthrough of all was the discovery of antibiotics in the 1920s. This new weapon minimized the threat from bacterial diseases such as pneumonia, tuberculosis and cholera which had previously ravaged human populations. We have also found new ways to affect and support the body's own defences against disease. We can now produce serums of various kinds which will make our bodies build up resistance to infections without having first to be laid low by them.

Consideration of the rapid progress of the last hundred years inevitably makes us optimistic about the next hundred. So far, there has been a big difference in complexity between the biologically active compounds we have been able to make in the laboratory and those which are inside the body. Most of the important structural and functional

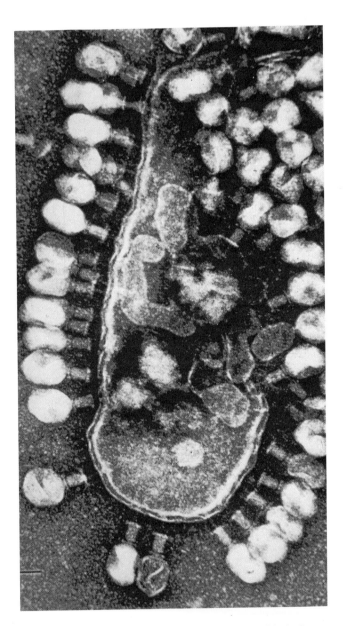

Biotechnology is providing us with many new ways of combating disease. Here, viruses called bacteriophages are attacking an *E. coli* bacterium which can cause disease in humans. Treatment with viruses, known as 'phage' therapy, may be a very useful alternative to antibiotics in dealing with bacterial infections – particularly those caused by strains of bacteria which have become resistant to antibiotics. Genetic engineers could design viruses to deal with specific infections.

molecules out of which we are made are proteins, and until the advent of the techniques of genetic engineering described in Chapter Two we had no way of manufacturing proteins easily and in bulk. Now the means are available, and it only remains for us to see what can be done in building up an entirely new pharmacopeia. There is no reason in principle why we should not be able to use such techniques to manufacture any and all of the proteins which are routinely made and used in human bodies; nor is there any reason why we should not go beyond that to manufacture all the proteins which exist anywhere in the biosphere, and all the potentially useful proteins which the processes of mutation and natural selection have not yet established within the biosphere.

It is astonishing that medical scientists have achieved so much in the past century with the limited tools at their disposal. The prospect of a new medical science based on a much more extensive understanding, and much more sophisticated techniques of control, of the actual chemistry of life is an exciting one. Medical science stands ready to be completely transformed by this revolution in biology. Medical applications will provide the main motivation for the development of particular techniques and the shaping of particular projects in which the techniques will be applied. The application of these new techniques may allow

medicine not only to catch up with our expectations of it, but actually to exceed them. One day it may even be realistic for us to demand as a right that we should always be in good health, and that any damage our bodies sustain can be efficiently repaired. Then medical science might be less concerned with protecting and repairing us than with improving on nature's endowment.

MICROBIAL INVADERS
Although vaccination and antibiotics have greatly helped in the fight against viruses and bacteria, there are many unsolved problems associated with them. For instance, a major problem with using antibiotics to fight bacteria on a large scale is that this subjects disease-causing bacteria to an extremely rigorous regime of natural selection. Every now and again a mutant bacterium appears which is resistant to a particular antibiotic, and it inevitably enjoys a tremendous advantage over its predecessor. The resistance can be transferred from one bacterium to another by plasmids, which means that it can spread very quickly. There are already

This monkey foetus was removed from its mother's womb to be tested for deficiencies and infections. It was then returned to the womb and born normally. This technique could enable life-saving surgery to be done on human babies before birth.

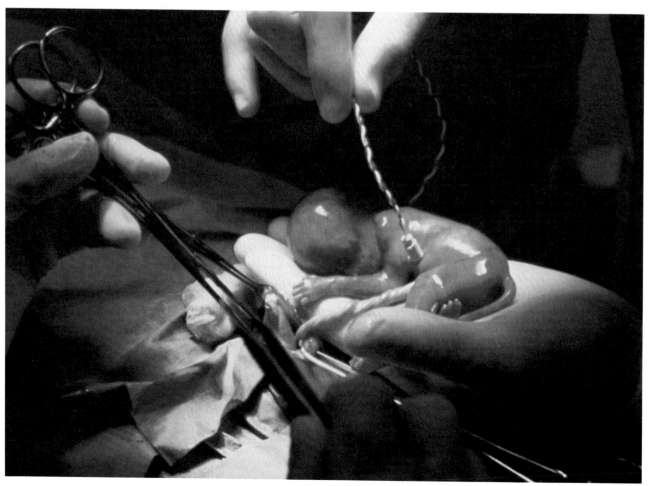

many penicillin-resistant bacteria. The problem was accentuated for some years by the practice of feeding antibiotics to domestic animals to keep them disease free. This turned our farms into a breeding-ground for resistant strains of bacteria. Nowadays, we deliberately give animals different antibiotics from those we use on people, so that resistant strains of bacteria produced in livestock will still be vulnerable to attack if they infect humans.

There are currently about 50 antibiotics in common use, some of them highly specific in destroying only a few types of bacteria, others much more general. At present, if a bacterial infection will not yield to the first antibiotic used against it, the second or third will surely get it. As time goes by, though, resistance to various antibiotics is bound to spread through bacterial populations. We will try to keep ahead by finding more and more new antibiotics, and will very probably do so. Whatever the biochemistry of the new bacterium is, there will be some way to disrupt it, but the job will never be quite finished.

A new approach to fighting bacteria has already been tried on animals. Bacteria have their own diseases, including viruses which attack them, known as bacteriophages. Strains of virus can be produced to attack specific disease-causing bacteria, and some success has resulted from treating stomach infections in animals induced by *E. coli* bacteria with 'phages' designed to attack the bacteria. There are problems in using this technique as a routine therapy for humans, but these will soon be overcome. For diseases where the requisite virus has not been evolved by nature, genetic engineers might turn their attention to designing such a virus.

Diseases caused by viruses are much more difficult to cope with than diseases caused by bacteria. Bacteria are whole organisms, each one with its own complete set of biochemical mechanisms for reproducing itself. Viruses, by contrast, are not whole organisms, and in order to reproduce themselves they ingeniously hijack the biochemical mechanisms of other living cells. This means that anything which will stop them will also stop the functioning of the tissues they infect.

A virus is a small packet of DNA (or sometimes RNA) enclosed in a protein envelope. The simplest viruses carry very few genes in their DNA, including one which codes for the protein of their coat. Sometimes the coat is made up of several proteins, or is surrounded by a membrane studded with other proteins. More complicated viruses may have up to 200 genes, and may produce many enzymes of their own as well as using those already existing in the cells of their hosts. Infection begins when a site on the surface of the virus binds to a 'receptor' on the surface of a cell. The virus pierces the cell membrane and injects its own DNA, causing the cell to make many new copies of the virus. The cell then bursts, releasing the new viruses, which go on to infect more cells.

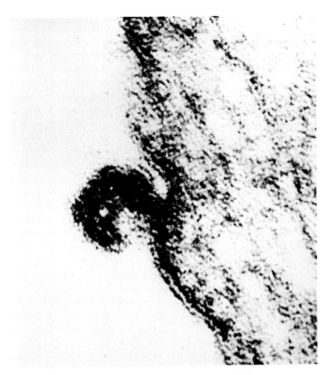

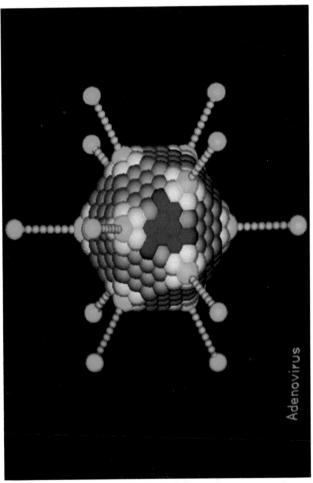

Adenovirus

(**Above**) This computer graphic image shows the complex proteins on the coat of an adenovirus.
(**Top**) An influenza virus attaches itself to the membrane of a cell before injecting its DNA (magnification: 4,000 times). The cell makes more copies of the virus and bursts, releasing them.

61

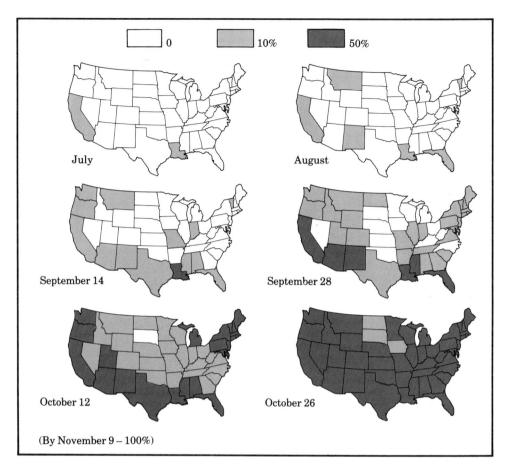

July

August

September 14

September 28

October 12

October 26

(By November 9 – 100%)

	0		10%		50%

The fast rate of mutation of viruses means that a strain sometimes appears to which no-one is immune. This series of maps shows the startling progress of Asian flu sweeping across America in the second half of 1957. The shading shows how the percentage of counties in each state reporting outbreaks of influenza increased as the weeks went by.

The body already has its own defence against infection, which can be effective against both viruses and bacteria – the immune system, controlled by the thymus gland. Foreign proteins, such as those in the outer membrane of a virus or bacterium, carry clusters of molecules known as antigens, which provoke the immune system into manufacturing antibodies. These are complicated molecules, made in the spleen and other organs of the lymphatic system, which attack foreign bodies by locking on to the antigen sites on their surface. Each antibody is precisely shaped so as to fit the antigen site at which it is 'aimed'. The locking action releases chemical signals which travel in the blood to other parts of the body, summoning cells which destroy or remove the invaders. In the case of viruses, the locking action stops the virus from attaching itself to the receptors on the host cells, thus neutralizing it.

The process is a complicated one, and tends to be a little slow in responding effectively to a new virus invasion. The first encounter with a virus may have devastating effects before the immune system can gain control. Second invasions are then usually impotent, which is why we usually only catch virus diseases once. In the past, medical technology has concentrated on attempts to induce immunity in people by making them form antibodies without subjecting them to the worst effects of the disease. This can sometimes be done by injecting them with a closely related but less dangerous virus – the

technique used by Jenner, who injected people with the cowpox virus to make them form antibodies which would protect them against smallpox. Nowadays we sometimes use an 'attenuated' virus, which is too weak to cause a bad illness but will nevertheless provoke antibody formation; or sometimes a dead virus will do.

Polio is an example of a serious virus disease which has been brought under control by mass immunization. Vaccination is also used against some bacterial diseases, such as diphtheria and tetanus. The poisons, or toxins, produced by the bacteria are proteins, and can therefore act as antigens. For vaccination, the toxin is treated to make it harmless, but it still provokes the formation of antibodies which will protect against the disease.

At the moment, the safety of a vaccine made to combat a virus cannot be guaranteed. Even an attenuated virus may mutate into a more dangerous form. Viruses used to make vaccines have to be grown in a living medium, such as cultured cells or fertilized eggs, and the medium may be contaminated, perhaps with another virus. For this reason, great interest is being shown in the production of 'synthetic vaccines'. Instead of containing whole viruses, they contain short protein chains, synthesized in the laboratory, that are the same as an antigen site on the virus's protein coat. The tiny protein chain alone can provoke the production of antibodies as well as, or better than, the whole virus. Besides promising safer vaccines, the very specific antibodies produced in this way are important investigative tools, especially in genetic engineering, where they help scientists discover what protein is produced by a particular gene.

However safe the vaccine can be made, some viral diseases are almost impossible to treat by vaccination, because the viruses occur in thousands of different variants, with many different kinds of protein coat. The viruses that cause influenza and the common cold are multifarious, and new mutants are appearing all the time. We make antibodies for the particular mutant we happen to have caught, but they are ineffective against other variants. Thus, the fact that we catch colds every year does not prevent us catching more colds in the future, and every now and again a new influenza virus appears, to which no-one is immune, and causes a great epidemic.

Another intractable problem is that once the virus gets to the wall of a cell, it tends to leave its coat outside; and once the DNA is free it is much more difficult to deal with, because the immune system is not very efficient at distinguishing viral DNA. DNA from a virus can sometimes remain within the body, occasionally being reactivated, even though there are antibodies on patrol to deal with its protein coat every time it puts it on. Thus, some diseases can become established within the body for ever, recurring at irregular intervals. This is the difficulty faced by sufferers in the recent epidemic of genital herpes.

IMPROVING OUR DEFENCES

A good deal of progress will undoubtedly be made in the fight against particularly troublesome viruses simply by using present techniques to study them closely. We need no new breakthroughs to enable us to do this kind of work – merely a good deal of care and patience in exploiting the knowledge and techniques we already have. The more we know about viral proteins and the enzymes that they make once inside host cells, the more chance we have of finding a point of vulnerability which will make them easier to attack.

One promising line of research is concerned with making antibodies outside the body instead of having to stimulate their production inside it. If we could have supplies of pure antibody ready to inject into the bloodstream of someone affected by a virus, this might at least help to alleviate the symptoms while the body musters its own resources. Antibodies are difficult to harvest from the blood of people or animals, simply because any particular individual will be producing so many different ones. Nor is it easy to grow antibody-producing cells in tissue-culture. It has been found possible, though, to

People with combined immune deficiency have no defences against infections, and would die if exposed to the outside world. They are therefore confined to the sterile atmosphere of a plastic isolation 'bubble'.

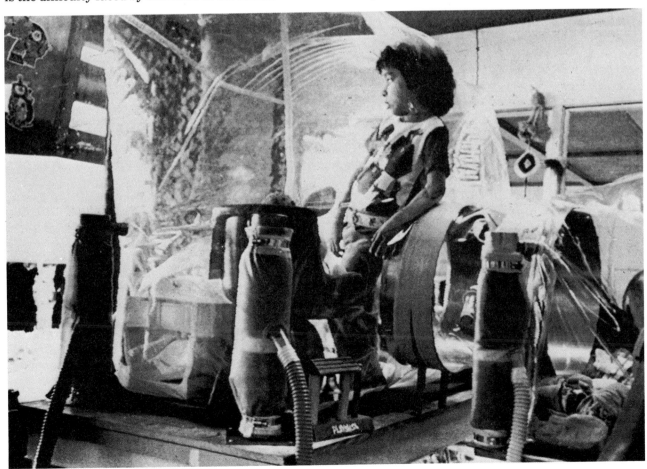

apply an ingenious kind of biological engineering to the problem.

There are ways of persuading two distinct cells to fuse into a single one. Cesar Milstein hit upon the idea of fusing a cell from the spleen, making the desired antibody, with a cancer cell, which has the capacity to keep on dividing. The new cell continues to reproduce itself, and produces a 'clone' of cells all making one kind of antibody. Antibodies produced in this way are called monoclonal antibodies. By developments of this technique, a specific antibody – one targeted on a particular antigen – can be made in any quantity.

Monoclonal antibodies have already found many uses in the new techniques of biological engineering. Their ability to lock on to a specific protein or part of a protein molecule is useful in purification processes, for instance in the purification of interferon made by genetically engineered bacteria. At one time it was thought that they could be used in the treatment of cancer, by making antibodies which would lock on to cancer cells, and attaching a lethal 'warhead' to the antibody such as an anti-cancer chemical or radiation. This has not proved as promising as it once seemed, but monoclonal antibodies are being used in diagnostic tests which might help in the early detection of cancer. They have also been used in an experimental treatment of bone marrow cancer, to attach tiny magnetic beads to the tumour cells in extracted bone marrow. The tumour cells could then be removed with magnets and the marrow returned to the patients.

A burgeoning technology is now devoted to finding new applications for monoclonal antibodies. This may eventually lead to the production of antibody serums that will help to counter the symptoms of many different diseases, including many virus diseases. It will not, however, solve all the problems of virus-induced disease. There will still be the same difficulty in keeping up with the rapid mutation of some kinds of virus, and it will still be the case that once the virus DNA gets into a host cell it is almost impossible to stop it hijacking the cell's manufacturing processes.

Another line of research, therefore, is concentrating on the attempt to develop defences which will enable cells to react generally against all virus invasions, rather than relying on an immune response to particular ones. Most of the interest in this line of research focuses on the class of compounds called interferons. Interferons were first identified in 1957 by Alick Isaacs and Jean Lindenmann, though it took some time for their results to be accepted by other workers. They are substances produced in minute quantities by cells, in reaction to viral or other infection, and have the effect (no one is quite sure how) of making the cells resistant to attack by other viruses. Because they

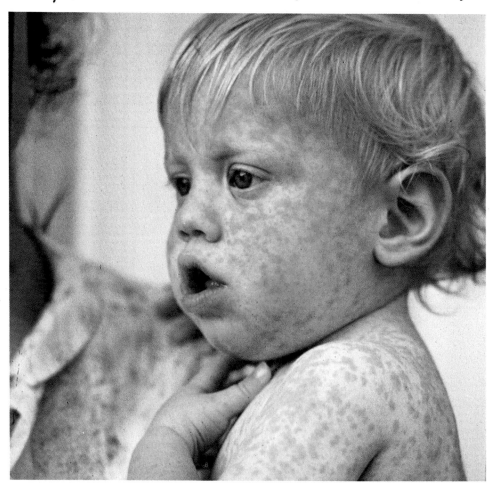

(**Right**) This baby has the familiar red spots of measles, one of the more common virus diseases. In many countries babies are vaccinated against this disease as a matter of course.

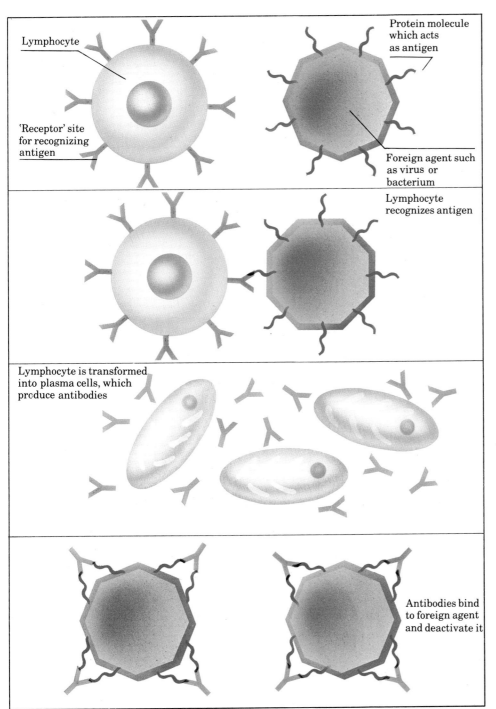

Lymphocyte

'Receptor' site for recognizing antigen

Protein molecule which acts as antigen

Foreign agent such as virus or bacterium

Lymphocyte recognizes antigen

Lymphocyte is transformed into plasma cells, which produce antibodies

Antibodies bind to foreign agent and deactivate it

Immunity

Cells called B-lymphocytes react to foreign molecules or 'antigens' by making antibodies. There are millions of lymphocytes patrolling the blood and lymph systems at any one time, each one designed to recognize a different antigen. If the antigen is encountered, the lymphocyte produces daughter cells which secrete antibodies to bind to that particular antigen and deactivate it. Antibodies can be made to protein molecules on the surface of viruses or bacteria, to bacterial toxins or to foreign body cells. Other lymphocytes, known as T-lymphocytes, do not produce antibodies but cause reactions such as the rejection of transplants.

are produced in such very tiny amounts and because only human interferons will operate in human cells, it was very difficult and enormously expensive to experiment with interferons until it became possible to manufacture them in bulk using cultures of bacteria with transplanted human genes.

Early experiments with interferons indicated that they could dramatically inhibit the growth of some cancers. More recently, attention has been partly diverted from that kind of application to the possibility of providing defences against types of virus which mutate rapidly, such as influenza and the common cold. At present we are still in an experimental phase because we do not yet know

exactly what interferons do, in biochemical terms, that allows them to have these potentially useful effects.

It would be nice to believe that interferons might prove very useful in our attempts to combat viruses and cancers, but there are some grounds for thinking that they may only be one more way of temporarily alleviating the symptoms of various illnesses. Our bodies already produce interferons: we already have the genes to provide this kind of defence. If successful defence against viruses were simply a matter of producing *more* interferons, one might expect our cells to do just that. (This is a very different situation from that involving antibiotics, which cannot be produced naturally by the body.)

It seems probable that interferons work by inhibiting the replication of DNA in cells, thus limiting cell division and the functioning of specialized cells. The net results of this will be good for the body when the inhibition is stopping cancers from growing, or stopping viral DNA from turning out vast numbers of copies of itself, but not when it is stopping the body's own cells from going on with their business. If this is the correct interpretation of what is happening, it is easy to see why cells are so discreet in their natural production of interferons: they are only able to hurt the invading virus DNA by hurting themselves as well.

This implies that if we are to use interferons to fight afflictions of the body we must be prepared to be discreet too. Obviously, if the body is threatened by death from a virus or a cancer, circumstances will justify setting all other priorities aside until the threat is alleviated, but in more commonplace circumstances it could be that interferons are simply too generally devastating to unleash. It might prove to be the case that using interferons against common cold viruses might be akin to amputating fingers to combat warts.

It seems unlikely at present that any of this research will lead to a 'penicillin for viruses' – a substance which will kill off a wide range of viruses soon after injection, in the same way as a shot of antibiotic will clear up a bacterial infection. But we can hope for more progress in making people immune to particular diseases, and better ways of handling the crises which develop when people do get the diseases. Thus, we may expect that in the future viruses will gradually lose their power to hurt and kill people. By finding out more about the immune system itself, we may also be able to improve its responses in areas where they are deficient.

Although the immune system is an instrument of great complexity and sensitivity, there are some circumstances in which it goes wrong or is ineffective. All cells in the human body carry various identification markers so that the immune system can recognize them and leave them alone. There are several 'auto-immune' diseases, including arthritis and (possibly) multiple sclerosis, in which the immune system begins attacking the body's own cells. On the other hand, if the body begins to manufacture the wrong proteins, or to produce cancer cells, the system sees the cells as 'self' instead of 'not-self', and leaves them alone. There are also difficulties connected with hypersensitivity, when the immune system over-reacts to invasion. The most common over-reactions are allergic reactions, when the presence of minute quantities of foreign proteins will provoke massive releases within the body of substances such as histamine.

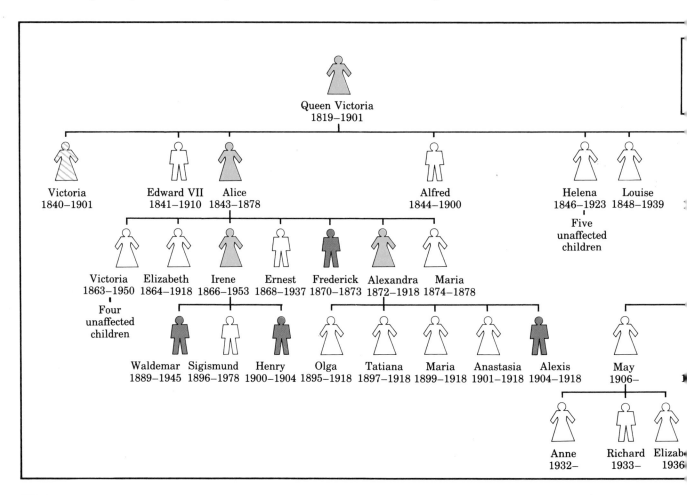

This usually causes symptoms such as rashes or hay fever, but in rare instances the over-reaction can be great enough to cause death.

The fundamental question underlying future research into improving the body's capacity to defend itself against viruses and other non-cellular invaders is whether the immune system can be made to react swiftly and unerringly against dangerous invasions – including viral DNA – while not interfering at all in the smooth functioning of the body's own tissues. At present it is hard to see how this kind of extremely fine tuning would be practical. The immune system is, however, a fairly recent invention in the evolutionary timescale. All vertebrates have such systems, but invertebrates do not. It is conceivable that the fallible system evolved by natural selection could one day be improved by future genetic engineers.

GENETIC FLAWS

Not all diseases are caused by invaders from outside the body. A good many are 'built-in flaws' caused by absent or faulty genes in the package that is passed on from parents to their children. If a gene coding for a really vital protein is missing, of course, it is unlikely that a child will ever be born. The egg which is missing the vital gene will not be able to develop even into an embryo. However, a missing or faulty gene can begin to hit a developing individual at more or less any time after conception. Some genetic deficiency diseases only begin to manifest themselves as adults grow old. Huntington's disease, which came briefly out of obscurity when it killed the singer Woody Guthrie, is a slow degenerative disease of the nervous system, with symptoms which rarely appear until late adulthood. On the other hand, Tay-Sachs disease, a disease of the central nervous system, usually kills children before they reach the age of seven. Sufferers from sickle-cell anaemia may not die until they are old, but they live all their lives with the handicap of inefficient blood which makes them perpetually weak.

Modern medicine has allowed some sufferers from genetic deficiency diseases to live more normal lives by supplying them with external sources of the protein which they cannot manufacture, or otherwise compensating for the effects of its lack. The prospect of curing people who suffer from this kind of disease by transforming cells in their bodies in order to enable them to produce the missing protein is obviously attractive. Martin Cline's unsuccessful attempt to work such a cure – described in Chapter Two – was undoubtedly premature, but there is a high probability that doctors will soon be able to succeed where he failed. The first genetic engineering of human beings will almost certainly be carried out in order to save them

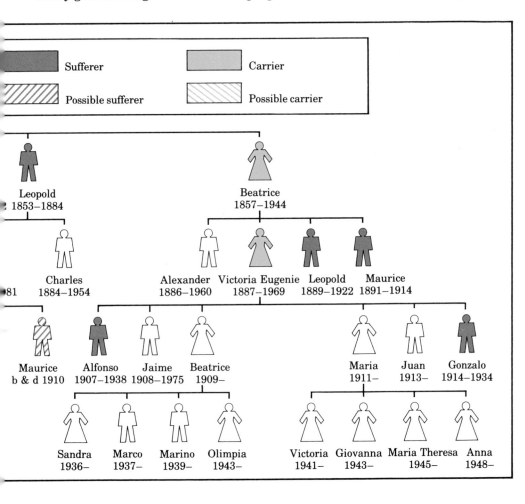

Sufferers from haemophilia lack the gene for making a vital blood-clotting protein called Factor VIII. The disease is hereditary and sex-linked: women can be carriers but usually it is men who suffer from it. A female haemophiliac would have to inherit the gene from both parents, and male haemophiliacs rarely survive long enough to have children of their own. Queen Victoria was a carrier, and passed on the disease to ten of her male descendants. Until recently, Factor VIII for treating haemophiliacs could only be obtained at great expense from donated blood. Genetically engineered Factor VIII has now been made and could eventually replace that derived from human blood plasma.

from dying because they lack important genes.

Scientists are now beginning to locate some of the genes that cause such deficiency diseases. With Huntington's disease, we are close to being able to use a process of 'genetic probing' – using small sections of DNA which will stick to the relevant gene – to test reliably whether or not someone has the gene. We still do not know how the gene causes the disease, but more accurate probes will allow us to work out the base sequence of the gene and take us nearer to discovering a treatment or cure. It should be possible soon to find tests for the presence of many other gene defects.

Only one person in a thousand suffers from an obvious genetic deficiency that is likely to prove imminently fatal, but that does not mean that the rest of us are perfect. Every single one of us is carrying around a hereditary package which contains flawed genes – even potentially lethal genes. The reason that we can carry these genes while remaining perfectly healthy is that we each have two full sets of genetic information: our chromosomes are paired. This arrangement allows individuals to get away with having one non-functional gene in each pair, because the functional partner will usually produce enough protein to keep the body adequately supplied.

Generally speaking, it is better to have two good genes than one, but it is relatively rare for one not to be enough. (The gene involved with Huntington's disease is one of the exceptions; one bad gene is enough to cause the disease.) Every individual gene package can therefore tolerate a few bad genes, and because of this bad genes are not entirely weeded out of the gene pool by natural selection. They persist, in hiding, so that two healthy parents who each carry the same bad gene without suffering any ill effects can occasionally produce children unlucky enough to inherit the bad gene from each parent.

The situation is further complicated by the fact there there are degrees of badness. Many mutant genes do not simply produce nothing at all, but produce different versions of the protein that they code for. In many instances the mutant protein is straightforwardly less efficient, but sometimes it can carry both costs and benefits. Sometimes there

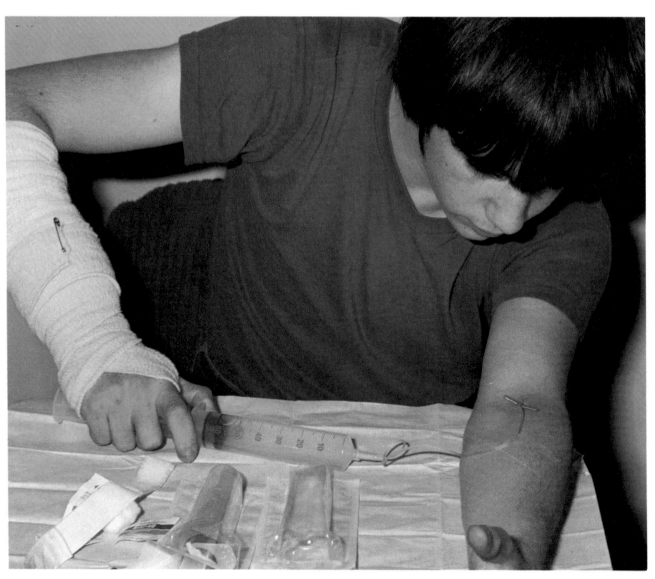

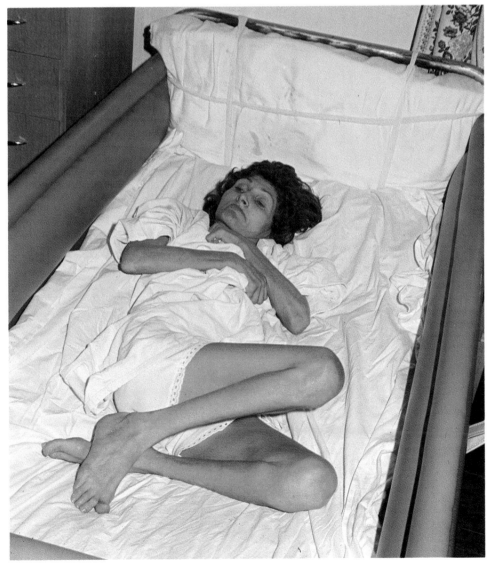

(Top) The characteristic sickle shape of red blood cells in sickle-cell anaemia. This inherited disease affects a high percentage of people of African or Indian origin, partly because it is linked with resistance to malaria.

(Bottom) This woman's weak, wasted limbs are caused by Huntington's disease, a debilitating genetic disease which strikes in early middle age. By this age the sufferer may have had children, who have a 50% chance of inheriting the disease.

(Left) Today haemophilia sufferers can inject themselves at home with the missing blood-clotting factor.

are even benefits attached to severely debilitating genes – thus, for instance, sickle-cell anaemia flourished in India because a side-effect of having one sickle-cell gene was a relatively high immunity to malaria.

Only today are we beginning to realize the subtlety of the effects that our genes have upon us. We now know that susceptibility to many diseases is subject to genetic influences, so that the presence or absence of certain genes may affect the probability of our dying of some particular cause without there being any direct determination. Possession of a particular gene may have a whole range of effects within the body which affect the pattern of its vulnerability without our being able to say simply that it is 'good' or 'bad'. It is because of this that we are seeing the growth of 'genetic counselling', in which examination of the patterns of death within several generations of a family tree can allow the risks faced by individuals to be assessed. People susceptible to certain kinds of illness can be advised to avoid the circumstances which might act as triggers. People can also be advised about the possible combinations of their genes that may emerge in their children with unfortunate consequences.

While new biotechnology may soon give us better ways of treating genetic deficiency diseases, the prospect of eliminating such diseases altogether is a very different matter. Even to eliminate straightforwardly lethal genes from the gene pool would require *every* fertilized human egg cell to be subjected to complicated genetic engineering techniques. This is hardly a likely prospect, even in the far future, though it will probably be technically possible to do it one day.

There is, however, another possibility. By engineering a few selected human egg cells, we could produce a population of 'genetically perfect' individuals who could preserve their perfection across the generations by marrying one another. This kind of possibility is one of those against which people tend to react strongly. We can certainly see the point of trying to eliminate some bad genes from a particular pool (whether it be the whole human gene pool or some specially protected enclave of it), but we become uncertain when we ask how far we should go. Even before we consider those genes which, in different variants, have different positive and negative effects, we will face awkward questions about how desirable it is to subject a whole population to genetic typecasting.

In the distant future, people may decide that it is, indeed, worthwhile to pursue some kind of genetic optimization programme for a special population of individuals. But they would be subject to the influence of mutation, just like the rest of us, so that mutant genes would reappear spontaneously among them. They would also probably be continually reabsorbed into the greater gene pool by marrying outside their own kind. It is unlikely,

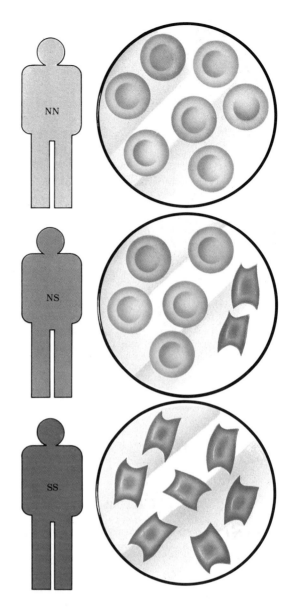

therefore, that any such new race of supermen and superwomen will displace their less-favoured cousins whose genetic packages remain slightly spoiled.

CANCER

Some diseases result from things that go wrong with the body's normal functioning. The most important kind of malfunction is cancer, which has become increasingly common as a cause of premature death now that infectious diseases are so rarely fatal. Cancer is still one of the most frightening of killing diseases. Statistics tell us that about one in four of us can expect to develop cancer and very probably die of it.

Cancer involves the unrestricted division of abnormal cells within the body's tissues. Tumours which begin in a specialized tissue may initially consist of cells which resemble those of the parent tissue, and they may even remain partly functional for a while, but eventually the tumour cells will take

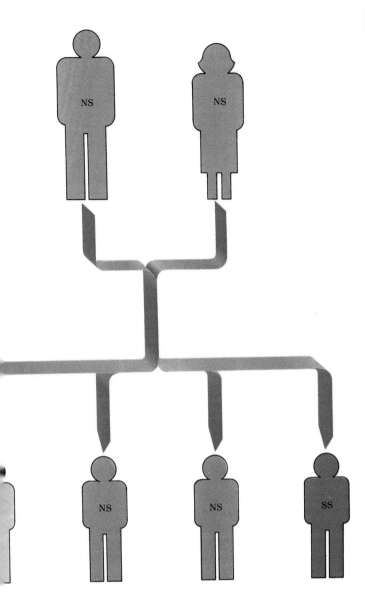

Sickle-cell anaemia
Sufferers from this disease have red blood cells which are inefficient at carrying oxygen. Their haemoglobin, the oxygen-carrying substance, is abnormal.
The disease is inherited through a single pair of genes. Here N is the normal gene, and S the sickle-cell gene. People who inherit two S genes usually die soon after birth. People who inherit just one S gene have the disease mildly, and can pass the gene on to their children. They also have increased resistance to malaria, possibly because malaria parasites cannot develop fully in sickle-shaped blood cells.

are associated with viruses, some with genetic factors. Injuries sustained by tissues can start cancers, and both the likelihood of developing cancer and the likelihood of recovering from it are affected by psychological factors.

Although cancer cells are abnormal, they are nevertheless the body's own cells, and hence tend not to be recognized as dangerous by the immune system. Sometimes the immune system appears to destroy tumours, as in cases of 'spontaneous remission', but it is not clear how it manages to respond. Some scientists believe that cancers are much more common than we think, but that most of them are obliterated by the immune system before detectable tumours develop. Much attention has recently been paid to the role played by personality and attitudes in the control of cancers, but until we know more about the biochemistry of spontaneous remission it is unsafe to conclude that people can really 'instruct' their immune systems to attack their cancers.

It seems logical to assume that cancers result from faults in the control mechanism which governs the differentiation of cells into particular types and the organization of those types into complex tissues. Presumably, something goes wrong with the 'switching mechanism' which instructs a specialized cell as to which of its genes are to be operational and how fast they should be working. Thus, a cell which should be performing some particular function and dividing fairly rarely suddenly begins dividing rapidly and stops being that particular type of cell. There are certain special genes implicated in cancer, called 'oncogenes', and it seems likely that some of these are related to the genes coding for proteins which regulate cell growth and specialization.

Until recently, all this was largely conjectural, but new discoveries have supported the hypothesis. It has now been found that one oncogene, already known to exist in a virus which causes cancer in animals, has the same base sequence as a gene coding for a protein called PDGF (platelet-derived growth factor), which is made by some cells – including human cells – to stimulate growth in certain tissues. PDGF is usually released by special blood cells called platelets, which use it to stimulate repair in damaged tissues, and perhaps on a more regular basis to facilitate normal cell replacement. Some human cancers begin when tissue cells begin producing their own PDGF, presumably because that gene – which would normally be inactivated

on a character of their own. Some tumours, generally called 'benign tumours', remain encapsulated within a membrane of connective tissue, isolated from the rest of the body, and although they may become a nuisance if they grow too large simply because of their bulk, they do not impair the working of the body. Malignant tumours, by contrast, are not imprisoned in this way. They gradually spread through a tissue, displacing functional cells, and may begin to eat into neighbouring tissues. Worse still, they may break up, shedding groups of cells which are carried through the body in the blood or lymph to start cancerous colonies elsewhere. This process is known as metastasis, and once a cancer has metastasized after this fashion it is completely beyond control.

Cancer is a condition, not a specific disease, and it has many different causes. Some chemicals are strongly carcinogenic, including many derivatives of coal tar, asbestos and various compounds in tobacco smoke. Radiation is also carcinogenic. Some cancers

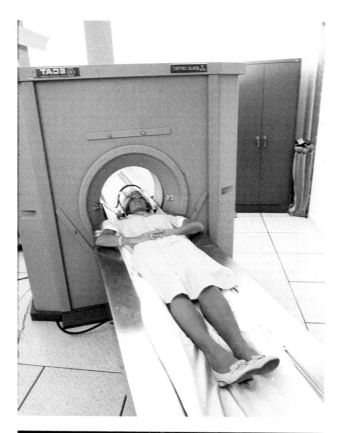

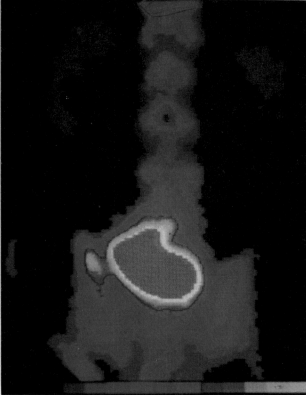

Techniques of detecting cancer in its early stages are improving rapidly. The PET scanner (**top**) can give detailed information, as seen in the scan (**above**) revealing a massive lesion in the sacrum caused by a tumour and secondary deposits. This type of scan involves placing radioactive substances in the body by inhaling or injecting them – a danger which the newest generation of scanners aims to avoid.

within them – has accidentally been switched on.

Other oncogenes may result when a gene coding for a protein connected with cell growth is changed slightly by a mutation, and produces a slightly different protein which makes the cell cancerous. In one known example – a gene implicated in bladder cancer – one single base change, the replacement of guanine by thymine at one place in the 5,000-base normal gene, is enough to turn the gene into an oncogene. In other cases, cancers are thought to be caused by the interaction of several oncogenes.

Some viruses apparently cause cancer because their DNA carries – along with genes to make particular enzymes – one or more 'viral promoter genes', which are genes instructing the cell's factory system when and where to start work. When the virus-DNA is taken up by the cell's DNA, these viral promoter genes occasionally switch on lengths of host-DNA which are normally inactivated. Mutations within the cellular DNA, especially mutations which involve the breakage of chromosomes or the relocation of DNA within a chromosome, might also move promoter genes next to genes which are normally deactivated. This is probably one of the reasons why radiation causes cancer.

This knowledge of how cancers begin is not yet complete, and there will undoubtedly be more discoveries made in the near future about what other oncogenes do and what kinds of chemical accidents within the cell cause tumours to start. How much more power this will give us to treat cancers successfully it is hard to say, but the new research seems to promise an explanation of how so many different agents can cause cancer, and to hold out hope that rational therapies based on knowledge of cancer's causation will become possible, instead of our present hit-or-miss methods.

At present there are several kinds of cancer treatment, but they all use the same strategy. The idea is to locate a tumour as early as possible in its development, before it has metastasized, and to obliterate it. Sometimes the tumour is excised by surgery. Sometimes the cancer cells are killed by radiation, or even by lasers. Sometimes it is necessary to use chemotherapy, which involves attacking the tumour with poisons that are somewhat more deadly to cancer cells than they are to normal cells. In all these methods, some healthy tissue gets destroyed along with the cancer. The idea is to kill off as little normal tissue as is compatible with the certainty of getting *all* the cancer cells. If any cancer cells remain, the tumour will simply start growing again; even if they are all dead, the patient still has to recover from the damage to the functioning tissues. Unfortunately, the trauma suffered by the tissue might itself become a factor in making a new tumour begin.

Given that this is at present our only strategy in fighting cancer, it is easy to see why metastasis is so dangerous. Once the cancer cells have begun to

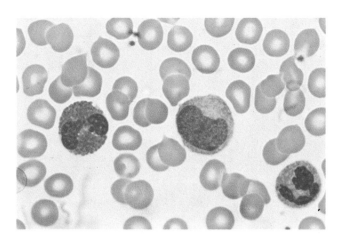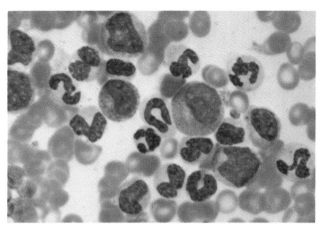

(**Above**) In leukaemia, a form of blood cancer, the shape of blood cells is drastically changed (right). Normal blood cells appear round (left). (**Below**) A patient receives radiation treatment for cancer. The cancerous cells are burned out by this process, but so are the surrounding cells. As with chemotherapy, the severe treatment may well kill the patient as well as the cancer. Scientists are working on ways of improving these crude techniques of combating cancer.

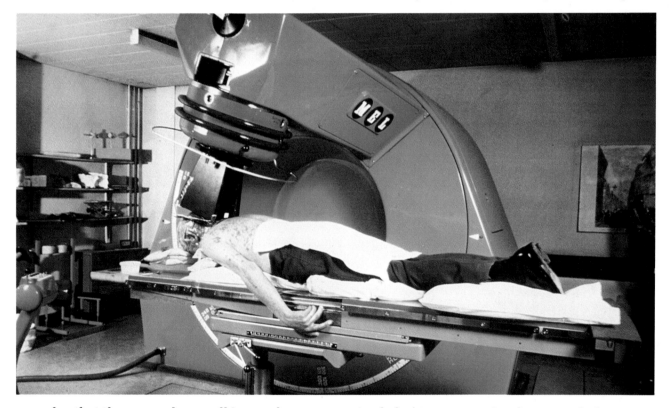

spread so that they are no longer all in one place only drastic chemotherapy can possibly destroy them, and the more drastic chemotherapy is the more likely it is that it will kill the patient as well as the cancer.

Present-day developments that are doing most to help fight cancer are those which help us to look inside the body to search for tumours. Body-scanners help us to spot tumours early, sometimes before painful symptoms actually develop, and they also allow tumours to be located without exploratory surgery, which may be very damaging in itself. The first generation of body-scanners were those which took X-ray cross-sections through the body, using computers to integrate an image from several different X-ray pictures. These CAT scanners (CAT stands for 'computer-assisted tomography') were replaced by PET scanners that used radiation emitted by substances inhaled or injected into the body. (PET stands for 'positron-emission tomography'.) They can give a cross-sectional image of metabolic activity in the tissues rather than simply a picture of the harder structures.

Shooting X-rays through the body, and injecting radioactive substances into it, are things which cannot be done lightly because they may themselves trigger the development of tumours. A new, safer body-scanner has now been developed called an NMR (nuclear magnetic resonance) scanner, which records magnetic fields set up inside the body when it is placed within a larger magnetic field. NMR scanners give better information than the scanners using radiation, and help doctors to distinguish between benign and malignant tumours and even possibly to determine the degree of malignancy. The time may come when everyone will subject themselves to regular body-scanning.

When we look to the future it is very difficult to believe that we could find a way of preventing tumours from ever getting started. Many cancers start from random accidents and there is probably no way to guard against such accidents. Perhaps genetic engineers in the far future could tackle the job of completely redesigning the chromosomal system so that it would not be so vulnerable to breakdown. If that were so, then a race of men very nearly free of the danger of cancer might ultimately be created. The more modest task of protecting ordinary people against cancer, though, is bound to occupy biological engineers for some time to come. There will be further refinement of our present techniques for destroying cancers while inflicting minimum damage on the healthy tissues that contain them. But hope for a really substantial breakthrough must rest on our finding out much more about the control mechanisms that switch genes on and off inside cells, and on discovering much more about the ways in which the immune system can be 'educated' into recognizing cancers as enemies and nipping them in the bud.

If there is cause to hope, it lies in the fact that many patients whose condition has seemed to doctors to be hopeless have actually recovered – or have survived much longer than expected. It seems that the body does have at least some resources of its own to draw upon in the fight against cancer, and if the resources are there our task is to learn how to use them. What we need is an intimate knowledge of what actually happens, at a biochemical level, in cases of spontaneous remission. Then, perhaps, we will be able to work the trick ourselves.

SELF-INFLICTED DISEASES
It would be wrong to consider the maintenance of good health entirely in terms of applying treatment to the body after something has gone wrong with it. Nowadays we recognize that good health is something that has to be carefully cultivated. It is not only new drugs and new surgical techniques that save lives but also a better diet, better sanitary conditions and more health education.

Diseases are very rarely self-inflicted in the direct sense. No-one deliberately injects himself with germs or carcinogens just for the hell of it. But the great majority of people in the developed world regularly take in poisons such as tobacco smoke or alcohol, knowing them to be dangerous. Smoking increases the likelihood of dying of lung cancer by a factor of four or five, and heavy drinkers are dramatically increasing the probability that their livers will eventually fail. Abundant recent work has suggested that people in those same countries prefer a diet which is far from being the most

healthy one. There is fairly solid evidence that we take in too much sugar, too much salt and too much fat, and that this greatly increases our chances of dying of heart disease of various kinds.

If people cannot be persuaded to give up these habits, there are several ways in which the new biotechnology might assist the situation. We might look to it to provide better ways of treating the various diseases that result from habitual self-abuse of this kind. The more control we can exercise from without over the metabolism of our bodies, the more power we will have to protect ourselves from the effects of a bad diet. As we find out more about the metabolism of fat, for instance, we might come up with a technique either for preventing the body from laying down excessive fatty deposits in its tissues or for helping it to get rid of such deposits once they are formed.

Another possible application of the new biotechnology is to control the taste of food, so that the most nutritious foods offer the most appealing experiences. The problem here is that individual people differ so widely in their preferences, but we can already see elementary steps being taken in this direction. Much effort has gone into the attempt to find a substitute for butter that will taste much the same without containing as much fat, and substitutes for sugar which retain the sweetness but not the calorific value. New products of this type come on to the market at regular intervals. We might also look for a compound which has the same intoxicating effect as alcohol without causing cirrhosis of the liver, or a better non-carcinogenic substitute for tobacco.

It will not be easy for food scientists to persuade us that the substitutes which they develop for harmful substances will really taste as good as or better than things we already like, but as their skills become more highly developed they will have increasing success. At present we are rightly suspicious of many of the things that are put into food to preserve it, to help it look nice, and to make it taste pleasant, but as biotechnology progresses it ought to be possible to achieve all the ends we think desirable without using compounds that have harmful side-effects. Another possibility is to work on ourselves instead of on the food. If there is a biochemical basis to our preference for some tastes, it might one day be possible to re-order our own taste preferences by genetic engineering so that, for instance, we find sugar less attractive.

A DISEASE-FREE WORLD?
Looking back at our achievements and hopes in dealing with different sorts of disease, we are forced to conclude that it is highly unlikely that the world of the future will be one where no one will ever be infected by a virus and no one will ever develop cancer. If it ever happens, this world certainly will not come into being in a matter of decades or centuries. It might be possible for genetic engineers

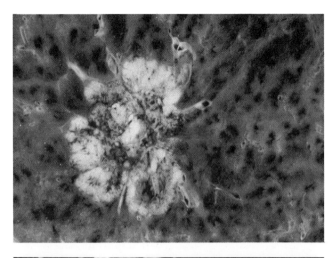

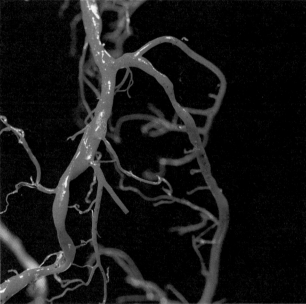

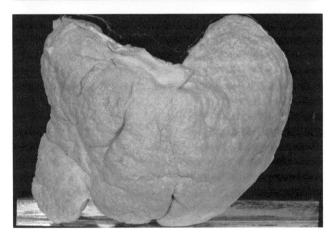

in the far future to produce a race of men immune to such invasions and failures of function, but they would probably have to redesign the immunity system and the cellular factories which make proteins to the instructions contained on our chromosomes. That kind of task could not be contemplated until our biotechnological skills were much more highly developed.

If, on the other hand, we are hoping for a world in which the vast majority of us can look after ourselves effectively – if we have the desire and the will power to do so – where any accidents of nature that do afflict us can be quickly controlled and where no one need be prematurely killed or crippled by disease, we have grounds for believing that progress in biotechnology will create such a situation at some stage. It will arrive more quickly in the developed countries than in the Third World, but there is room to speculate on the possibility that as medical biotechnology becomes more sophisticated, the financial cost of medical care might gradually be reduced.

The major hurdles which we have yet to jump are obvious enough. We need ways to combat the effects of viruses – to defend our own DNA against invading DNA – and we need ways to control the growth and spread of cancers – to be able to discipline our own DNA more rigorously. We already have a great asset in the body's existing defence mechanisms, particularly the immune system, and as we learn more and more about the ways in which these defences function the prospect of giving them a helping hand gets better all the time.

The advent of antibiotics encouraged people to think in terms of miracle drugs that could cure all manner of ills as though a magician were waving a biochemical wand; but this was naive. It is unlikely that we will ever be able to cure arthritis, the common cold, multiple sclerosis, heart disease or cancer simply by administering a single injection or a course of tablets. The problems are far too complicated to permit such a casual mode of response. Nevertheless, there will be techniques which will allow us to control the development of these diseases, and to ameliorate the suffering that they cause. Many people now living and suffering will undoubtedly find themselves losers in their particular races against time, but we can legitimately believe that with every year that passes the life-and-death lottery into which our children are born allows them better odds on success.

Many of the diseases we suffer from could be avoided if we were prepared to give up smoking and drinking and change our diet and lifestyle. (Top) A cross-section of the upper lobe of a smoker's lung, showing a cancerous growth 5cm across.
(Centre) Coronary arteries, some of which are blocked by deposits, often caused by a diet with a high fat content. Such blocking can cause heart attacks, paralysis and strokes. (Bottom) The liver of a chronic alcoholic patient. Typical signs of cirrhosis are present: the liver is shrunken, tawny in colour and covered with fine, regular nodules.

Chapter 5

Spare parts for people

Many of the most spectacular advances in modern medicine have been concerned with the development of 'spare part technologies': organ transplants, artificial organs and prosthetic limbs. The new biotechnology will almost certainly cause more sweeping changes in this kind of medicine than in the fight against disease.

The catalogue of our achievements so far in repairing damaged bodies is impressive. The methods by which surgeons can now restore function to broken arms or legs are wonderfully clever. Today's mechanical arms and legs, which are used to replace amputated limbs or limbs which never develop because of damage to an embryo, are very capable in comparison with artificial limbs of the past – wooden legs and hooks for hands. It is now possible to go inside the body to implant metal pins to strengthen long bones, plastic artificial joints and plastic heart valves.

We have not been so successful in compensating for the failure of major organs in the body. Severe damage to a vital organ may well be fatal unless medical teams can intervene quickly to provide a technological substitute for the injured organ's function. Nowadays we can quickly replace blood that is leaking away, and we have heart-lung

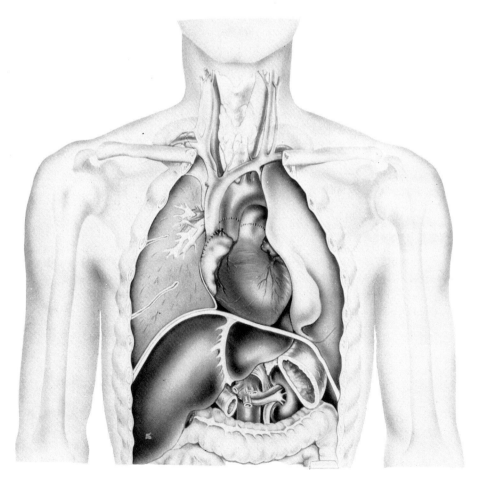

(**Opposite**) The donor heart is held above the open chest and measured for size in a heart transplant operation. The heart is trimmed and sewn in place (see over). (**This page**) A cutaway diagram shows the stitching joining the new heart to the main blood vessels.

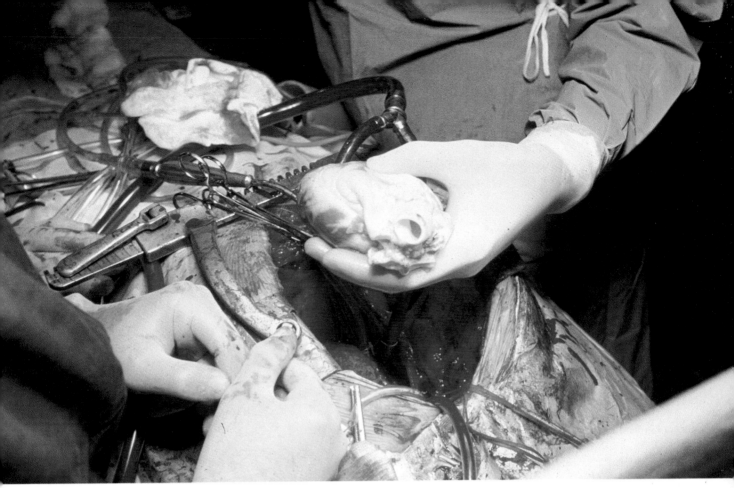

machines which will keep the blood circulating and supplied with oxygen. These are basically stopgap measures: at present, we have no permanent artificial substitute for the heart, the lungs, the liver or any major part of the digestive system. The artificial kidney developed by Willem Kolff during World War II remains our most impressive success. Modern kidney machines can keep people alive for long periods of time, although they are rather cumbersome to use.

Surgeons can now sometimes help patients needing new organs by using ones taken from other people. Kidney transplants have become almost routine, and there have been notable successes too in the grafting of skin and the transplanting of bone marrow. Skin for grafting is usually taken from another part of the patient's own body; bone marrow tissue can be taken from live donors without harming them. Hearts, lungs and livers have to be obtained from people who have just died.

Medical spare part technology seems at present to be at an awkward stage – we can see the scope of its possibilities, but its rewards are relatively meagre. However much admiration we feel for the surgical teams transplanting hearts, we can hardly avoid disappointment as we see so many operations fail, or succeed only in procuring a few more months of life for their beneficiaries. Inevitably, there is a heavy demand for a dramatic improvement in performance of these kinds of techniques.

Certain basic problems underlie the whole business of providing spare parts, which we must look to biotechnology to solve. In transplanting

organs, we face the problem of tissue compatibility – making the host body accept the new organ instead of rejecting it by a reaction of the immune system. We also face problems of securing an adequate supply of organs to be transplanted. If we are to make better mechanical systems which can duplicate the functions of particular parts of the body, ideally they should be as compact as the organs which they aspire to replace, and subject to control by electrical signals transmitted through nerves or by chemical signals carried in the blood by hormones.

There are good reasons for supposing that new biotechnology will be able to help us with all these difficulties. We will learn to achieve a better integration between biological systems and mechanical ones – so that, for instance, information collected by an electronic eye might be transmitted into and decoded by the brain, or a mechanical arm might be controlled directly by the brain. However, there is a sense in which neither the development of artificial organs nor the improvement of transplant surgery can be regarded as the ideal answer to the problem of repairing bodies. The best possible way to replace a damaged organ or limb would be to make the body grow a new one. The ultimate aim of this branch of medical technology must be to help the body to extend its powers of self-repair and regeneration. This, too, may be within the scope of future biotechnology.

ARTIFICIAL ORGANS
Some body parts are easy to replace, because the

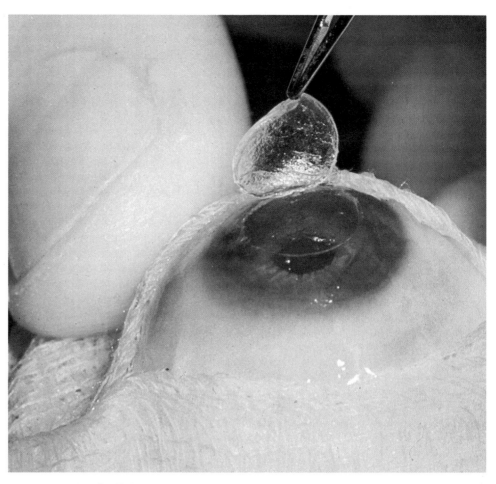

Corneas are among the organs that can now be transplanted successfully, due to improved techniques of tissue-typing. Every cell in the body carries complex 'markers' which can cause an immune reaction and rejection of the transplant. The markers of the donor and the recipient have to be matched as exactly as possible.

functions which they perform are very simple. False teeth have only to be the right shape, resistant to wear and firmly held in place. Artificial bones are difficult to insert in the right place, and they may have to be articulated with other bones at the joints, but otherwise their function is purely structural. Substituting a machine for an organ which is routinely active, such as the heart, is much more difficult.

At first glance, the heart seems to be simple enough as organs go. It is a four-chambered pump equipped with valves, which sends blood to the lungs and back so that carbon dioxide can be removed from it and oxygen taken in, and which then pumps oxygenated blood into the arterial system which will deliver it to the organs where oxygen is needed.

We already have mechanical substitutes for certain bits of the heart. Battery-operated pacemakers can be implanted under the skin to administer electric shocks that control the rate of the heartbeat, and they are now sophisticated enough to adjust the shocks to the needs of the heart, so that they only work when it starts to beat too fast or too slowly. Inserting a whole artificial heart is, however, fraught with problems.

First, the artificial heart must link up to the two sets of blood vessels that connect it on the one hand to the lungs and on the other hand to the rest of the body. Second, it is necessary that the walls of the artificial heart should not injure the delicate blood cells which are constantly being forced to surge through it. It is now possible to make reasonably good connections between blood vessels and plastic tubes, and the problem of damage to blood cells can be overcome. The problem that remains is putting the whole artificial heart into the chest cavity with its own power supply. Pacemakers can be powered by batteries because they only have to deliver a tiny electrical signal, but the amount of electrical power needed to keep something the size of a heart constantly in motion is considerable. Everyone who has ever owned a battery-operated toy knows how quickly the batteries run down.

Artificial hearts are used temporarily to assist patients in surgery, but these are devices outside the body which are powered simply by plugging them into the mains electricity supply. More recently developed artificial hearts place a simple pump in the chest cavity which is still powered by a unit outside the body. One patient in America agreed to have his own failing heart replaced by such a device, but he was so ill before the operation that he did not survive it more than a few months. One reason why an external power supply creates difficulties is that the point where the tubes go into the chest is extremely vulnerable to infection. The experimental animals on which these artificial hearts are tested can survive for several months, but generally succumb to multiple infections.

Willem Kolff, the father of modern artificial

78

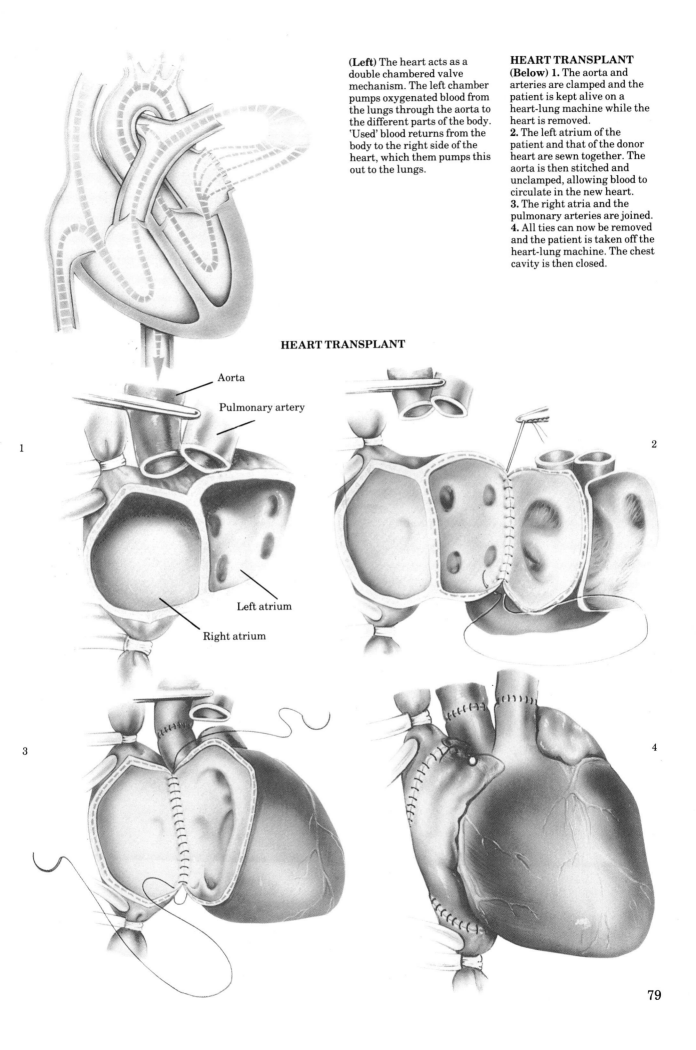

(Left) The heart acts as a double chambered valve mechanism. The left chamber pumps oxygenated blood from the lungs through the aorta to the different parts of the body. 'Used' blood returns from the body to the right side of the heart, which them pumps this out to the lungs.

HEART TRANSPLANT
(Below) 1. The aorta and arteries are clamped and the patient is kept alive on a heart-lung machine while the heart is removed.
2. The left atrium of the patient and that of the donor heart are sewn together. The aorta is then stitched and unclamped, allowing blood to circulate in the new heart.
3. The right atria and the pulmonary arteries are joined.
4. All ties can now be removed and the patient is taken off the heart-lung machine. The chest cavity is then closed.

HEART TRANSPLANT

Aorta

Pulmonary artery

1

2

Left atrium

Right atrium

3

4

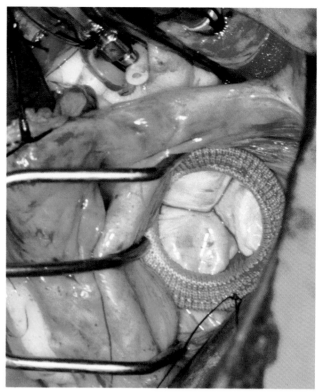

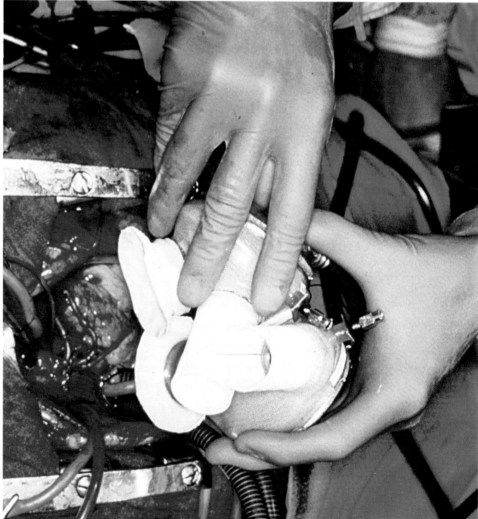

Faulty hearts can be aided or
even replaced with mechanical
devices. **(Above left)** This
valve can be inserted **(above
right)** to replace the heart's
own faulty valves. A complete
artificial heart **(right)** can be
implanted in the body. These
devices are still at an
experimental stage. The main
problem is infection, since they
have to be connected to an
external power source through
a permanent breach in the
chest wall.

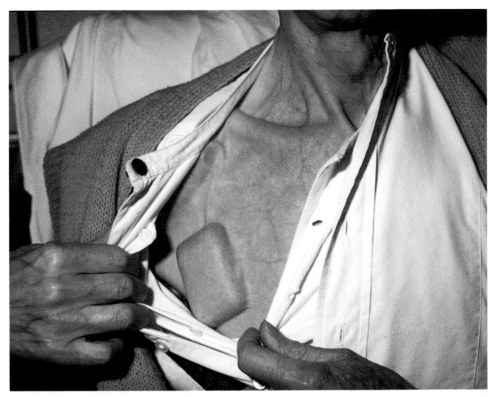

Probably the most common spare part is the pacemaker which regulates the beat of the heart by tiny electric shocks. A control device is inserted beneath the skin. A pacemaker can be severely damaged by external electronic impulses such as those emitted by anti-theft devices in stores.

organs, once suggested that the only plausible way to put the power supply inside the patient was to give him a tiny nuclear engine, in which the energy required to drive the heart would be supplied by decaying plutonium. Experiments have been done with a prototype which showed that only a direct hit with a bullet broke open the casing, but not many people would want such a powerfully radioactive substance inside them, and others might be reluctant to live in close proximity to such a person. People with plutonium-powered hearts would also be ready-made kidnap victims for terrorists wanting to get their hands on a useful weapon.

In the immediate future we will probably see more experiments with externally powered artificial hearts, and these may succeed within their limitations once the problem of infection has been tackled. If people are ever to walk around with artificial hearts inside them, though, one of two innovations must be devised. The more likely innovation would be a battery-powered artificial heart whose battery could be recharged at regular intervals from the mains. This would involve giving the patient a permanent socket in his chest where he could plug in. Here, too, steps would have to be taken to alleviate the constant threat of infection at the site of the socket. The better innovation would be a 'biological motor' which would use the same energy supply as a real heart – the energy of the body's own metabolism. There is no reason why we should not ultimately develop such energy-producing and energy-using systems as we gradually learn more and more about building our own organic artifacts, but it is probable that we would not be able to consider this as a practical

project for a very long time. What we would effectively be doing would be not so much *making* a new heart as *growing* a new heart, and if we could do that we would probably find it more convenient (and perhaps simpler) to make one grow inside the body, from its own tissues, rather than grow one outside that we could then patch in.

The problems associated with the development of other artificial organs are much the same as those associated with the heart. External kidney machines now pose few problems in use. Patients are plugged into a dialysis machine for several hours at a time, about twice a week, while all their blood is circulated through the machine so that its waste products can be removed. Because connection to the body is a relatively simple matter of inserting sterile hollow needles into blood vessels, the dangers of opening potential channels of infection are minimal. Although some patients have been fitted with their own 'sockets' (not electrical sockets in this case, of course) to enable them to plug themselves into their kidney machines more easily, this is really unnecessary. Some patients now keep their dialysis machines at home and need hardly any assistance to use them. A new kind of dialysis machine is beginning to come into use which provides what is known as 'continuous ambulatory peritoneal dialysis' (CAPD for short). Here the patient remains permanently plugged into the machine, which is small enough to allow him to walk about. The logical next step is to make artificial kidneys that are small enough to go inside the body, and to find some way of powering them; but here the real difficulties begin for precisely the reasons discussed in connection with putting

81

artificial hearts inside the body.

BIOSENSORS

Organs whose function includes the supply of a particular chemical compound, such as the pancreas, pose a different problem. An artificial organ would have to be equipped with the appropriate 'biosensor' – a device which can monitor the body's need for the compound and control the release in accordance with it. Such biosensors are now being developed, and could bring into existence a new generation of artificial organs. For instance, some research has been devoted to constructing an 'artificial pancreas' for diabetics. It is easy enough to insert plastic bags full of insulin into the body, and not too difficult to enclose them in some inert substance which will stop the body from reacting adversely to their presence, but it is not easy to regulate the release of insulin from such implants so as to meet the body's requirement for it. Scientists at the Cranfield Institute of Technology in America have recently developed a biosensor for measuring blood sugar level, and it is hoped eventually to integrate this into a device which could release an appropriate flow of insulin into the bloodstream of a diabetic patient.

An artificial heart might use a biosensor to tell it when to beat faster because an increased oxygen supply is required. Biosensors are already being incorporated into control devices for heart pacemakers. A model soon to be produced can respond to levels of adrenalin – the chemical that makes the heart beat faster when we are frightened. The next generation of sensors will respond accurately to changing levels of chemicals in the heart's muscle, adapting the signals from the pacemaker to the needs of the heart as it changes with different physiological conditions.

Another field in which intensive research is going on involves attempts to make artificial sense organs. Here, too, there are problems in establishing 'communicative links' between the body and the artificial organ. The brain's millions of nerve cells, or neurons, communicate by a combination of chemicals and electricity: an electrical signal in one neuron is passed on to the next neuron by transmitter chemicals which cross the tiny gap, or 'synapse', between them. In the future it may be possible to make biosensors that will be implanted in the brain, creating a chemical pathway for communication from the outside. This technology might be used to connect the brains of blind or deaf people to artificial eyes or ears, or it might one day become possible to link the brain directly to a computer to gain access to information. At present, artificial sense organs rely on stimulating the brain electrically – the signals carried in metal wires are transmitted to living nerve cells across a metallic/organic synapse.

It has always been very difficult to make such junctions between electronic devices and nerve cells, because our electronic devices have always been very crude by comparison with nature's electrically active systems. Until very recently the thinnest wires we could make were many times thicker than nerve threads. Now we are making such rapid progress in micro-miniaturization, it is becoming feasible to create such metallic/organic synapses

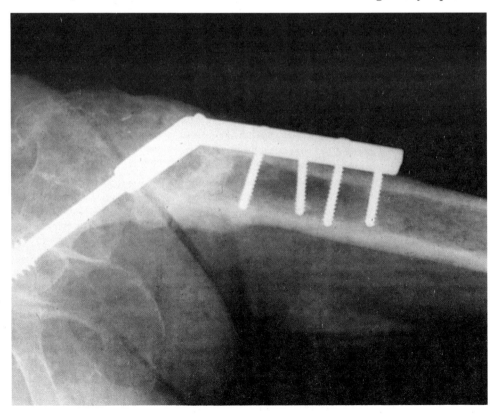

Joints which have degenerated through disease can now be replaced by artificial ones, as in this X-ray showing a replacement shoulder joint. Artificial joints are at present made from polyethylene (a nylon compound) and titanium (an aluminium alloy) cemented to existing bone with acrylic glue. Future improvements may include better materials for the bearing surfaces, and attachments to the skeleton by using electromagnetic stimulation to encourage bone growth.

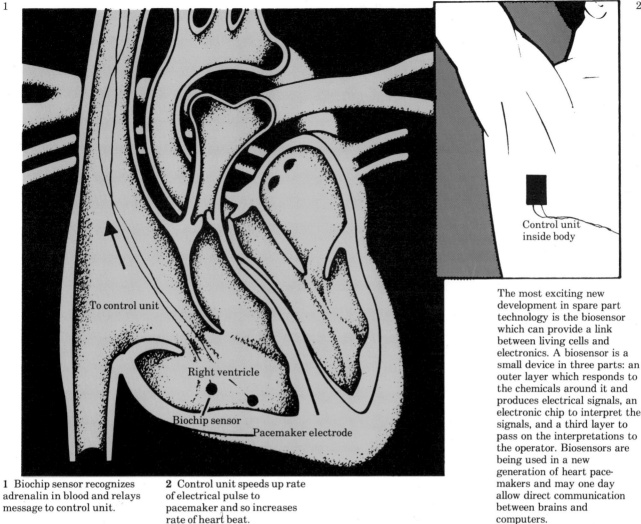

To control unit

Right ventricle

Biochip sensor

Pacemaker electrode

Control unit
inside body

1 Biochip sensor recognizes adrenalin in blood and relays message to control unit.

2 Control unit speeds up rate of electrical pulse to pacemaker and so increases rate of heart beat.

The most exciting new development in spare part technology is the biosensor which can provide a link between living cells and electronics. A biosensor is a small device in three parts: an outer layer which responds to the chemicals around it and produces electrical signals, an electronic chip to interpret the signals, and a third layer to pass on the interpretations to the operator. Biosensors are being used in a new generation of heart pace-makers and may one day allow direct communication between brains and computers.

and to hope that we can feed information into living nerves in a form which will allow the brain to decode it. Teams of researchers in America and Australia have developed artificial 'ears' whose task is to receive sounds through a microphone, convert the sounds into electrical signals, then transmit those signals via the auditory nerve to the brain. The Australian version of the artificial ear at present has an array of 22 electrodes making contact with the auditory nerve. This is impressive, but still very crude by comparison with the 30,000 nerve fibres that nature provides. The artificial ear is still a long way from providing a substitute for a real working ear, but it does open up a channel of auditory communication between the brain and the outside world which can carry *some* information.

Attempts have also been made to give blind people artificial eyes which can relay information to the optic nerve in much the same fashion. Electrodes are passed through the skull and implanted in the optic nerve – a process which causes no pain. Again, the discrepancy between the number of electrodes in an artificial eye and the number of nerve endings in a real one is very great, but it does allow a channel of communication to be opened. Patients with

artificial eyes cannot yet see as ordinary people do, but they can perceive flashes of light, known as phosphenes, and can 'read' signals transmitted by manipulating the phosphenes. Some researchers in America have managed to transmit Braille patterns in this way, so that blind people can read with their optic nerve instead of their fingers. The advantage is that they can do it very much faster.

Artificial synapses are not only required to carry information into the brain from artificial sense organs; they are also required to carry information *from* the brain to artificial arms and legs. This is the main limitation on the development of prosthetic limbs. Because artificial limbs are fairly large, and worn externally, it is easy to give them their own power supplies – usually rechargeable electric batteries. Contemporary engineers are sufficiently competent to design artificial hands that will grip, and artificial legs that will make all the movements necessary for walking (or even running). The big problem is that the person wearing the prosthetic limb must have some way of telling it what he wants it to do. Ideally, the means of instruction should be so efficient that he can move the limb without having to think about it.

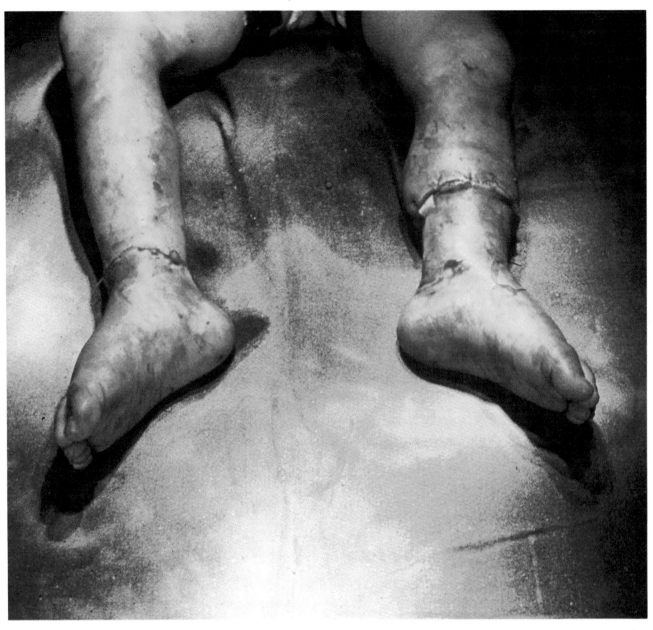

This Russian girl had both her feet cut off in an accident. **(Above)** The feet are stitched back on by techniques of microsurgery. **(Right)** She takes her first steps on the rejoined limbs.

At present, some patients can be given more able artificial limbs than others, if, for instance, they have vestigial limbs which, although no good for gripping or walking, can be controlled well enough to manipulate a control system in the prosthetic limb. Some present-day systems make the limb responsive to twitches in the muscles. The twitch of the muscle causes an electrical impulse which is picked up and amplified, then used to control the limb. People with artificial limbs are becoming more and more competent: TV broadcasts periodically bring us pictures of a boy with an artificial leg playing football, or a boy with an artificial arm playing snooker. These items are testimony to the rapidity with which progress is being made.

With the advent of computers, a new branch of spare part technology has opened up which aims to replace some of the functions of damaged nerves. The artificial eyes and ears mentioned above use computers to translate the incoming information into signals that can be interpreted by the recipient. The latest artificial limbs now have an inbuilt microcomputer to interpret whatever movements are available and use them to control the limb.

Ideally, though, it would be better to be able to link the control systems inside prosthetic limbs directly to the nervous systems of the bodies to which they are attached, so that the brain could instruct the limb automatically. Recent research is directed towards implanting a device under the skin which would pick up signals coming from the brain and transmit them to the control mechanism of the limb. The biosensor will have a role to play here too. The perfecting of such connections between a mechanical device and organic nerve cells is basically a technical problem. The challenge is one for our bioengineers to meet, and eventually they will succeed, through ingenuity and artistry.

TRANSPLANTS

While it remains impractical to supply artificial substitutes for damaged organs, medical scientists are making every effort to improve techniques for using nature's own spare parts. Many people who die prematurely – especially those killed by head injuries in road accidents – have organs which are in perfectly good working order. It is sound, if somewhat macabre, economics to try to make use of such organs by giving them to people who need them.

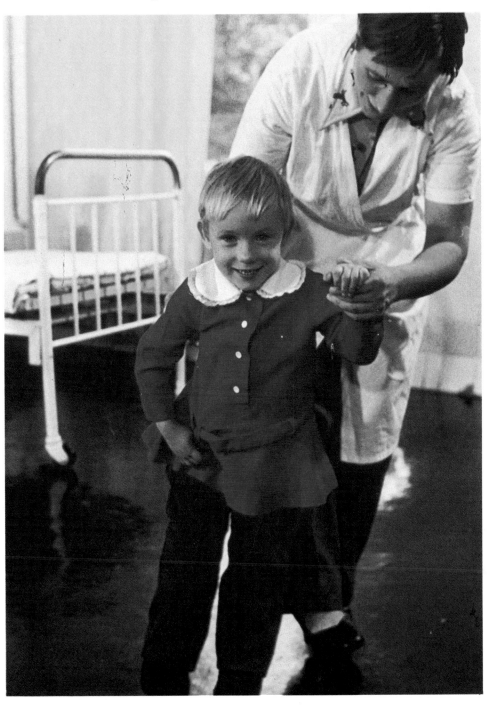

The big problem which transplant surgeons have to overcome is the fact that their patients' immune systems tend to react against transplanted organs in much the same way as they react against invading bacteria. Surgeons are now very skilled at connecting up the new organ to the relevant structures in the host body, but such connections may be easily broken again as the patient rejects the transplanted tissue.

The first successful kidney transplant, in 1954, was carried out in special circumstances which allowed this problem to be sidestepped. The kidney is a paired organ, although the body can in fact get by with only one, and the patient in need of the transplant had a genetically identical twin brother, who volunteered to surrender one of his own kidneys. Because of the genetic identity, the transplanted kidney was not deemed alien by the recipient's immune system and was accepted without difficulty.

In the early days of heart transplants, when Christiaan Barnard was doing such operations in South Africa in 1967–68, he tried to cope with the problem of rejection by using drugs that suppressed the activity of the immune system. This allowed the transplanted hearts to be accepted, but rendered the patients highly vulnerable to other infections. Barnard's first heart transplant patient died of double pneumonia after 18 days.

Things have improved dramatically over the last 15 years because of sophisticated techniques of tissue-typing. In order that the immune system can distinguish the body's own cells from invading cells, every cell carries a set of identification markers.

There are four series of these 'histocompatibility' markers, each one of which exists in up to 40 different variants. If transplanted tissue has a set of markers similar to those of the recipient, there is a much greater probability that it will be safe from attack.

Hospitals now keep a record of the pattern of markers on the cells of each kidney patient, so that when a kidney becomes available it can be checked against a central record to find which of thousands of potential recipients would be least likely to reject it. These computer-held central records are now being extended internationally. We have already become used to the idea of conducting a worldwide search for a potential donor when a child is in need of a bone marrow transplant. Because bone marrow can be taken from live donors, anyone whose tissue-type has ever been recorded can be matched against the patient for compatibility. It may soon be the case that we will all be asked to have a record of our own tissue-type placed on file.

Tissue-typing has allowed kidney transplants to become common and has helped other such operations, including transplants of the corneas of the eyes which can restore sight to some blind people. Heart transplants carried out nowadays are much more successful, and often give the recipients years of extra life instead of mere weeks. In Britain and America there are now heart transplant

Complex tasks such as carpentry or drawing are possible with today's artificial arms and hands. The most advanced prosthetic limbs are controlled by tiny electrical impulses in the muscles. Future artificial limbs might be linked directly to the nerves.

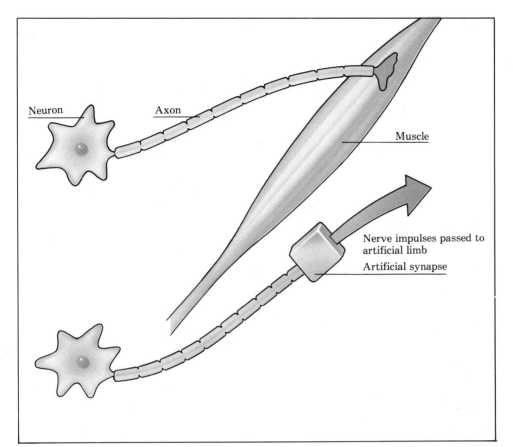

To move a muscle, a neuron sends an electrical signal along its axon to the muscle tissue. With an artificial organo-metallic synapse, it will be possible for a prosthetic limb to be controlled directly by nerve impulses coming from the brain.

patients who have been released from hospital to resume their normal lives in the community.

Unfortunately, due to the complexity of the histocompatibility markers mentioned above, tissue-typing has not solved all the problems of rejection, and immuno-suppressive drugs still have to be used in many cases. Even with these techniques, some transplanted organs, such as pancreases, are usually rejected. Biotechnology may be able to help here with further applications of our new ability to produce specific antibodies outside the body – the monoclonal antibodies described in Chapter Four. Researchers at the Washington University School of Medicine have developed a technique for transplanting the insulin-producing islets of Langerhans from the pancreas without causing rejection. They use antibodies to destroy the particular cells in the pancreas that spark off the rejection. They have been successful with mice, and a treatment for human diabetics will soon be tested. Bone marrow transplants may soon become easier with a similar method.

The one part of the body which is not subject to normal immune reactions is the brain. 'Transplanting' a whole brain will probably never become practicable – it would mean severing all the major nerves and therefore complete paralysis of the body. It will not be feasible, either, to transfer memories or aspects of the personality by transplanting parts of the brain. Grafting of small amounts of brain tissue has, however, been performed in animal experiments for many years,

and recently a medical application has begun to seem a possibility.

There are several diseases which appear to be caused by loss of function in brain cells. Parkinson's disease, a disorder of movement from which many old people suffer, is caused because brain cells no longer produce enough of a compound called dopamine. A drug called L-Dopa is given to patients with Parkinson's disease, which the body converts into dopamine, but its level does not correspond to the needs of the brain; the treatment is only partially successful, and the patients may become psychotic. Surgeons have already attempted to correct Parkinson's disease in human patients with tissue grafted into the brain from the adrenal gland, which also produces dopamine. (We have two adrenal glands, but can function with just one.) In some experiments with rats, transplanted adrenal gland cells have produced more dopamine than they do in their normal site, showing that they are responding to the brain's needs. If this can be achieved in humans, such grafts would be a great advance over present drug treatments.

Some kinds of senility, such as Alzheimer's disease, seem to be connected with the lack of a brain chemical called acetylcholine. Because brain tissue is less prone to reject foreign material than other tissues, cells to make acetylcholine could be taken from monkeys' brains or from human embryos. At present there is great resistance to the idea of using aborted foetuses in medical research, but this attitude might change.

It would be useful to give man the ability of some invertebrates and small animals to regenerate damaged limbs. (**Right**) This earthworm is growing after having been sliced in two. Starfish have a similar capability (**opposite**). Regeneration is shown taking place from a single leg (**top**) and from a set of three legs (**bottom**). A whole new organism will result.

The problem of supply is an acute one in all kinds of transplant. The number of people who might benefit from a kidney transplant is much larger than the number of available kidneys in good working order. At present, the situation is further complicated by the need to have permission before kidneys are removed for transplantation. If this has to be obtained from the next of kin, it sometimes takes too long: to be useful, the kidney must be removed within hours of death or it begins to deteriorate. This is why we are now asked to carry kidney donor cards with us, giving permission for our kidneys to be removed without delay in the event of our death. In Austria, Denmark and France an 'opting-out' system is used, in which the dead person is taken to have given his consent to the removal of organs for transplant unless he carries a card stating that he has not. Systems such as this are likely to become more common, or else a computerized record might be kept of each person's consent or refusal.

Several suggestions have been made for improving the supply of transplantable organs, including the setting up of deep-freeze 'organ banks'. It has been argued that the business of having to seek permission to remove organs from dead people is archaic, and that all dead bodies should routinely be 'broken up for spares', with any usable organs being automatically saved for future use. More adventurous versions of this kind of scheme suggest that whole limbs might be preserved for grafting.

It is fairly easy to construct some rather gruesome future scenarios on this premise. If organ banks are to be run as businesses, operated by rival corporations, living people might promise their organs to a particular company in return for a guarantee that if they needed a transplant themselves their needs would be met. The corporations would ensure that their banks remained full by importing organs from poorer countries, where people are more likely to die prematurely. Newspapers have already carried stories – probably based on rumour, but possibly not – about the establishment of a trade in kidneys from the Third World. It is possible to imagine a society in which murder or other crimes would incur the death penalty, and the dead person's organs would be re-used, perhaps on the grounds that in this way the criminal was paying his debt to society. When everyone's tissue-type is recorded on some central file, this might even provide an incentive to murder, since it will be possible for an unscrupulous person in need of a transplanted organ to find out whose death would be most convenient.

Fortunately, there are good reasons for believing that such possible futures will not come to pass. Organ transplants can best be seen as a stopgap measure – a way of holding the fort until reinforcements arrive in the shape of better artificial organs. The eventual mission of the biotechnologists must, however, be to make both transplants and artificial organs redundant.

REGENERATION

What is really needed when a heart or a kidney fails within an otherwise healthy body is not an organ borrowed from another person or a mechanical substitute but a way of making the body repair itself. If a man loses a leg in an accident, it would be infinitely more convenient if he could simply grow a new one instead of having to put up with an artificial one.

It is for this reason that we really need an intimate knowledge of the processes of cell

differentiation, and of the way that amorphous groups of dividing cells become organized into structures, as soon as possible. Such knowledge, and the control that will come with it, can be applied in many areas – we have already discussed its potential in food production – but it is the need to keep our own bodies in good repair that is most urgent.

There are many organisms that have remarkable powers of regeneration. Whole plants can be grown from single cells. The ability of plant cells to differentiate into all the component parts of a complex organism is not, however, matched in the animal world. Animals that can regenerate tend to be relatively simple ones, where the functional differentiation of cells is limited, and the integration of different kinds of cells into systems is not too complex. If a planarian worm is sliced into several pieces, each piece will grow into a new worm. Starfish will also regenerate in this way. When higher animals have some powers of regeneration, they can usually only regenerate simple structures of limited functional range. Some salamanders can re-grow lost limbs, and lizards which can shed their tails when they are attacked by predators can grow them again, but birds and mammals have very limited power in this regard. Young children can regenerate fingertips, but not whole fingers, let alone whole arms.

There is already intensive research into the mechanisms of regeneration which some animals already have, and various methods are being tried to enhance the powers of self-repair of human tissues. There are, apparently, two stages in the process by which limbs are re-grown in animals which have this ability. Blood-corpuscles and other cells that migrate to the site of the wound first become 'de-differentiated', generating an amorphous bundle of cells called a blastema. This cell-mass begins growing, and the dividing cells are co-opted back into the functional tissues as they proliferate, becoming re-specialized according to the appropriate pattern.

It is still not known how this process is controlled, but it has been found that electrical stimulation seems to aid it. What we need before we can hope to induce and control this kind of process in human beings, though, is a detailed knowledge of the switching process by means of which the genes in the cell nucleus are selectively activated and deactivated. A blastema is effectively a kind of 'controlled cancer' which is deliberately formed and then converted into a structure of functional tissues. It seems probable that techniques controlling tissue regeneration will come hand-in-glove with methods of controlling cancerous tumours.

The prospect of achieving this kind of fine control over dividing cells seems awesomely difficult, but when we remember that a tiny piece of a sliced-up planarian 'knows' how to build itself back into a whole animal in much the same way as an early embryo 'knows' whether to turn itself into an ostrich or a shark or a giraffe, it is clear that such things can be done. Once we know how this kind of 'knowledge' is incorporated into the cells of the body, we should be able to exploit it. It seems possible that the potential for repair of damaged tissues and regeneration of lost limbs is already there in human cells, but needs help in order to become effective.

Even limited gains in our knowledge of how to stimulate regeneration of damaged tissues could have important consequences in the next decades. People with injured spines often find themselves partly paralysed even though a relatively small amount of tissue has been damaged. This is because nervous tissue has very little power of regeneration, and chains of nerve cells which are once broken almost never reconnect. Experimental scientists have already reported some success in stimulating nerve cells to divide in the laboratory, and it may be only a matter of time before such techniques of stimulation can be applied to the nerve networks of living organisms. This would be the first step on the road to a technology of regeneration. Further hope is offered by the fact that occasional instances are known where nerve tissue has spontaneously regenerated (though the regeneration has not always been associated with a recovery of function). Giving some capacity of renewal to the tissues in ailing brains might also be a better way of treating Parkinson's disease, Alzheimer's disease and other similar dysfunctions rather than grafting in new tissue.

As we learn more and more about how to control the growth of cells, we might be able to grow new organs in tissue culture, starting with cells taken from the potential recipient's own body. Science fiction writers have already considered very extensively the possibility of cloning people by taking cells from their bodies and using these as substitute egg cells from which to grow whole new individuals. This may become possible in the relatively near future, though it is not altogether clear why anyone would want to make whole new individuals in this way. It may, however, be convenient to make new organs by this method if for some reason it is easier to grow them *in vitro* rather than inside the body. It might be an advantage for the sick person to be kept going by the existing organ while a new one was taking shape in the laboratory.

In the fullness of time, technologies of tissue regeneration may well displace the other strategies of repair which are presently important. Even before they reach that stage, though, they could prove very useful in coping with certain kinds of injury and illness. In this area perhaps more than any other we may look to new biotechnology to bring about a radical change in medical treatment and practice.

THE PURSUIT OF PERFECTION

At present we do not expect very much of artificial

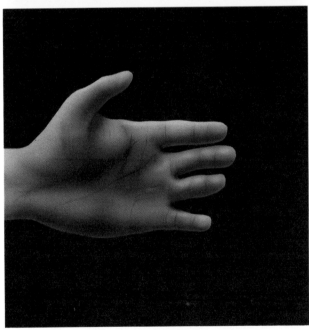

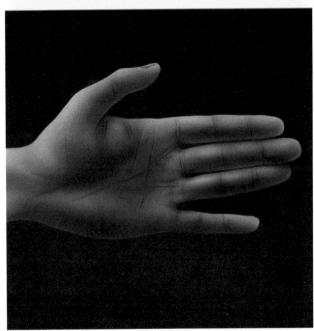

body parts. No one expects that a prosthetic limb will work as well as a real one; we are apt to marvel if such a device can allow its user to live anything approaching a normal life. As future technologies of this kind become gradually more sophisticated, though, the possibility must arise that we will be able to make artificial body parts that work better than natural ones.

The TV series *The Six Million Dollar Man*, which featured the adventures of a man made super-human by his artificial legs, arm and eye, has already introduced us to the idea of artificial limbs and organs more powerful than the ones which nature has seen fit to give us. It seems plausible that fingers of steel might grip harder than fingers of flesh and bone, or that electrically powered legs might allow us to run faster than ordinary ones.

Once we have fully understood the mechanisms that switch genes on and off, we should be able to regenerate damaged limbs. A damaged hand would regenerate in a similar way to the development of a foetal hand: first the palm, then the stumps of the fingers and finally the entire organ would reform. Such an ability would render more clumsy artificial body parts redundant, unless mechanical substitutes were significantly stronger or more capable.

In the future, advances in spare part technology might allow us to create banks of spare organs culled from cadavers. An injured person could be given a matching replacement organ of the right size, blood group and tissue-type. Storage in liquid nitrogen at a temperature well below zero would keep the organs free from infection.

Each of these thousands of masks was made from the face of a person about to undergo cosmetic surgery in a specialist hospital in Japan. As our artificial organs and surgical techniques improve, our willingness to undergo major operations for purely aesthetic reasons could increase.

The artificial eyes and ears which exist today are relatively feeble devices, but when we can make sensors which will feed information into the optic and auditory nerves as cleverly as natural sense organs do, there is no reason why that information should be precisely the same. If the day ever comes when artificial eyes are noticeably more competent than natural ones, the demand for them might not be restricted to the blind. Some sighted people might want to trade in their own good eyes for better, artificial ones. Perhaps they might also be tempted to trade in their own frail limbs for more powerful ones devised by electronic engineers.

It is hard to imagine that anyone would ever want to go in for self-mutilation of this kind, but it is not unknown for people to have healthy teeth extracted on the grounds that a set of false ones will look nicer. Many women, especially in America, are quite prepared to have sacs of silicone implanted in their breasts on cosmetic grounds. Some people undergo even more extensive processes of restructuring in order to alter their sexual identity. It is possible to imagine future societies whose members pursue a curious kind of 'perfection' in having the fleshy parts of their body replaced bit by bit, until they end up with a brain and spinal cord connected to a powerful and indestructible carcase of steel and electronic wizardry. This might not even look like a human body – it might resemble (indeed, might *be*) a giant computer, a tank or a spaceship. Such visions have almost become commonplace in modern science fiction. But as with the more exotic scenarios associated with the future of transplant surgery, the possibility of doing very peculiar things

with mechanical technology may well be overtaken by the possibilities inherent in organic metamorphosis.

When it does become possible to make lost limbs grow again, it will presumably become possible also to exercise some degree of control over how they will grow. There are already techniques available by means of which people can try to reshape themselves. Lightweight weaklings, if they are prepared to work very hard at it, can turn themselves into muscular 'he-men'. People who are grossly overweight can slim down to more desirable proportions. The ability to make cells de-differentiate and then re-form into a new cell structure would give us much more sweeping power over the human form. There would be no need for silicone breast implants if breast tissue could be made to grow exactly to the mass and shape required.

It is probable that if and when we do want to become artists whose medium is human flesh, and seriously set about the business of improving on nature, the kinds of things discussed here will play only a minor role. More ambitious improvements and wholesale transformation will surely be carried out by genetic engineering of human egg cells. Such radical redesigning of the human form will be discussed in Chapter Seven. Nevertheless, the scope and utility of tissue regeneration – and even of organ transplants – should not be set aside as trivial. Any technology which gives us the power to enhance the means of self-repair that the body already has must be reckoned a significant improvement on nature.

Chapter 6

Aging

Our lifespan has been reckoned since Biblical times as 70 years, and although two thousand years of scientific advancement have allowed many more people to reach that term, scientists have so far done nothing to extend it. We have looked at the ways in which new biotechnology might help us to resist and overcome the various kinds of disease and damage which threaten to shorten our normal lifespan. We will now consider the question of whether future biotechnology will assist not only in restoring the sick to health, but also in transcending normality by allowing us to extend youth and vigour far beyond the traditional span.

The more we learn about the biochemical systems within the body, and the way that they are supervised and controlled by the genes, the more likely it becomes that we will find effective ways to prevent our slow decay into senility. Already there are optimists who think that a breakthrough in this area is imminent and who have proclaimed that ours might be the last generation to die. This might be asking a little *too* much, but it is quite clear that any significant discovery could have very profound effects on our society. Better ways of attacking disease and repairing injury will only allow us to do the things we are already doing a little bit better: they will not force changes in our lifestyle or our view of the world. The conquest of aging, by contrast, would make a very striking difference to the human situation. It would alter our most basic attitudes and would compel dramatic changes in social organization.

THE CAUSES OF AGING

The outward symptoms of aging are all too obvious. Our hair turns grey, and our skin becomes less elastic, shrivelling into wrinkles. There are many invisible symptoms too. We gradually lose our strength and stamina as our muscles become less capable. Our mental faculties are likely to decline. The control mechanisms which regulate conditions within our bodies become less reliable, making us more vulnerable to environmental stress, and more likely to contract diseases. Our bones become brittle, and there is a waning of our power to recover from injuries. The tissues of the body shrink as dying cells are no longer replaced, and the cells that remain

become senescent themselves, functioning poorly. Arthritis, cancer and hardening of the arteries hang over us like vultures, moving in to destroy us as our resistance weakens.

There is a common analogy which likens the aging process to a biological clock. It is easy enough to think of our bodies as having some kind of inbuilt timer which tells them, after 70 years or so, that their time is up. There are, however, two ways to construe this analogy which are rather different in their implications. We might be tempted to think of this timer as something like the time selector on an alarm clock. According to this way of thinking, we do not begin to age until a particular switch is tripped, at which point we begin to deteriorate. If this *were* the case, then the biotechnological conquest of aging would simply be a matter of finding this 'switch' and making sure that it was not tripped. Longevity might then be available as the reward for a single discovery.

Unfortunately, it is more likely that we should think of the inbuilt timer as something more like the tightly wound spring of an old-fashioned watch. Aging would then be like the slow unwinding of the spring, with the timekeeping of the watch becoming more erratic as the spring becomes fully unwound, ever more prone to stop as friction gets a grip on the complex workings of the mechanism. If this is the case, we must try to discover which biochemical systems in the body are analogous to the watchspring. Can these biological systems, like the watchspring of a clock mechanism, be 'rewound' in some way, so that the body can be kept running much longer – perhaps even indefinitely?

There is one contemporary theory of aging which suggests an 'alarm clock' mechanism rather than a 'watchspring' mechanism, and that is the one put forward by W. Donner Denckla of the Roche Institute of Molecular Biology. He proposes that there might be a single pituitary hormone which controls all the symptoms of aging. The evidence for this is based on similarities between normal aging and the symptoms of a hormonal deficiency disease associated with the thyroid gland. Denckla suggests that as we get older the pituitary gland (the 'master gland' at the base of the brain, which controls the activity of the other glands) begins to produce a

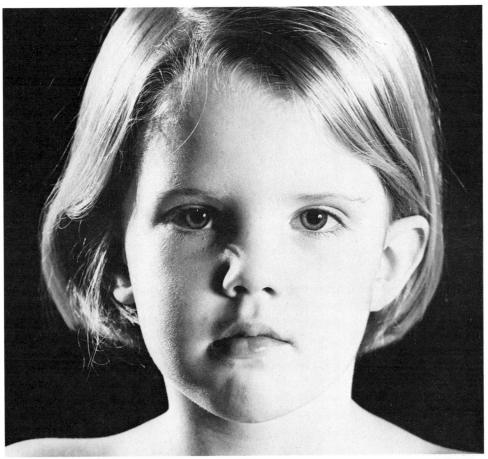

The familiar signs of aging –
wrinkled skin, greying hair –
are accompanied by gradual
deterioration in many of the
body's systems. The causes of
aging are still obscure, but
intensive research being
carried on at present may
permit us one day to avoid this
deterioration, or even to
increase our life-span. Living
to a greater age might involve
halting development – for
instance, by a very much
delayed sexual maturation.

95

hormone which blocks the action of the thyroid hormone, thus causing us to age and die.

If Denckla is right, then the conquest of aging might be quite simple. We might be able to stop the 'aging hormone' from being produced – thus altering the 'alarm clock setting' so that we can live on peacefully without being disturbed. Alternatively, we might find a way of blocking *its* action so that it can no longer block the action of the thyroid hormone. It would be nice to believe that the whole matter were as simple as this, but Denckla has not so far managed to isolate his hypothetical pituitary hormone.

One reason for believing that Denckla is very probably wrong is that if aging were, indeed, caused by a single hormone – presumably produced by a single gene – then one would expect to find occasional humans in whom the hormone was ineffective because of a mutation in the relevant gene. There would therefore be mutant immortals already among us. The fact that there is no sign of any mutation which protects people from the effects of aging strongly suggests that aging is a more complicated and more fundamental process than

Denckla proposes. It is very difficult to accept that aging might be an arbitrary process which has to be triggered, and which could therefore be overcome simply by deactivating the trigger.

Other theories of aging assume that it is a continuous degenerative process that does not have to be triggered because it is going on all the time. It may begin at birth or at conception rather than in maturity. It is when we are mature that we begin to notice our decline, but this may be because when we are young the aging process is screened out by the process of growth. It may be that we begin to die even before we are born, although it is only when we have reached the plateau of our physical development that the insidious process of gradual degeneration becomes evident.

There are several main candidates in the contest to establish which biochemical system is the 'watchspring' forever winding down inside us. R. L. Walford, one of the most experienced researchers in this field, has recently directed a lot of attention to the 'autoimmune theory of aging', which suggests that the body's immune system is the culprit. He proposes that the body becomes gradually less

(**Right**) The inhabitants of the Hunza area of Pakistan are reputed to live up to 120 years, though there are no official records to substantiate this. They subsist on a diet of apricots and fruits, with minimal animal fat, and continue to lead active lives well into old age.

Many plant species have maximum lifespans far longer than those of any animal. (**Opposite page, left**) The *Welwitschia mirabilis* of the South African desert lives for between 100 and 1000 years. Its strap-like leaves can be very long, though the ends become withered by the wind and by friction with the sand. (**Opposite page, right**) The bristlecone pine is one of the oldest trees, surviving for several thousand years. With other long-lived trees, it is used by archaeologists to provide a record of fluctuating radiocarbon levels in the past, allowing them to calibrate radiocarbon dates for other objects as far back as 7000 BC.

competent because its tissues increasingly come under attack from its own defence mechanisms. The main problem with this theory is that invertebrates, which do not have immune systems, are still prone to aging. Johan Bjorksten has suggested that important molecules within the body – proteins and nucleic acids – gradually lose their power to function because of 'cross-linkages' that occur inside them. It is known that structural proteins, such as the collagen which makes up a major constituent of connective tissue in the body, can decay because of these extra chemical bonds. (The process is rather like rubber perishing.) Leslie Orgel has suggested that the key mechanism is the accumulation of random errors in molecules of DNA as they are replicated over and over again, so that eventually the proteins that they produce become non-functional.

A good deal of interesting experimental work on aging has been done, without, as yet, suggesting that any of these theories is the true one. Leonard Hayflick found that cells grown in tissue culture could not go on dividing indefinitely. After approximately 50 divisions the cells became senescent. By trial and error he found a number of substances which, when added to the culture, increased this number, but it has not so far been possible to determine what biochemical effects these substances were having in order to achieve this result.

Diet is one factor which is known to affect lifespan. Experiments carried out in the 1930s by Clive McCay showed that rats fed on an adequate but highly restricted diet lived longer than rats allowed to eat as much as they wished. The rats on the restricted diet grew and matured more slowly, but lived up to twice as long. Walford has managed

to show that the development and efficiency of the immune system is affected by this kind of dietary regime, thus providing a connection with his autoimmune theory of aging, but the hypothetical causal chain still remains largely untested.

Other experiments on the effect of diet on longevity have shown that mice and rats live longer on diets low in unsaturated fats. This is alleged to provide support for another theory of aging, popularized by Paul Gordon, which holds that it is caused by chemical damage inflicted on our cells by highly reactive molecules called 'free radicals' produced during some metabolic cycles. Reactions between unsaturated fats and oxygen are 'free radical reactions', and it is alleged that we may be better off if we discourage such reactions within our bodies. Experimenters who have added antioxidants, which inhibit free radical reactions, to the diet of experimental animals have also managed to extend their lifespans. Vitamin E, which is one such antioxidant, was one of the substances which Hayflick used to increase the number of cell divisions which could take place in his tissue cultures.

The findings of this kind of research have inspired many people to take action in the interest of trying to live longer. Ordinary people are understandably not content to wait for complicated research to be conducted over many years – the moment anything turns up which *might* help to increase the length of their lives, they want to get what benefit they can. This phenomenon has been well known since the 1930s when Serge Voronoff, having observed that some of the symptoms of castration were similar to the signs of aging, contended that aging was mainly a matter of the failing of the gonads. He therefore tried to rejuvenate old men by transplanting into their bodies the testicles of monkeys. Nowadays, there are many people who wolf vitamin pills, take every other substance that has ever been associated with life extension, and keep the calories and unsaturated fats in their diet under strict control. It remains to be seen whether any new longevity records will be established as a result of these enthusiastic projects.

AGING AND THE GENES
We know very well that different creatures have different lifespans – and, for that matter, that men and women appear to have slightly different lifespans. This strongly suggests that the natural lifespan of any organism is determined by its genes, and that different genes would allow people to live longer. Hence, there might be a role for genetic engineers in modifying the human lifespan. It is unlikely, though, that aging is controlled by one or a few genes, because that would imply an 'alarm clock' type of switching system. Just as different kinds of clocks and watches are designed to run for different lengths of time after being wound, so different kinds of bodies are genetically designed to run for different periods, and modifying this time would probably require quite radical redesigning of the mechanism.

Man is already an exceptionally long-lived species. Small mammals such as mice grow old after two years, dogs and cats after ten. Some kinds of tortoises can apparently live much longer than we can, but it is unclear how representative of the species the record spans are, and it is possible that the average is much less than the reported maximums. In the plant kingdom, many species – mostly trees – regularly do better than man, but they have a very different and less taxing lifestyle.

This long lifespan must be the result of evolution acting on our genes. Presumably, our apelike ancestors must have grown old faster than we do, just as our contemporary cousins – chimpanzees and gorillas – still do. It seems clear that the extension of the human lifespan was connected with the evolution of neoteny – the extension of the developmental phase of growth and maturation. The human infant is born at a relatively early stage in its development, and takes a long time to grow to maturity. This is an advantage, in evolutionary terms, because it makes the human child capable of much more sophisticated kinds of learning than any animal infant. It is on the foundation stone of this capacity for learning that our essential humanity – all that distinguishes us from the animals – is built.

Because human infants take so much longer to grow into adults, they require a greater measure of parental care than any other creatures. In order that their phenomenal talent for learning may be fully exploited, it is desirable for them to remain in intimate association with older and wiser humans even after they have become mature enough to reproduce themselves. In most animal species there

is no need – in evolutionary terms – for individuals to survive once they have reproduced. In higher animals such as birds and mammals, where there is a substantial measure of parental care of offspring, individuals must survive long enough to see their children through to the time when they become capable of independent life. In humans, it is advantageous for individuals to live even beyond the point when their children are physically capable of looking after themselves and rearing children of their own; the advantage is dissipated only when the children become intellectually as well as physically mature.

If natural selection can increase our lifespan from about 10 years to 70 years in the course of 10 or 20 million years, there is no reason why biotechnologists – once they figure out how the trick was done – should not help us to increase it still further. If nature could redesign the human clock so that its watchspring would animate it for seven times as long, there is no reason why biological engineers should not design it even more cleverly.

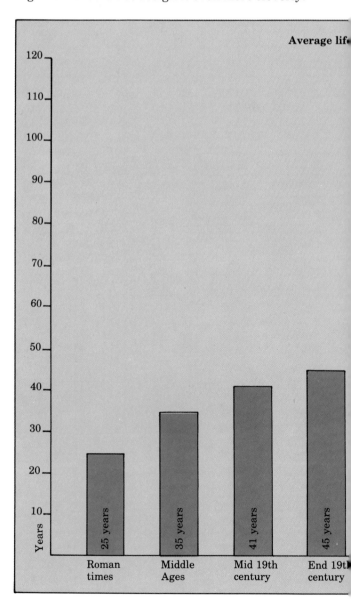

Average life

	Roman times	Middle Ages	Mid 19th century	End 19th century
Years	25 years	35 years	41 years	45 years

Nor is there any reason why biotechnologists should not find chemical 'keys' which we can insert into the mechanism to rewind it. Perhaps neither project will be easy, but there is certainly room for hope on both scores.

CONTROLLING THE LIFESPAN

There are already lots of ways in which individuals can prolong their youth – that is to say, can maintain their mental and physical vigour against the forces of decay. A sensible diet is an excellent defence against bodily degeneration. Exercise to keep the body fit is very useful too – systems decay much more readily if they are not regularly used. The same appears to be true of the mind: the best defence against senility is to keep the brain busy by using it to think, to reason and to remember. Above all else, if you want to live a long time you must refrain from poisoning yourself: smoking and heavy drinking give generous assistance to the processes of bodily decay.

The main problem with these defences against aging is not their ineffectiveness, but the unwillingness of people to comply with their prescriptions. People like doing the things that are shortening their lives unnecessarily, and are reluctant to give them up. What people actually want from biotechnologists is a breakthrough that will produce miracle cures for old age, and pills that can be taken three times a day to guarantee eternal youth. It *is* possible that such easy remedies might be found, although there may be several different ways in which they would take effect.

We might be able to produce drugs that would eliminate some of the debilitating effects of aging, without having much effect on the normal lifespan. This would be the case if aging were a complex process involving several different kinds of chemical decay. For instance, if aging were a matter of the combined effects of free radical damage, error accumulation in DNA, cross-linkages in structural molecules *and* autoimmune damage, we might be able to counter the first and third without being able to interfere with the second or fourth. Thus, people

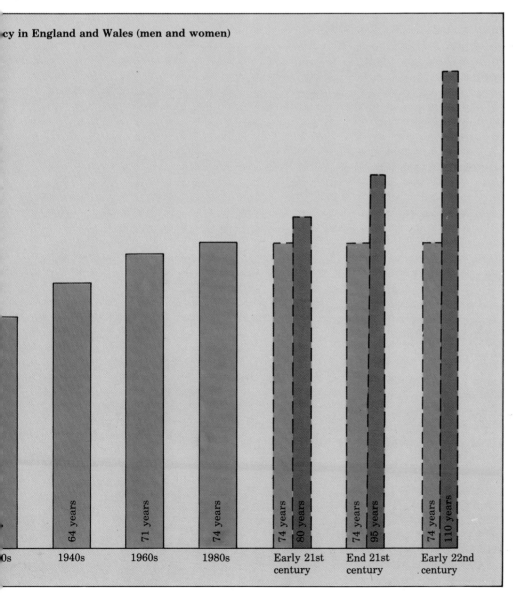

cy in England and Wales (men and women)

	1940s	1960s	1980s	Early 21st century	End 21st century	Early 22nd century
0s	64 years	71 years	74 years	74 years / 80 years	74 years / 95 years	74 years / 110 years

As medicine makes more progress against disease, average life expectancy is continuing to increase. Finding better treatments for the typical illnesses of old age – such as cancer and heart disease – can, however, make only a small difference. To raise life expectancy still further, or to increase the maximum lifespan, we need to find out more about the root causes of aging.

Hibernation is a state of 'suspended animation' in which an animal uses very little energy and can survive without eating for several months. The golden-mantled ground squirrel is one of many small mammals which hibernate during the winter. The animal's body temperature drops, all metabolic processes slow down, and the heartbeat and breathing slow to about a tenth of the normal rate. If men could hibernate, entering this state might become an option for prolonging life. It might be undertaken by those awaiting medical advances to cure their illnesses, or by astronauts on long space journeys.

over 60 might be able to retain more of their youthful appearance and physical strength while still vulnerable to the typical diseases of old age. This is perhaps the most likely contingency for the immediate future: we will discover drug treatments which will conquer some of the symptoms of old age, but which will not postpone the inevitable end.

On the other hand, we might be able to slow down the aging process as a whole. We might be able to produce a drug which would actually inhibit the winding down of the chemical watchspring. We could do this if it were ultimately to transpire that there is one particular kind of biochemical degeneration which is the root cause of all the others. Our chances of finding such a treatment would, however, depend on what kind of root cause this was. It is not too difficult to imagine our finding a treatment to help prevent free radical damage, or to break up cross-linkages in structural molecules, but if the root cause of aging is error accumulation in DNA molecules this would be much more difficult to counteract.

If aging is primarily a matter of the failure of inbuilt repair mechanisms, we might be able to accomplish the rejuvenation of the old. We have always been attracted to the notion that old bodies might be rejuvenated if young flesh could somehow be incorporated into them – such thinking led not only to the bizarre monkey gland experiments of Serge Voronoff but to even more outlandish activities, such as the Countess Bathory's reputed predilection for bathing in the blood of virgins. It is not beyond the bounds of possibility that biotechnologists may find out how some such process of renewal might actually be accomplished. As we saw in Chapter Five, transplant surgeons have already considered trying to restore certain functions to aging brains by importing tissue from the embryonic brains of aborted foetuses.

If the real root cause of aging is of the kind indicated by Orgel's theory and Hayflick's experiments, it may be that cells, once they become specialized, can only reproduce themselves a limited number of times before error accumulation in the DNA (or some such process) renders the descendant cells incapable of performing their function. We know, though, that the body can keep its own fundamental identity and integrity as a whole while individual cells are continually dying and being replaced. If we can find some way of replacing the cells in the body not by their own defective daughter cells, but by new cells which could reproduce themselves dozens of times before deteriorating, then bodies *could* be rejuvenated – and perhaps, by serial rejuvenation, kept going for ever.

There are many difficulties attached to such a scheme. Where would we get the young cells from?

Could we persuade the body to accept them? Could we guarantee that the new, young cells would colonize and take over the organs of the old body, eventually *becoming* the body? It is highly probable that any rejuvenation treatment along these lines would be far more complicated than a mere injection or course of pills. Possibly, people wishing to preserve their option to be rejuvenated in this fashion might have to assure themselves of an adequate supply of transplantable tissue, compatible in type. This could involve taking steps not too far removed in their moral dimension from those which the Countess Bathory took, such as the growing of cloned embryos as a source of compatible cells.

All these hypothetical methods of lifespan control involve trying to preserve individuals who already exist, working with their natural genetic heritage. It is possible, though, that the only practical way to produce very long-lived people would be to tamper with their genetic heritage, just as natural selection tampered with the heritage of our remote ancestors. When techniques of genetic engineering advance to the stage when it is possible to transform human egg cells creatively, then it may be possible to engineer a new race of long-lived humans. This is not, though, something that we can expect to happen soon. For the next few hundred years we will have to hope for treatments that can be applied to mature individuals, or at least to children.

If we are lucky, the fundamental aging process will turn out to be a kind of biochemical

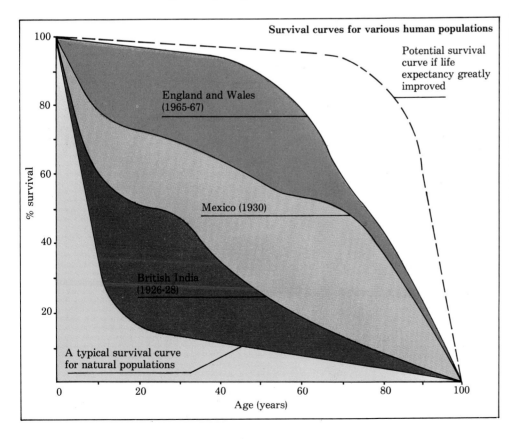

Survival curves for various human populations

100
Potential survival curve if life expectancy greatly improved

England and Wales (1965-67)

Mexico (1930)

British India (1926-28)

A typical survival curve for natural populations

% survival

80

60

40

20

0   20   40   60   80   100

Age (years)

'Survival curves' for different populations show the effects of increased life expectancy. For instance, the curve for British India in the mid-1920s indicates that infant and child mortality was very high, with 50% of people dying before 20 years of age. The curve for England and Wales in 1965–7 shows greatly decreased infant mortality. The 'survival curve' for developed countries will approach the upper curve as a larger percentage of people reach the maximum age.

The loss of function with increasing age occurs at different rates in different organs and systems. Graphs here show the loss as a percentage, with the level of function of a 30-year old representing 100%. The fall-off ranges from 9% (brain weight) to 57% (lungs).

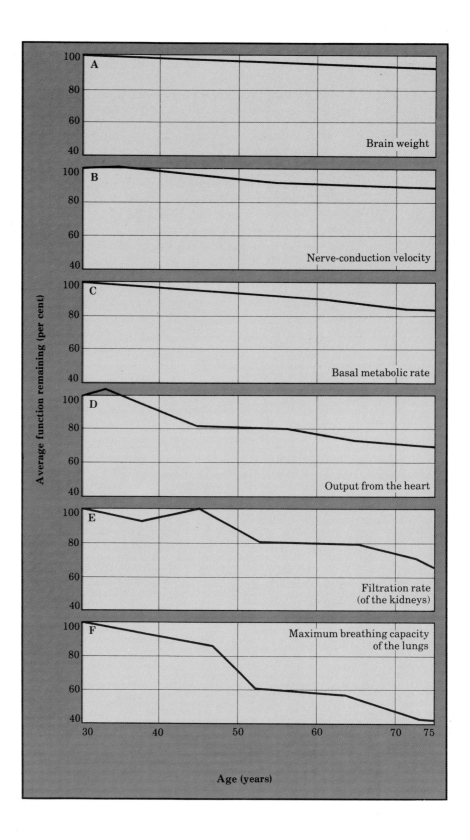

deterioration that can be counteracted, slowed down or prevented by some kind of drug treatment. If that is the case, then we could discover in the near future a way to maintain youth and vigour longer and perhaps also to add many years to the normal lifespan. If we are unlucky, then prolonging or renewing youth might be very much more complicated. It might even be impossible to make very substantial gains.

We must, however, consider the possibility that a cure for aging can and will be found, if only because the consequences of such a cure would be so far-reaching. The likelihood is that we will find ways to achieve some improvement in lifespan, even though it may fall far short of the immortality that men have always dreamed of.

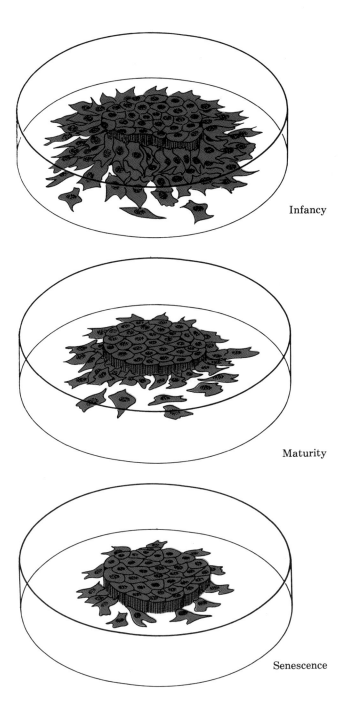

Infancy

Maturity

Senescence

The ability of cells to reproduce themselves diminishes with age. Tiny scraps of living tissue placed in a culture medium will continue to divide, but the older the tissue source, the slower the rate of reproduction. The cells undergo a variety of degenerative changes and then die. Some substances have been found which allow a greater number of cell divisions when added to the tissue culture. This research may result in a therapy for aging.

SOCIAL CONSEQUENCES OF LONGEVITY
The immediate effect of any technology of longevity would be to reduce mortality rates in the developed countries. How much the rates would be reduced would depend on the effectiveness of the treatment (i.e. how many years it could add to the average lifespan) and its cost. No doubt the treatment would also find a market among the richer people of the Third World, but they are relatively few in number. Very little mortality in the Third World can be ascribed to old age; the average life-expectancy at birth in many African countries is less than 40 years, and millions of poor people die in infancy.

If, in the next generation or so, we manage to find ways of distributing food and medicines more effectively to the poorest people in the world, there will be a dramatic change in world mortality rates. It would require a fairly spectacular breakthrough in longevity research to make a comparable difference. The present world population is nearing four billion, and will probably be over that figure by the year 2000. The capacity of the world food-producing system to accommodate a large expansion in population depends on many factors, one of the most important being the rate at which new biotechnology of the kinds described in Chapter Three can be introduced and exploited. Whatever changes occur, it is safe to say that the world already has a population problem, and will continue to have one for half a century or more, if not longer. The presence in the world of a technology of longevity is unlikely to make all that much difference to the problem on its grandest scale.

Within the developed countries, though, even a modest increase in the length of the average lifespan could make significant differences to the organization of society. We already have a situation where the average age of the population is increasing steadily, partly because of a decline in the birthrate since the post-war 'baby boom' and partly because better medical care already allows more people to live to the limit of their natural span. Any increase in the lifespan would raise the proportion of old people in the population still higher.

If, as expected, longevity comes hand in hand with the ability to cure some of the characteristic ailments of old age, many of the extra old people would be fit and able-bodied, but no matter when the natural lifespan reaches its end – at 100 years, 120 or even 150 – there will still be people approaching their end who require considerable health care.

It would be absurd, in such circumstances, to retain a standard age of retirement. There could easily be a situation where people who benefited from the treatment could look forward to a vigorous existence until they were centenarians. We already know that one of the aids to living a long time and preserving one's faculties is keeping busy, so it would seem absurd to use a technology of longevity on people who would then be forbidden to work. It is noticeable, though, that the developed countries already face something of a problem in finding employment for what they currently regard as their working population. It is possible that new political and technological situations will lead to the opening up of all kinds of new employment opportunities, but an increase in the number of people wanting work would not help.

Any substantial increase in the number of old people holding jobs – however fit and capable those old people might be – would be certain to cause frustration and dissatisfaction among the young. The better able the old are to preserve their own 'youth', the less the authentically young will be able to make of theirs. It is difficult enough to build a successful career when those at the top will not retire until they are 65; it would be very difficult indeed if even the people in the middle of the hierarchy could keep going until they were 90 or 100. A different pattern of life, with people changing jobs much more often, might have to become the norm.

The frustration and resentment felt by the young in this situation would be nothing, of course, to the frustration and resentment which would develop if there were to emerge a technology of longevity that was both highly effective and very expensive. If only a few rich people could obtain an extension of their health and vigour, this would create a new kind of inequality within society. We could find ourselves living in a future where there would be a widening rift between two new classes of people: the short-lived, who would continue to die routinely after 70 years or so; and the long-lived, who would become capable of living for 100 years, then 150, and perhaps finally for centuries. The kind of serial rejuvenation treatment imagined in the last section, involving complex transplant surgery, could have this kind of effect.

If a technology of longevity does become available, then eventually the world will have to adapt to it. Societies will have to overcome the initial disruptions and find a new balance in their way of life. It is difficult to speculate in detail about the possible patterns of adaptation, but there are some things that would be absolutely necessary. First and foremost, a society of long-lived people would have to control its birthrate very rigorously. This could be difficult if extended life were also to mean extended fertility. Societies in the past have successfully practised birth control, using methods such as sexual abstinence and infanticide. These methods are to some extent still employed today, but even in relatively poor countries more modern methods – contraceptives – have become commonplace. It could be necessary for a society of long-lived people to reverse the normal situation, though, and keep the majority of its population in a state of perpetual artificial sterility, restoring fertility only temporarily, in a carefully regulated fashion. We already have medical technologies which would make such a situation easy to achieve, given the political will.

It has been suggested by some writers that a technology permitting the easy selection of the sex of unborn children would function as a means of population control, because many Third World cultures place a much higher value on boys than girls. (Where infanticide is still widely practised it is not so much to control the numbers of children as to control the sex distribution.) It is unlikely, though, that a society of long-lived people would choose to control its own reproduction by choosing to limit production of women, even if that were an easily available option.

It would not necessarily be the case, though, that extended life would mean extended fertility. It might be possible to help women to live much longer, and stay active for much longer, while experiencing menopause – cessation of fertility – at the same point in their lives, around the age of 50. If this were the case, a society of long-lived individuals might contain a very high proportion of non-reproductive females. In a society where everyone can expect to live to be 150 it might not be too difficult for a late age of marriage to be established as the norm. In that case adjustment of the birthrate could be made by an adaptation of sexual mores rather than by universal artificial sterilization.

One more, rather bizarre, possibility that should be considered is that if longevity is a corollary of neoteny, longevity might be achieved by extending the human developmental stage even further. It could be, therefore, that we will be able to guarantee people a longer life if we can artificially delay maturation (including puberty). We tend to think of eternal youth as being eternally 21, because that is what would suit us best, but it is not inconceivable that if we want to be eternally young we might have to be eternally juvenile. That would certainly set aside any problems of birthrate control, but it would mean that the lives of people within the long-lived society might be very different from ours. Imagine a society where no one reached puberty until the age of 80 – a society of sexually immature sages!

It is tempting to argue that a society of long-lived people would be more stable than ours, politically protective of its *status quo*, with everyone anxious to prevent disruption so that they could live out their extended lifespans in peace and security. On the other hand, it might be that such a society would be violent and strife-ridden, precisely because violence provided the only means by which an ambitious man could displace others from positions of power. In a divided society, with a long-lived elite and a short-lived proletariat, the possibility of violence would surely be ever-present in the minds of the rulers. No technology of longevity can protect a man from an assassin's bullet, and it is conceivable that in a world where medical science will see to it that no man *needs* to die, other men will see to it that they die anyway. In most past societies, and in many present societies, the average life expectancy was and is much lower than the natural lifespan. Perhaps the same will be true in future societies where the attainable lifespan has been extended dramatically.

There is another way in which future societies may become divided according to the length of lifespan: it could happen that longevity – though not

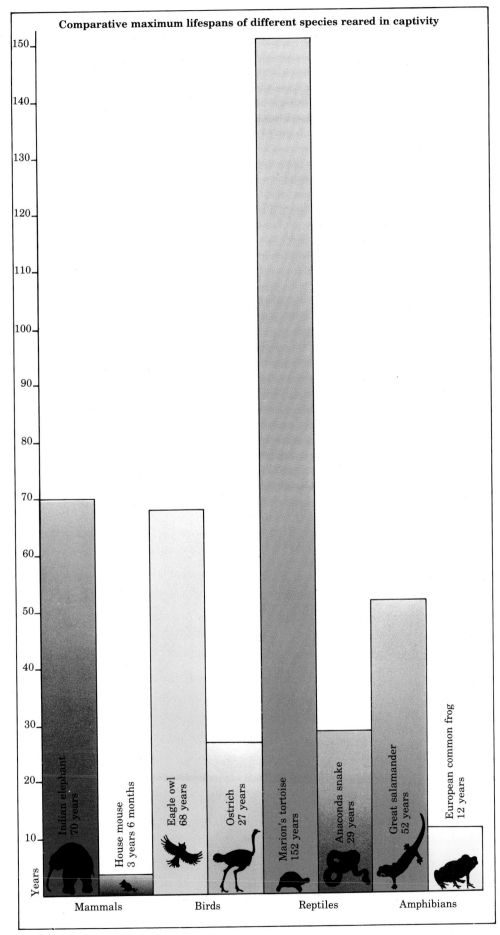

Comparative maximum lifespans of different species reared in captivity

Years

Mammals — Indian elephant 70 years; House mouse 3 years 6 months
Birds — Eagle owl 68 years; Ostrich 27 years
Reptiles — Marion's tortoise 152 years; Anaconda snake 29 years
Amphibians — Great salamander 52 years; European common frog 12 years

The lifespans of various species differ markedly, as shown in this chart. Lifespan thus seems to be determined by the genes, giving genetic engineers a good chance of being able to influence it. Variations in lifespan between species seem to be related to body size, though by this criterion man's lifespan is already exceptionally long.

105

expensive – requires constant and rigorous effort and self-discipline. Suppose that we *can* ensure that the biochemical watchspring inside us winds down very slowly, so that we may live to be 200 and preserve our fitness well into our second century – but only if we eat a very carefully controlled diet, follow a rigid regime of exercise and meditation, and by an effort of will keep our minds and bodies perpetually calm. If this were the case, people would have to choose between living for a long time and making the most of a shorter time with all manner of self-indulgence. This might lead to a divided society of a different kind, in which the long-lived would be retreatists rather than rulers: a class of stoical and ascetic seekers after knowledge, uninterested in pleasure or the exercise of power.

HOPING FOR IMMORTALITY

So far we have discussed longevity rather than immortality. It seems far more likely that we will develop biotechnologies to slow down aging than that we shall eventually banish its effects altogether. Nevertheless, the lure of immortality is so powerful that there are people prepared to take action in the hope of securing it. Dozens of Americans have already paid out large sums of money for their bodies to be deep-frozen after death, in the hope that there will one day be a medical technology capable of resurrecting them. Others have seriously considered the possibility of having themselves frozen before death, hoping that they can be revived at some future time when their diseases can be cured and their bodies rejuvenated.

The freezing of human bodies is known as cryonics, and there are several institutions in America actively involved in it. The movement of which they are a part originated in the 1940s, when the biologist Jean Rostand developed a technique for freezing and preserving frog sperms using glycerol as a cryoprotective agent to prevent damage to the sperms. The idea of using similar techniques on human bodies was first popularized by R. C. W. Ettinger in his book *The Prospect of Immortality*, published in 1964. The Cryonics Society of California began freezing newly dead bodies in 1967.

The argument used in support of the claim that what we currently call death might one day be reversible is based on the fact that there is no single moment of death. 'Clinical' death involves the cessation of heartbeat and breathing, but nowadays hearts can be made to start beating again if prompt action is taken, and there are hundreds of people walking around who have 'died' temporarily in ambulances or on operating tables. Because of this, we have substituted 'brain death' as a criterion of real death – a person is thus held to be dead when no brain activity can be detected, even though the heart and lungs can be kept going with artificial assistance. Unfortunately, there is a certain arbitrariness about this criterion, because we cannot be completely sure that brain function might not be restored, if only we knew how. It *could* be the case that a more developed medical technology could save people currently deemed brain dead, and might perhaps save anyone whose cells had not actually decayed to the point where they would no longer function.

The purpose of cryonic freezing is to preserve people from cellular decay, in the hope that they can thus be kept within the margin of possible resuscitation by courtesy of future discoveries. It may turn out to be the case that medical scientists never will be able to revive people who are currently certified as dead. Perhaps brain death really is the final and irreversible end. To the proponents of cryonics, though, any chance is better than no chance at all. Given that people cannot take their money with them when they go, why not spend it on the slim chance that they will one day be able to come back?

No one has yet been frozen while still alive, but it seems likely that someone will before long, if the legal difficulties can be sorted out. (No cryonics society would want to risk facing a charge of murder.) At present, no mature animal has been resuscitated after prolonged freezing at very low temperatures, but eggs and sperms can now be routinely frozen for later use – the technique is even used on human eggs and sperms – without any apparent loss of viability or intracellular damage. Early animal embryos have been successfully frozen and revived, and there does seem to be a possibility that we could develop cryoprotective agents effective enough to preserve whole bodies.

The Cryonics Society of California ran into trouble in 1981 when some of its stored bodies accidentally thawed out because of a power failure. A court ordered it to pay very heavy damages on the grounds that as the Society was charging tens of thousands of dollars for the slim chance of later revival, they must pay out commensurately when they failed to preserve that slim chance. Nevertheless, it seems likely that such projects will continue to gather support, and it is possible to imagine a future in which they would become important social institutions.

Even if freezing is not the answer, there seems to be no reason why we should not find some other way to put human beings into suspended animation. Many animals routinely go into such a state in order to hibernate, and although we have not yet figured out exactly how they slow their metabolic rate down so drastically, such a discovery may occur in the near future.

If it does become possible to put people into suspended animation, whether by freezing or by some kind of artificial hibernation, there will be a strong temptation for people faced with imminent death or decrepitude to take that option. It may be an option that remains open only to the rich, but if the technology becomes cheap it could conceivably become the right of every citizen of a technologically developed society. It might also be a possible response for whole societies facing a period of famine or a nuclear war.

We must consider, therefore, the possibility of a future society where hardly anyone ever dies, but where everyone eventually goes into cold storage. As stored bodies piled up, generation by generation, we would have to find space for them all. If the situation were to persist for more than 100 years we might well find it difficult to decide which would be worse: a medical breakthrough which would enable them all to be revived, multiplying the population of the world severalfold; or the failure to make a breakthrough, leaving the 'undead' to increase their numbers indefinitely.

This set of possibilities makes it clear that the potentialities of future biotechnology concern us here and now. If we really are convinced that a biotechnological revolution is under way, and that future medicine might become increasingly competent to deal with the ills that afflict us, then we should be prepared to take a serious interest in the technology of suspended animation. One of the modern prophets of immortality, Alan Harrington, subtitles his book *The Immortalist* 'An Approach to the Engineering of Man's Divinity'. If he is right, and biotechnology does eventually progress to the point where men can become godlike in their

relative invulnerability to death, then it may make very good sense to buy a ticket to that Utopia as soon as one comes on to the market.

We could go on multiplying the possibilities of a technology of longevity, and elaborating upon them, more or less indefinitely. Science fiction writers have been playing such games for years, and will continue to do so. Until we are in a position to say what the causes of aging actually are, it is difficult to estimate what biotechnology may achieve in preventing or reversing aging. Until we can guess more accurately what kind of control we can achieve, we cannot really say with certainty what social effects it is likely to have. What the above arguments attempt to show is that those effects might be remarkable. In the long term, an effective technology of longevity could alter the social and political order out of all recognition, by altering one of the most fundamental assumptions about what human life is like, and introducing new parameters into the question of how men ought to live.

A human body prepared for freezing is placed inside an insulated cryogenic storage capsule at Trans Time Inc. in California, to be stored in liquid nitrogen at a temperature of −196°C. People who arrange for their bodies to be frozen hope that future scientists will be able to resuscitate them when medicine has found cures for their diseases and solved the mystery of aging.

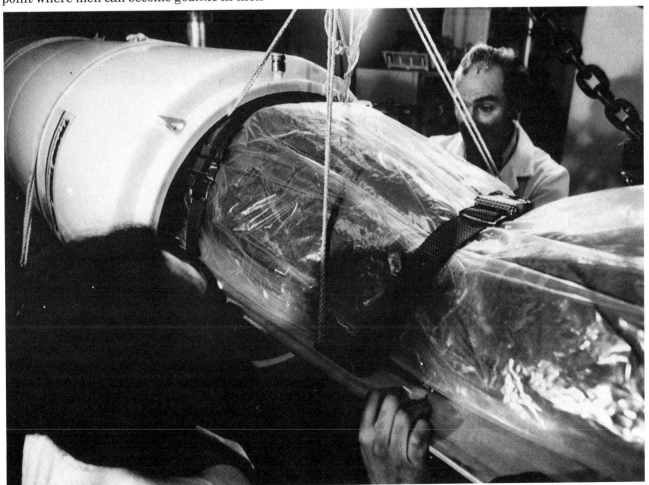

Chapter 7

Engineering people

Until now, we have had to be content with the image in which evolution has shaped us. Soon, we will have the capacity to remake that image in any way we choose. Many people find this a horrifying idea. Most of us would be prepared to sanction the use of genetic engineering techniques on human beings in order to repair damaged or diseased bodies, and even to extend our lifespan. But to many people, it would be a very different matter to alter men crucially in form and structure – to modify what 'nature' has determined and produce new kinds of human being.

The new kinds of people discussed in this chapter *are* unnatural, but so are we. Popular ideas of what is 'natural' and what is 'unnatural' are to some extent arbitrary. Everything that makes us human as well as animal is 'unnatural', the product of human knowledge and not of genetic destiny. Agriculture, cooking, wearing clothes, reading books, science, technology, medicine and even language can be seen as unnatural if observed with a dispassionate eye. Modern man is not the product of nature, but the product of his own attempts to remake himself and to reshape his life. What we are today is the result of millions of choices made by millions of men over the last few tens of thousands of years. If we have achieved relatively little in the way of altering the form of our bodies, it is because of the limitations of our power rather than the dictates of our collective conscience.

Even if we do not like the idea at all, we should still be willing to accept that when the technology does exist for transforming human egg cells in such a way as to produce new kinds of human being, it is likely to be used. As long as there are purposes to be served by such a technology, it will be put into practice; and it is not too difficult to imagine motives which the people of the future might have that would lead them to play at being God. No doubt the first individuals who decide they want to do it will meet powerful and outspoken opposition, but it is difficult to believe that in the long run such opposition can prevail. If there are any mankinds at all a thousand years from now, there will be many mankinds. There are no grounds for doubting it.

IMPROVING ON NATURE
In one of the most widespread modern hero-myths,

IMPROVING ON NATURE
One of the first major projects of future genetic engineers will be to eliminate the imperfections of the human body as evolved by natural selection.

Neck
At present, we are very vulnerable to accidents: we die if the brain is starved of oxygen for more than a few minutes. Small extra lungs, with a tiny heart and blood vessels of their own, could be added in the throat, to keep the brain oxygenated when the major blood-system is injured. The brain could thus be kept alive until medical help was reached and future techniques of surgery, transplantation, or regeneration could be applied.

Spine
The backbone might be made less vulnerable to strain or damage. Instead of interlinked bones separated by cartilage, a combination of stronger materials could be used. A surrounding network of extra blood vessels might be needed to supply the energy to alter the spine's plasticity as required.

Stronger materials could be similarly used throughout the skeleton, with further networks of blood vessels surrounding the long bones.

Hands
Parts of the body might be given the capacity to grow again if they were lost through injury, so that a severed hand could be regenerated in a matter of weeks.

Skin
The skin and body wall could be made tougher, especially in places such as the abdomen where inner organs have to be protected from harm.

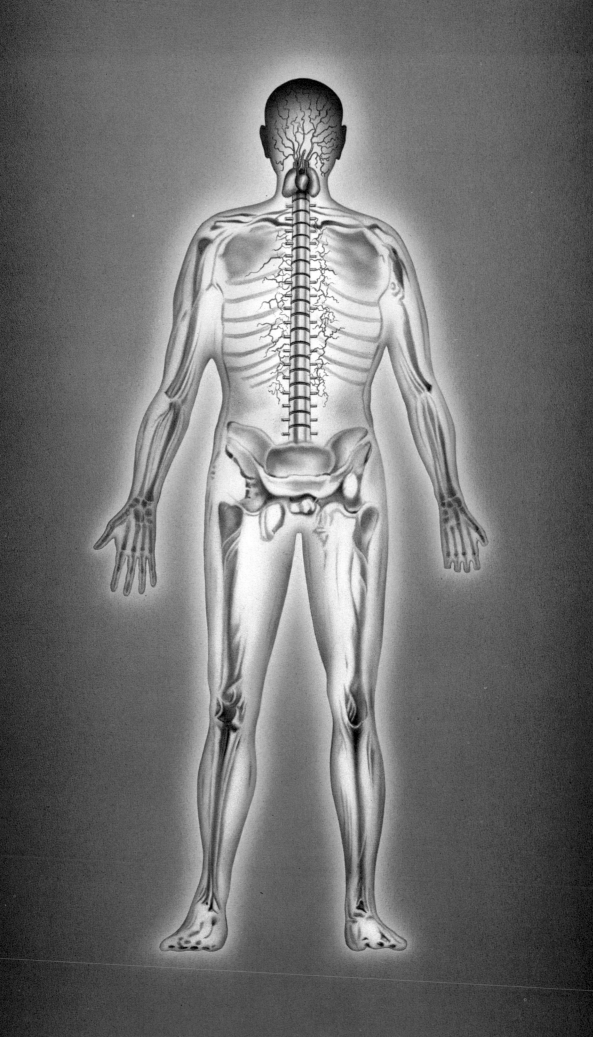

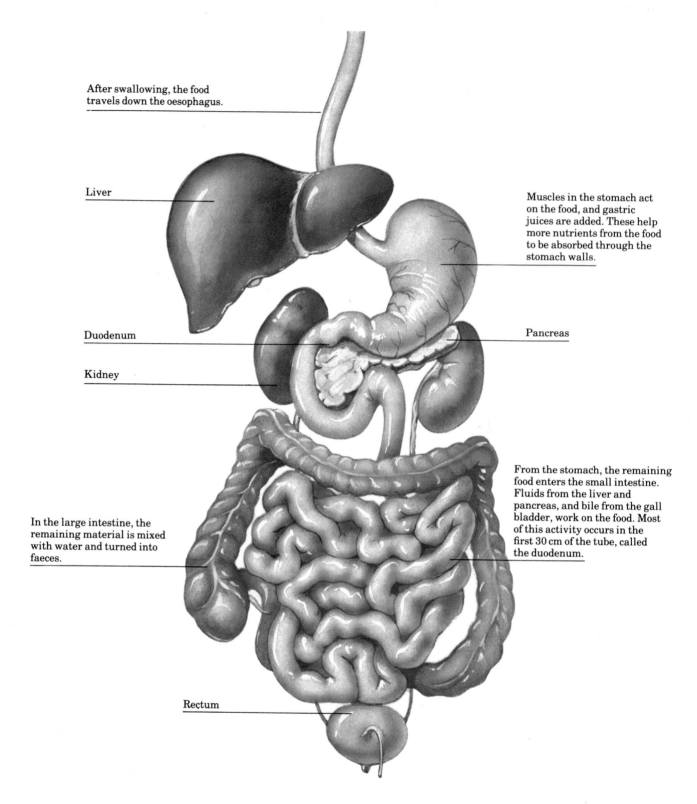

After swallowing, the food travels down the oesophagus.

Liver

Muscles in the stomach act on the food, and gastric juices are added. These help more nutrients from the food to be absorbed through the stomach walls.

Duodenum

Pancreas

Kidney

In the large intestine, the remaining material is mixed with water and turned into faeces.

From the stomach, the remaining food enters the small intestine. Fluids from the liver and pancreas, and bile from the gall bladder, work on the food. Most of this activity occurs in the first 30 cm of the tube, called the duodenum.

Rectum

The design of our present digestive system leaves plenty of room for improvement. For instance, we have about 7 metres of intestine although we could manage with only one. There are also many materials we cannot digest. Radical redesigning by genetic engineers might be preceded by a simpler strategy: engineering bacteria capable of digesting new substances, which could live in our stomachs much as cellulose-digesting bacteria live in those of cows. This approach would mean that, by replacing the bacteria with new ones, human beings of the future could adapt to new environments such as other planets.

110

an Everyman figure called Clark Kent harbours within an innocent disguise his true identity: Superman, the man of steel. The notion that a meek victim of circumstance can be transformed into an omnicompetent demigod is an appealing one; but designing new human species cannot give us the power of instant self-transformation, nor will it enable us to produce people invulnerable to injury, capable of levitation or possessing X-ray vision. Nevertheless, many improvements to our capabilities will be within the compass of the genetic engineers of the future, affecting not only the structure of our bodies, but also their metabolism and powers of perception. The desire to improve on nature will probably be one of the first motives to encourage them to design the seed of a new kind of man.

What appals us most when we contemplate the human condition is probably our frailty: the ease with which we can be damaged, and our vulnerability to disease. Nature, like contemporary commercial technology, seems overfond of planned obsolescence, and human bodies suffer the double disadvantage of being soft and brittle at the same time. If one were laying down specifications for a new kind of man, one would probably ask first that he should have flesh which would not tear so easily and bones which would not snap so readily. Next, one might ask that he be given the capacity to recover much more completely from inflicted damage, by regenerating tissues and regrowing limbs and organs.

Why, if regrowing damaged parts is such a wonderful idea, has natural selection not already endowed us with such a capacity? Partly, this is because natural selection usually works in the most economical way available. It makes good sense for an organism to maintain repair facilities for skin – skin is very likely to be torn or scratched, but such tears and scratches are unlikely to be fatal. On the other hand, organs deep within the body are much less likely to be injured, and if they are injured the likelihood is that the injury will prove fatal anyhow. The cost-effectiveness of endowing individuals with great powers of self-repair also has to be compared with the cost-effectiveness of simple replacement of a whole individual by another grown from a new egg. This does not mean, though, that such repair would be impossible.

It would undoubtedly be hard to give redesigned people the chance to regenerate completely if they suffer great damage. Regenerating bodies might not be too difficult, but regenerating minds is another matter: if the brain is starved of oxygen for only a few minutes, the person is destroyed, even though the cells can be revived. We will not be able to produce a race of people who could afford to be casual about massive blood loss or temporary heart failure, but it would be a significant step forward if a new kind of people could be given the power to seal off leaking blood vessels and the power to keep their hearts pumping even in the most difficult circumstances. This would allow time for sophisticated regrowing mechanisms to come into place, restoring lost limbs and smashed organs, or simply time to reach medical aid. The more effective our methods of medical care become, the more it will be to our advantage to adapt ourselves to make the maximum use of them.

Even when not subject to accident or disease, the human body is an imperfect structure made out of imperfect materials. For instance, people are especially prone to back trouble, because one of the weakest aspects of human bioengineering is the spine. Natural selection cannot be held entirely to blame for the design faults of the human spine, largely because it had such unpromising material to start with: there were limitations on what could reasonably be done in modifying our quadrupedal ancestors for upright life. The careful human engineer would surely try to do better in providing his creations with a backbone sturdy enough, yet flexible enough, to answer the various demands made of it.

The main function of a skeleton is to provide rigid support and protection for the soft parts of the body, while at the same time providing adequate jointing and manual dexterity. One wishes occasionally, though, that there were more freedom of action permitted by some of the joints, and that the rigidity of the long bones could be temporarily modified. If redesigned man could have the capacity to modify the properties of his skeleton (however slightly) at will, that might be greatly to his advantage.

A NEW METABOLISM

As well as modifying the body's structural properties, it would also be convenient to pay serious attention to its metabolism. An engaging notion would be to increase the range of substances which the body can utilize as food. There are all kinds of organic molecules which we cannot digest, because we lack the enzymes which would be necessary to break them down into smaller molecules that can be used directly for energy production.

One unusable substance of which we eat quite a lot is cellulose, the principal structural substance in plant tissue. It becomes the 'roughage' in our diet, passing all the way through our digestive system. There is no reason in principle why cellulose should not be a useful food; it is a long-chain molecule whose individual units are glucose. If our bodies could make an enzyme to break up the chain, the glucose units could then be handled very conveniently by metabolic apparatus which we already produce. Actually, there are no higher organisms which possess such an enzyme. As we saw in Chapter Three, herbivorous animals which live primarily on grass or leaves rely on micro-organisms which live in their gut to break down cellulose for them.

Adapting men to digest cellulose would be a very minor modification in biochemical terms – as long as the required enzyme could in fact be designed – but it would be of very considerable significance. It would be very difficult for such redesigned people to find themselves facing starvation. As long as there was live plant material around, they could get by.

Another long-chain carbohydrate molecule widely used in nature as a structural material is chitin, different versions of which are employed by insects and fungi. There is not nearly as much chitin about as cellulose, but the problem of adapting human beings to take advantage of it is much the same and might as well be solved at the same time.

An extrapolation of this line of thinking might suggest that there is a certain inconvenience in relying on other organic material at all. In eating plants we are only 'reclaiming' the energy of sunlight which the plants have patiently absorbed and converted into the energy of chemical bonds. If we can adapt human digestive juices to cope with cellulose, why could we not endow human skin with a photosynthetic apparatus to make direct use of solar energy?

The problem with this idea is a simple one of energy economics. Plants get by perfectly adequately on the solar energy which they fix, and lay down stores of organic treasure for human and other animals to plunder; but what counts as getting by for a plant is very limited by the standards of animals. Plants are sedentary: they do not move. Humans not only move about, but maintain a constant internal temperature. It is difficult to imagine human intelligence evolving under other circumstances. To keep one human being going day by day requires the energy-fixing capacity of large numbers of plants spread over a wide area. Every animal that exists has to be sustained by many times its own weight and surface area of plant material. Cutting out the middleman, therefore, simply would not work; there is no way any animal, including a human being, could photosynthesize enough carbohydrates to sustain its lifestyle. If it *were* possible, we would not be able to make the category distinction between animals and plants that we do: there would indeed be wayfaring trees with lower branches specialized for manipulation and brains in their trunks.

There are other aspects of metabolism which might be modified productively. Control of metabolic rate might be a useful talent to have. Routine hibernation is not something that would be useful to most human beings, but the ability to slow the metabolic rate voluntarily to suit particular situations could be valuable. The most frequently suggested use for such an ability is to allow people to sustain themselves economically through long journeys in interplanetary – perhaps even interstellar – space.

It is likely that none of these modifications would be very sweeping in biochemical terms. None of

Our present digestive system is extremely intricate. This shows the long finger-like *villi* that line the small intestine wall and are crucial in breaking down carbohydrates and proteins by secreting enzymes.

A NEW METABOLISM
Adapting the digestive system to make it more capable would probably not require much structural change, but existing organs could be modified to take on extra tasks.

Stomach and pancreas
If man could be given the ability to produce new enzymes, to break down molecules such as cellulose that are at present indigestible, many new food sources could be exploited. Such enzymes could be produced by glands such as those in the stomach and pancreas, which secrete the juices that digest food. Alternatively, clusters of cells could be added to the stomach wall to manufacture the new enzymes (inset right).

Small intestine
Evolution has equipped us with far more small intestine than we really need. Its length could be reduced considerably.

Large intestine
The original function of the large intestine – storing useless material to be eliminated – would be reduced in importance if we were able to digest a greater part of the food we eat. New structures could be added (inset left) to store some products of digestion, such as fats, as a source of energy when no food was available.

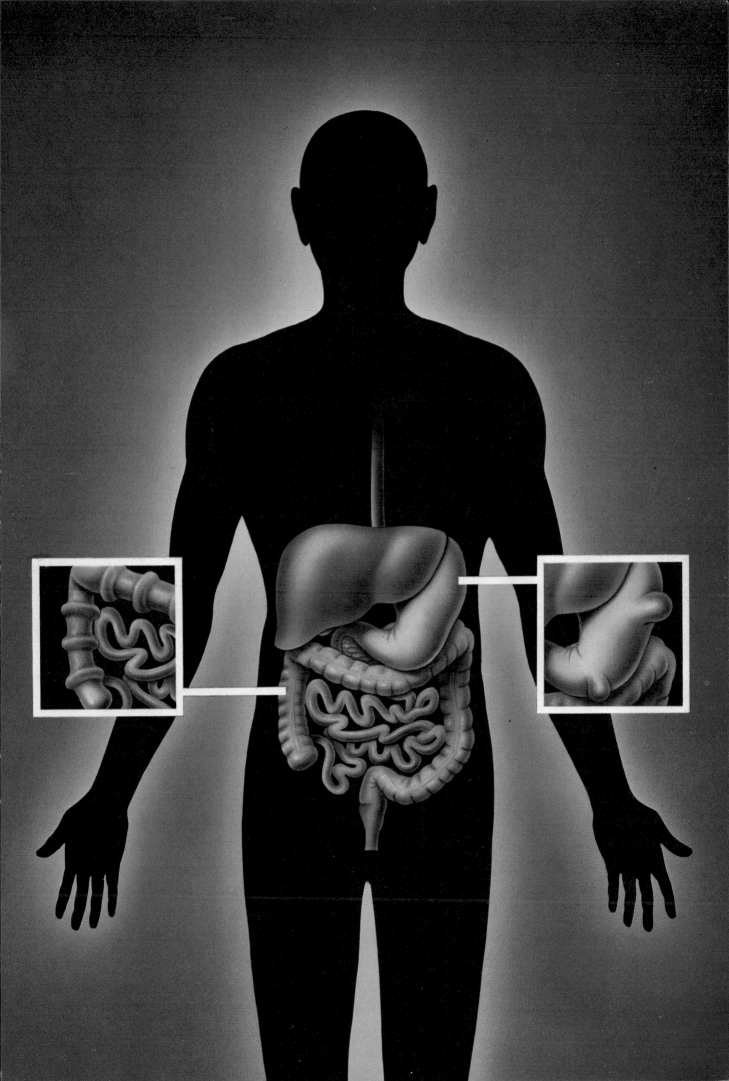

them would require the wholesale alteration of the system we have inherited; it is a matter of tinkering. The consequences of such changes, in terms of human abilities and lifestyles, would nevertheless be profound.

NEW PERCEPTIONS

The third general area in which modifications might profitably be made to human capability is the area of sensory perception. The information provided by the five senses about what is going on around us is the raw material on which our intelligence works, and any improvement in its quality would be an advantage.

It is easy enough to imagine our senses working better – clearly, we do not smell as well as dogs or hear as well as bats – but there is a catch in the naive argument that each and every one of our senses might simply be able to take in more information. There is such a thing as too much information; the brain's capacity to cope with it can be overloaded. The intelligent use of the eyes, for instance, involves the capacity to ignore most of what falls within the field of vision, and the intelligent use of the ears involves blotting out of consciousness most of the sounds that are actually there. The human sensorium has been 'finely tuned' by natural selection to pick out most of the information relevant to our decisions, while neglecting much that is relatively unimportant.

A simple increase in the sensitivity of one or more of the senses could easily be counterproductive, because it would throw out this delicate filtering mechanism. Optimizing the capabilities of the five senses is therefore a much more complicated matter than it might initially seem. Even taking these arguments into account, though, there are some additional facilities for recovering information

which it would certainly be useful to have.

One point which immediately calls itself to mind is that humans are not good at seeing in the dark. There are many animals which are better at making use of low levels of light than we are – cats, for example. It would be very useful to enhance the ability of humans to see by night, provided that any modifications made to the eyes for that purpose are not prejudicial to the ability to see by day.

There are two ways by which night-vision might be enhanced. One strategy would be to rearrange the proportion and distribution of the receptors in the retina. The retina contains different kinds of light-sensitive cells – rods, which perceive dim light, and cones, which discern fine detail in bright light and are used in colour vision. In man, cones are concentrated in the centre of the retina and rods predominate round the edges. By this means the human eye can adjust moderately well to very different light intensities. Improving night-vision by rearranging the receptors might, however, have a detrimental effect on daytime vision.

The second strategy would be to increase the spectrum of radiation to which the eye is sensitive. If the eye were sensitive to radiation in the infra-red range, it would have far less difficulty in discriminating between objects in the dark – especially living objects which are radiating heat in those wavelengths. Again, the problem would be one of improving night-vision while not harming day-vision. In daylight, infra-red sensors might simply be overloaded. Some kind of internal 'switch' would be required which could activate some receptors and deactivate others, so that the eye could operate in one mode by day and another by night. How such a mechanism could be biochemically designed is not clear, but something along these lines might be managed. Another solution to the problem would be

Modified man might take several lessons from nature. Insects such as this horsefly have compound eyes which consist of many small visual units or facets. Their sensitivity to polarized light and ultraviolet rays, if transplanted to man, would greatly increase his ability to survive in areas of low light intensity.

The flashlight fish has light organs below its eyes which are colonies of living luminous bacteria. They are used for seeing, communication, hunting prey and confusing predators. A similar in-built lighting mechanism would enable future man to see in low light environments – underwater, in space and at night.

This long-eared owl is able to see and hunt in less than one tenth of the illumination needed by humans. It can also hunt in total darkness, by relying on its acute hearing, with ear openings positioned asymmetrically to locate the source of sounds. The discs of feathers around the eyes concentrate sound rather like the 'receiving dishes' on radiotelescopes.

to have the night-vision eye, or eyes, separate from the day-vision eyes. This is the strategy followed by a certain kind of snake which has heat sensors as well as eyes.

The eyes are not the only sense organs which can be recruited to solve the problem of getting around in the dark. Bats find their way around not by using their eyes, but by using their ears, and some marine mammals which have to cope with the murky ocean depths use a similar system of echo-location. Sonar and radar are technological versions of this method of sensing which we have found extremely useful in extending our powers of perception artificially.

It might conceivably be possible to equip redesigned human beings with some kind of system akin to that used by bats. This would involve whole new anatomical structures being added to the head, and it would mean also that people so equipped would have to learn to make use of a new kind of incoming information. There might well be problems of compatibility involved in maintaining that kind of echo-location sense and retaining normal hearing too. We use our ears almost entirely

for heeding warning sounds and listening to speech, and it is possible that other kinds of auditory signals would interfere with these uses. On the other hand, dolphins – which use echo-location to scan their environment – also appear to exchange complicated sound signals of some kind. One might argue that if we can use the five senses we have more or less simultaneously, integrating the various kinds of information, we ought to be adaptable enough to take in a sixth channel of information given time to practise.

Another sense which may be fairly well developed in some animals, although humans hardly make use of it at all, is a sensitivity to magnetic fields. Those bird species which are exceptionally good navigators – many migratory species and homing pigeons – apparently orientate themselves partly by means of the Earth's magnetic field, and can recognize certain anomalies introduced into the field by geological features. It is probable that humans do possess some capacity for this kind of sensing but are not normally conscious of it – many individuals do appear to have a 'sense of

115

NEW SENSES

Our redesigned descendants could have many capabilities that we lack at present; in particular, the ability to see and work in the dark.

Eyes

Infra-red vision would enable man to 'see' different heat intensities (this page). New heat-sensitive or radiation-sensitive cells could be incorporated into the rods and cones of the retina or added as a separate organ. Night vision could also be improved by simply increasing the number of rod-cells – those which respond to low light intensity.

Ears

A large receiver in the centre of the modified ear would enable future man to receive high-frequency signals. These would then be relayed along a fine electrical wire to an organo-metallic synapse, where they would be transmitted by the nerves to the brain.

A smaller transmitting device in the top of the ear would allow man to send signals in a similar way.

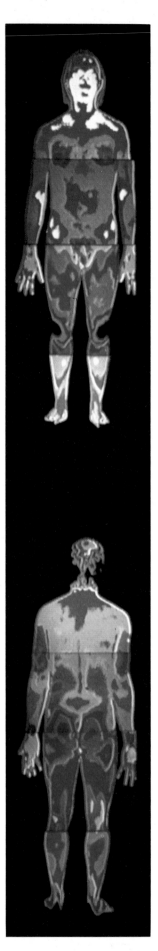

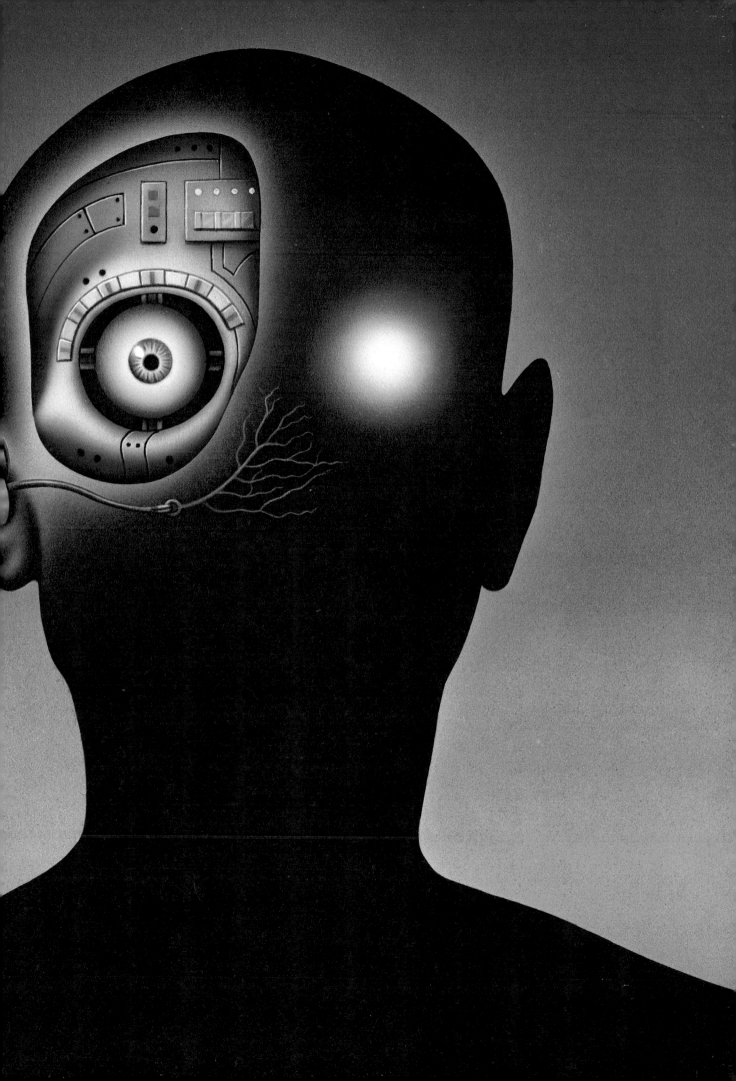

Genetic engineers may be able to increase man's range of perceptions by imitating nature. **(Left)** The jackrabbit's long ears give sensitive hearing which is particularly useful at night. **(Right)** Rattlesnakes use the heat-sensitive pits above their jaws to detect predators. **(Below)** The American moon moth has tiny hairs on its antennae which detect smells.

direction' which functions subliminally. If this is the case, then the sensory capacities of redesigned people might be enhanced along these lines.

There have been many other claims about extra senses which people either have already or are potentially capable of developing. The idea of telepathic communication – the shifting of coherent information directly from one mind to another – is one which exercises a powerful hold on the human imagination. The idea of being able to 'read' another person's thoughts has fascinated us for centuries. But the notion of 'extra-sensory perception' is in fact a contradiction in terms. *All* perception is sensory, and if information is to get from one place to another it *must* be physically incarnate in some way, as a movement of actual molecules or some kind of electromagnetic disturbance.

While it may be possible, therefore, to give redesigned humans better versions of the five senses we already know, and perhaps extra ones based on other kinds of signals, we can be reasonably certain that we will not be able to endow them with telepathy, clairvoyance or precognition. The power of levitation and other psychokinetic abilities are out of the question for similar reasons. They are 'plausible impossibilities', akin to the convention of cartoon artists that characters run off the edges of cliffs but do not begin to fall until they realize they are no longer supported.

MAN MODIFIED TO LIVE UNDERWATER

We are already aware of some of the very modest modifications to the human physique – such as changes in skin colour, or the shape of the eyelids – by which natural selection has helped men to live in different climatic conditions (see Chapter One). Human engineers would probably feel that they could do a better job of modifying men for life in extreme climatic conditions than natural selection has. It might be possible to enhance our powers of water conservation to make it easier to get by in arid places, or to adapt us better to life at high altitudes. These matters would, however, be trivial compared to the real challenge: that of extending the human domain into new environments.

Adapting human beings for life in the sea would probably be a fairly simple exercise of this kind. The fact that numerous mammal species such as whales, dolphins and seals have 'regressed' to aquatic life is testimony to the ease with which mammalian characteristics can be so modified. The primary requirements are better protection against cold and some kind of physiological protection against caisson sickness ('the bends'). It would not be necessary, at least in the first instance, to replace or supplement lungs with gills: dolphins and seals get by perfectly well breathing air.

Protection against cold is easy enough to provide: all that is required is a layer of subcutaneous fat (blubber). There would have to be corollary changes in the properties of the skin, however, to make it tougher and oilier – effectively, the skin would have to take over the functions served by the wet-suits used by scuba-divers. Protection against caisson sickness would be more difficult. The disease is caused by the fact that changes of external pressure affect the gases dissolved in the blood, so that if a diver comes up too quickly bubbles of nitrogen tend to appear in the blood vessels. These cannot be absorbed quickly enough by the tissues and tend to accumulate in the joints, causing severe pain and restriction of mobility. Bubbles in the nervous system can cause paralysis or convulsions; bubbles in the heart can cause death. Aquatic mammals achieve protection against the disease partly by collapsing the lungs before a dive and partly by greater facility in nitrogen uptake by the tissues.

No mammals which have regressed to the sea have actually traded in their lungs for gills, and this reflects the fact that it is difficult to keep a warm-blooded system going with the amounts of oxygen which can be extracted from water. Total dependence on air does, however, have its disadvantages; it puts a severe restriction on the time that an aquatic mammal can stay submerged. There would probably be no benefit in creating a race of men who have gills *instead of* lungs, but there would be considerable attraction in the notion of creating a race who have gills *as well as* lungs, who could therefore operate as genuine amphibians. Such people could stay beneath the surface for long periods – perhaps indefinitely, provided that they were not too active while relying purely on oxygen taken in through the gills. They would thus be able to do some kinds of work underwater – which would, after all, be the main purpose in creating such a race. Periodic visits to the surface would be necessary if the full capabilities of the body were to be exploited, or if active work were being done, but these visits might be less frequent than those which dolphins are compelled to make.

Equipping a human body with gills would seem to be an awkward problem in human engineering, but it should be capable of solution. It might involve adding a new structure to the upper torso, thickening the neck considerably and reducing the size of the lungs so that the space occupied by the uppermost part of the lungs could be given over to a set of gill filaments. As well as being reduced slightly in size, the lungs might have to be further modified in order to allow them to be collapsed and reflated easily. The gills would have to be supplied with an extra pair of blood vessels equivalent to the pulmonary artery and the pulmonary vein which carry blood back and forth between the heart and the lungs.

Adding these gills to the human body might not be so very difficult, given that the human embryo, like all mammal embryos, goes through a stage where it has gill-like structures – curious 'phantoms' of the evolutionary past. Adding the genes to exploit this potential, making the gills develop and grow instead of disappearing as the embryo develops, probably represents a modest problem in genetic engineering. It is a matter of addition rather than of large-scale replacement. Once we understand how it is that the structure of

MAN MODIFIED FOR LIFE UNDERWATER
Future genetic engineers could come full circle in the process of evolution and adapt man to live underwater.

Breathing
Underwater man would need a second breathing apparatus to complement the existing lungs which can only take oxygen from the air. Feathery gill structures could be developed in the neck to extract oxygen directly from water. The oxygen would then pass along new blood vessels in the thickened neck to a modified heart.

The lungs and other tissues could be altered in order to absorb free nitrogen and prevent caisson sickness.

An internal blocking mechanism in the nose would allow man to alternate between air and water breathing, giving him more flexibility in his choice of habitat and means of transport.

Skin
The skin would be toughened and scaly with an additional layer of fatty tissue for protection against the cold. Membranous structures could be added to the feet for swimming, but their size would be restricted so as not to hinder locomotion on land.

New senses
In the murky underwater environment, man's eyes would give him little advantage, but he would retain them for use on land. An echo-location system similar to that of bats and dolphins could be incorporated; alternatively, a lateral line of chemo-receptors like those of fish would enable man to detect chemical changes and the presence of other organisms around him.

Underwater communication would differ from the conversation of today. A sign language developed from that of present day divers could be supplemented by a system of radio receiver and transmitter implants.

Further adaptations
The spine would be both strengthened and given maximum flexibility for sinuous underwater movement.

The lower abdomen would be modified so that the genitals could be withdrawn into the body for protection.

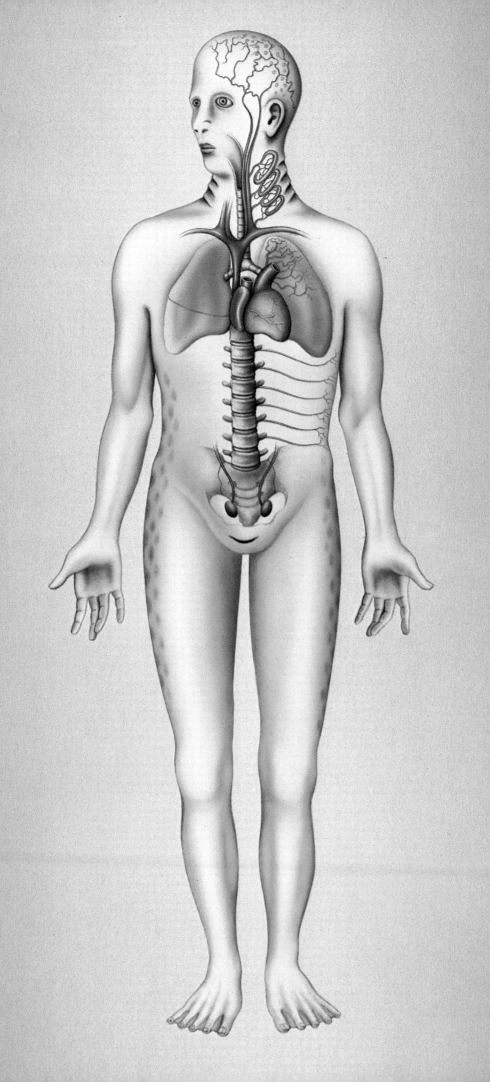

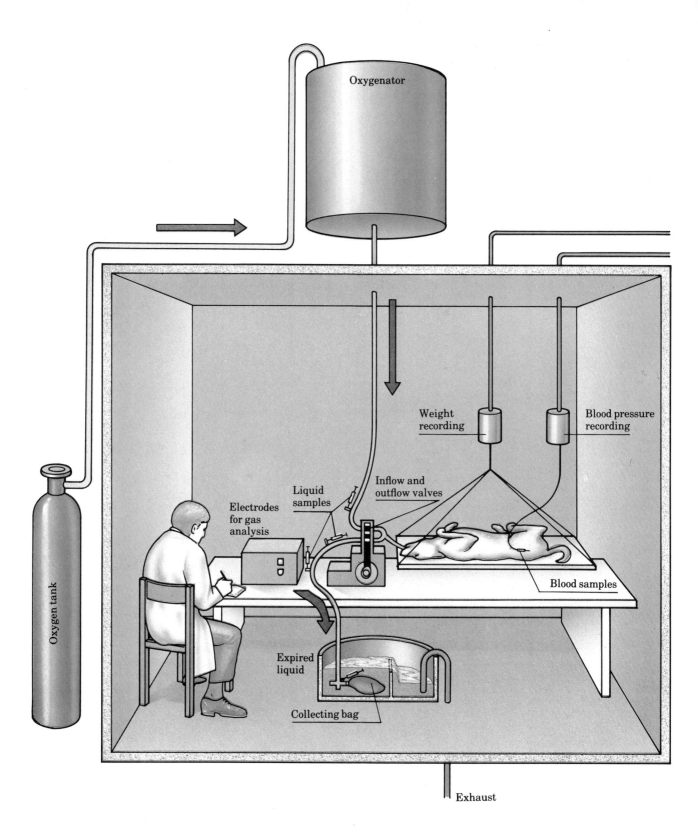

Oxygenator

Weight recording

Blood pressure recording

Inflow and outflow valves

Liquid samples

Electrodes for gas analysis

Blood samples

Oxygen tank

Expired liquid

Collecting bag

Exhaust

It may not be necessary to engineer new gill structures to enable man to breathe underwater for short periods. Experiments have been carried out in which animals have inhaled sufficient oxygen from water to survive for up to 24 minutes.

In this experiment, extra oxygen was pumped into the water, while the dog's oxygen requirement was reduced by anaesthetizing and cooling. The used water flowed out of the dog's lungs by gravity. The main difficulty was the expulsion of carbon dioxide, which accumulated gradually inside the body: this problem could easily be overcome by future genetic engineers.

the body and its organs is determined by the genes, and once we can transplant genes and construct whole chromosome systems at will, then such design projects must become possible. Their accomplishment becomes merely a test of ingenuity and artistry. There would, however, have to be plenty of practice on animals before an attempt was made to transform a human ovum in this way. (The actual engineering work would, of course, be carried out on egg cells, not on mature individuals.)

After these basic alterations, there would be numerous other modifications to the human frame which would be either necessary or highly desirable as adaptations for underwater life. The gill slits which permit water breathing would have to be sealed when the adapted men were breathing air; similarly, the nostrils used in air breathing would have to be sealed while under the surface. This would require alterations to the structure of the nose, which would probably be flattened, with slit-like nostrils.

One big problem faced by men modified for aquatic life would be that of sensory adaptation. Human eyes are geared to seeing in bright light, but in the depths of the sea there is little or no light to convey visual information. Although some marine creatures – notably octopuses and squids – have well-developed eyes, most invest heavily in other senses. Dolphins use echo-location, and most fish use sensitive chemo-receptors arranged along their bodies in a 'lateral line'.

It would probably make sense to modify the eyes of aquatic men so as to make them more suitable for underwater use, although one would not want to go so far in doing this that the eyes became useless for seeing above the surface. At the same time, though, providing an extra sensory apparatus more suited to the submarine environment would be an attractive option. It might be easier to provide aquatic men with lateral-line systems, but echo-location systems would undoubtedly be more useful for a varied and active life. Provided that the brain could cope with such a spectrum of information inputs, it would be best to have both.

The most obvious adaptation which aquatic mammals have undergone as a consequence of their regression to the sea is that they have lost their legs. Even myth-makers, creating imaginary aquatic humans, give mermaids fishy tails instead of legs. The logic of this is easy enough to appreciate: legs are specifically suited to locomotion on land and support against the pull of gravity. Underwater locomotion demands sinuous wave-like motions of the whole body, and support is not an issue. However, the designer of an aquatic human race would probably be most reluctant to copy the natural selection which shaped seals and dolphins. For one thing, he would want to preserve if possible the amphibian potential of his new humans, and would not want them to be as helpless out of water as are seals. For another, the aquatic men would be

working and living mainly on the seabed, where, although legs would not be vital for support, their capacity to act as levers in moving and manipulating large objects could be very important.

Genuinely amphibious animals tend to keep their legs, although the ones that spend a good deal of time in water tend to modify them somewhat to facilitate swimming. There are basically two strategies that can be followed – the one employed by frogs, which go in for large flipper-feet, and the one employed by newts, which go in for very short legs and very big tails. For humans, the option favoured by frogs looks by far the better bet – it would be inconvenient for aquatic men to go on all fours if and when they do come on to the land, and short limbs are much less useful for purposes of manipulation.

We would expect, therefore, that men modified for aquatic life would keep their legs, but would be equipped with large feet and webbed toes. These would not be too exaggerated, however, lest they should make walking too difficult when the aquatic men emerge on to land. The arms and hands would not be modified in the same way – the manipulative potential of the hand and arm would have to be preserved at all costs.

Other anatomical modifications to be made would be slight. The alteration of the properties of the skin would probably imply the absence of body hair, or the modification of that hair to form something like a seal's pelt. The skin might be coloured, either defensively (dark on the back, light on the belly to be less noticeable to predators and prey) or – perhaps – with a distinctive warning coloration as in killer whales. One particularly noticeable change would be the reduction of external genitalia. Aquatic mammals generally keep their genitals hidden within their bodies and their apertures sealed, except when they are actually in use. It would be prudent for aquatic humans to do likewise. The breasts of the female might also be expected to be less exaggerated, in the interests of streamlining. Sexual differentiation in contemporary versions of *Homo sapiens* is orientated almost entirely to visual perception, but aquatic men, especially if equipped with lateral-line systems, might make more use of pheromonal signalling. These relatively trivial alterations complete a package which will one day constitute the specifications upon which a new human species will be constructed.

LIFE UNDERWATER
How would people adapted for aquatic life actually live? We may take it for granted that they would not live as savages of the sea, hunting and gathering with fish-spears and baskets of seaweed. Theirs would be a sophisticated and industrialized culture. They would work with machines, and would undertake the extensive transformation of the seabed into an artificial environment. They would

be submarine agriculturalists, cultivating crops for food and sale, and they would invest in elaborate animal husbandry. They would, of course, be prolific exporters of seafood to the land, and would probably export raw materials too: they would be miners of the seabed, extracting fossil fuels and metal ores. They would be forced to import most of their finished technological products from the land, but they would be able to establish a reasonable trading position.

These sea-people would live in houses, not so much because they would need shelter in their weatherless environment but because they would value personal space, as we do, and would need artificial environments both for work and for comfort. Houses are places to store up possessions and places where particular social functions are located. Underwater houses would not be shaped like houses on land, however; they would be rounded rather than angular. They might well have 'air rooms' within them, because there are many operations that can be performed in air much better than in water, and the apparatus maintaining the oxygenation of these air rooms would be one of the most important which the sea-people possessed.

The main disadvantage of water as a habitat for intelligent life is that it is a fireless environment. Maintaining machinery without fire presents many difficulties; the routines of submarine cookery might well present a host of practical problems. A second major disadvantage of sea-water is its corrosiveness. Delicate machinery is difficult to protect if it is to be permanently submerged. Once the need exists, however, such technical problems can be overcome.

A further difficulty would arise in respect of communication. Water will conduct sound, but it does not transmit words produced by human vocal chords; nor is the human ear adapted to underwater hearing. If the sea-people are to be amphibious, they will want to retain the voices and ears which they have for communication out of water, and may therefore have to develop a new code of signals for their own use in their new environment. Divers use sign-language, but this has awkward limitations, especially bearing in mind the poor visibility of the submarine world. What possibilities there would be for developing a new language would probably depend on the specific innovations which had been introduced into the sensorium of the adapted men; sound communication might still be the best option

Life underwater
The colonization of the seas opens up new possibilities for future life. With underwater houses and factories made of non-ferrous materials, our descendants might have little cause to visit the land of their ancestors. Two separate worlds and races could develop, coming into contact only near coasts and shipping.

124

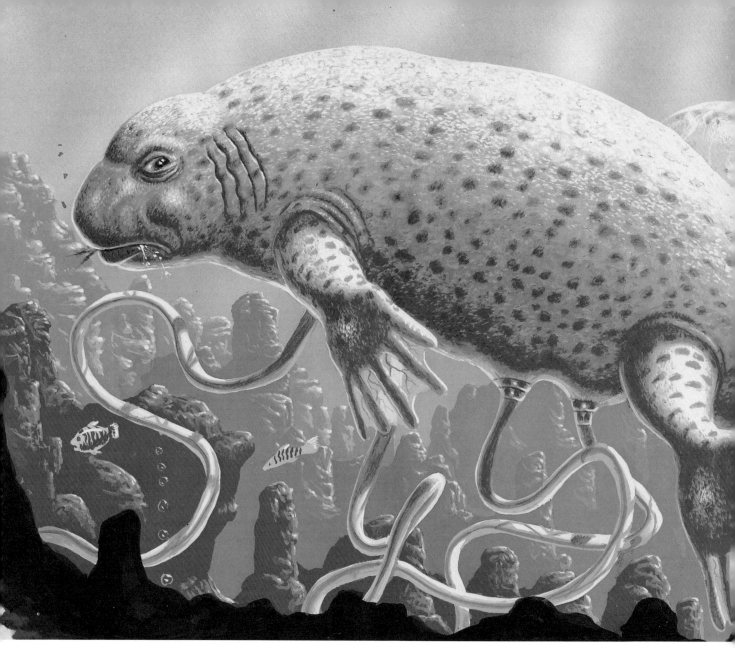

Underwater agriculture
Man living underwater will apply techniques of genetic engineering to other species as we do today. A sea-cow would be engineered to make maximum use of its environment.
Designed to eat the plankton and seaweeds of the oceans, and adapted for underwater motion, these walrus-like creatures could be milked or slaughtered in underwater farms, supplying fresh agricultural produce to the aquatic population.

if some kind of signal-transmitter and receiver could be built in. It would be possible to use technological devices to facilitate communication, and even though this would make mechanical malfunctions very inconvenient it might be the most sensible course.

The crops cultivated by the underwater farmers, and the livestock which they keep, will very probably be products of genetic engineering just as they are. They may well go in for the cultivation of oyster-beds, and for the breeding of lobsters, as well as trapping fish and milking whales, but in most cases they will be working with specially adapted species – just as our domestic animals have been specially adapted (so far mostly by selective breeding) to our purposes. Perhaps the sea-people will also take sea-sheep and sea-cattle into their new world with them.

Initially, at least, the sea-people would colonize the continental shelves rather than the ocean depths. They would probably first establish themselves in warm waters. The best place for them to begin in Europe would be the Adriatic Sea,

hope for future human progress, might pass to the people of the sea rather than their land-based cousins.

It is difficult to guess what kind of attitude the sea-people might have to the land-people: there are no analogous situations to which we might turn for inspiration. It is possible that they would not be entirely grateful for having been created, and might be resentful on account of not having been made in the image of their makers. Perhaps they would not be ready to take the place prepared for them and would want to make their own choices about how and where to live. Some sea-people might not want to live in a way that integrated them – albeit peripherally – into the technological civilization of the land-based cousins. And there always remains the possibility of conflict between different races.

The moral propriety of this whole kind of engineering enterprise is questionable. It is arguable that the people whose contribution to that moral debate will be the most crucial of all must be the first engineered people. They – and perhaps only they – will be in a position to estimate whether what has been done in creating them is good or bad.

MAN MODIFIED TO LIVE IN SPACE

The extension of the human domain to the continental shelves, and eventually to the deeper waters of the Earth's oceans, is a parochial matter. It might be of negligible significance in future human history if we can extend the human domain in the other direction which is open to us: beyond the atmosphere, into the wilderness of space.

In order to go into space we have to take pieces of our habitat with us: little capsules of Earth's atmosphere or some breathable substitute, enclosing all the systems required to feed us and tend to our needs. The human colonization of space, at least in the first instance, will be remarkably akin to the fishy colonization of human homes, by means of aquaria. Because they will take their environment with them, our descendants who go out into space will not need radical changes in the human sensorium. They will not need extra layers of fat, or special apparatus to enable them to breathe.

There is, however, one aspect of the Earthly environment that they cannot take with them, and that is Earthly gravity. In an orbital spacecraft, or a spaceship travelling between the planets, people will have no weight at all. If space stations and space colonies can be spun, then weight can be simulated by centrifugal force, but the spin has to be very rapid if that force is to be equivalent to Earthly gravity. On the surfaces of other worlds, people would have weight, but that weight would depend on the size of the world. On the surface of the Moon a person weighs about one-sixth of what he does on the surface of the Earth. A whole Moon habitat cannot be spun around in order to provide its inhabitants with the illusion that they are living at home.

provided that the pollution problem which currently afflicts the whole Mediterranean could be solved. Other seas that seem ripe for such colonization are the Yellow Sea, between Korea and China, and the Timor and Arafura Seas north of Australia. Australia also has the extensive shelf on which the Great Barrier Reef is situated, and might well be the country from which the project will be launched. The eventual expansion into colder and deeper waters will probably be led by the search for natural resources rather than *lebensraum*, but it is likely to be a carefully measured progress.

The civilization of the sea-people will certainly in the first instance be dependent upon that of the land; were the new race to strike out for self-sufficiency, they would find a high level of technology almost impossible to maintain. If the support of the world system were removed, however, a small group of sea-people would find it easier to cope than a land-based community in a similar situation. It is possible to imagine circumstances – a nuclear war among the land-people, for instance – in which the heritage of human knowledge, and the

Adapting a space habitat to our physique by spinning it is only one of the options which will be open to us; it might be more convenient to adapt our descendants to weightlessness. It would almost certainly be desirable, if people are to live on the Moon, to adapt them for low-gravity life.

It is not immediately obvious why weightlessness should be problematic – and, indeed, we know that astronauts can live in orbit for fairly long periods of time without suffering any dreadful consequences. The reason why damage can occur is that the body's systems are geared to a particular workload. The pumping rate of the heart is adjusted to the 'assumption' that it is pumping in a gravity field of a particular strength. The rate adjusts spontaneously to circumstances, but the system can become confused by different conditions.

The effects of weightlessness are several. Decreased circulation of the blood may reduce the supply of oxygen and nutrients to particular organs. Water retention in the tissues is reduced and there is a constant danger of dehydration. Slow, cumulative changes may take place in the skeleton, particularly the long bones, which may eventually be considerably weakened. Bringing a body back from a low-gravity environment to a normal one subjects it to strains to which it has to re-adjust, and if a long time has been spent in the low-gravity environment the body may not be able to re-adjust before suffering serious damage.

If people are to commute regularly between the surface of the Earth and low-gravity or zero-gravity environments, these are medical problems which have to be countered by treatment. If, however, there are to be people in the future who will spend entire lives in space or on the surface of the Moon, these problems might be met by improving the body's ability to adapt itself to new circumstances, or by redesigning it to suit them much better. Some of the features of the human anatomy are things which we need only because we live where we do; if we were living in orbit, our needs would be different, and it would make sense to remodel human anatomy to meet these new needs.

The fact that human beings stand erect against Earth's gravity poses certain problems which have been solved by skeletal modifications. Basically, we have big, fairly thick legs to support our bodies, and a spine which has to support the head and permit us to use our arms to carry loads.

In a weightless environment, strain would no longer be put on the spine by erect posture, and heavy supportive legs would become redundant. One consequence of this, in redesigning people for life in orbit, is that much more use can be made of the lower limbs. Because they would no longer have to perform the supportive function, they would be available as an extra pair of 'arms', bearing manipulative extremities like hands. Modifying the legs into a second pair of arms would be particularly useful because one of the problems of working in a

128

MAN MODIFIED TO LIVE IN SPACE
The ability to survive temporarily in the void without the cumbersome apparatus used by today's astronauts would require far-reaching modifications to the human frame.

Eyes
In a vacuum all apertures would have to be tightly sealable. A protective outer lens with adjustable transparency could keep the eyeball moist and act as a double glazing device.

Lungs and stomach
Two new lungs would act as an internal reservoir for oxygen and a store for waste carbon dioxide. These would have valve connections with the other two lungs, which would themselves be modified, with muscular walls to control their expansion and collapse.

An extra organ close to the stomach could store food reserves, perhaps in the form of fatty deposits.

Skin
The skin would have to be thickened and strengthened to protect the tissues from the effects of zero pressure.

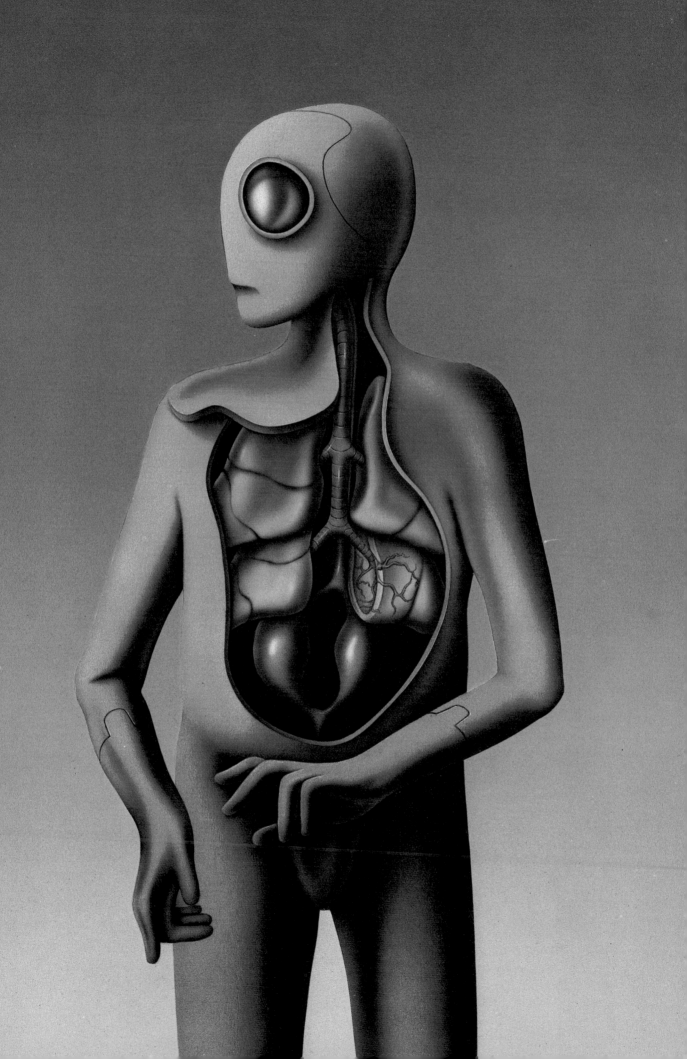

weightless environment is anchorage. There are
many science fiction stories in which men who live
in space wear magnetic boots so that they can
adhere to smooth steel 'floors', but it would be much
simpler if the floors were railed instead of smooth,
for gripping by one or both of an extra pair of hands.
(This would also help to solve the problem of
securing *other* objects within the weightless
environment; simple clamps could be used instead of
magnets.)

It is not merely the form of the bones that might
be modified, but their structural properties as well.
As the bones no longer have to perform a supportive
function in a weightless environment, they do not
need to be so rigid; they can afford to be more elastic.
The limbs will still have to act as levers, and
therefore the ribs will still have to protect the soft
organs of the torso against impact injury. The spine,
with its supportive functions redundant, might be
redesigned to be more efficient as the major
component in a system of levers.

It would be convenient if people adapted for life
in zero gravity were also capable of operating in low
gravity, such as might be associated with asteroids
or moons, and this would mean retaining some of the
features and capacities of the skeleton adapted for
life on Earth. One would not want to go too far,
therefore, in taking advantage of the concessions
made by weightless environments. Nevertheless, it
seems eminently reasonable to suggest that the
people we dispatch into space, to explore it and to
make their livelihood there, will be somewhat
different in physical appearance from ourselves, and
will constitute a race apart: a new species of man,
like the people of the sea.

Are there any further modifications which
human engineers might profitably make in adapting
men for life outside the Earth? Coping with low
gravity is probably a minimum condition of setting
up house elsewhere in the solar system; but
ambitious engineers might want to go further in
equipping men to cope with the airless void.

There is no question of adapting men to survive
indefinitely in the void; animals need a ready supply
of energy in order to be active, and that energy has
to come from the metabolism of appropriate food.
The presence of oxygen is usually necessary for the
release of that stored energy. To contemplate
changing such a fundamental aspect of biochemistry
would be altogether too ambitious.

What can be considered, however, is the
possibility of making men who could survive
unaided in the void for some time, returning only
periodically to their artificial Earth environments.

Two kinds of modifications would have to be
made. There would have to be some kind of oxygen
store incorporated into the body to allow metabolism
to continue for periods of time when no external
supply is available. There would also have to be
modifications to allow the body to cope with the
absence of external pressure. Neither task in itself

seems particularly formidable, but both
modifications would require considerable ingenuity.
Establishing an oxygen store inside the body is
difficult; even aquatic mammals, which have a
strong vested interest in being able to go without
fresh air for as long as possible, have to rise to the
surface in a matter of minutes. In the context of the
body's biochemistry, oxygen is highly reactive, and
cannot last long in its native state once it is in the
bloodstream. What would be needed is a kind of
'third lung' into which pure oxygen could be secreted
while it is freely available, but whose walls are quite
inert. Then, when the external supply of oxygen is
shut off, this extra lung could slowly deflate by
expelling its contents gradually into the actual
lungs. The system would also need some means of
disposing of the carbon dioxide which would build up
and could not be exhaled; perhaps this, too, would
require its own container: a 'fourth lung'.

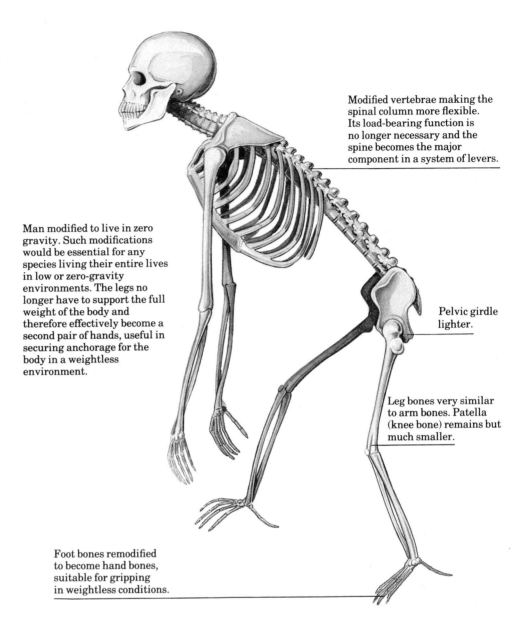

(Left)
Future advances in genetic
engineering will make today's
space technology seem
comparatively tame.

Modified vertebrae making the
spinal column more flexible.
Its load-bearing function is
no longer necessary and the
spine becomes the major
component in a system of levers.

Man modified to live in zero
gravity. Such modifications
would be essential for any
species living their entire lives
in low or zero-gravity
environments. The legs no
longer have to support the full
weight of the body and
therefore effectively become a
second pair of hands, useful in
securing anchorage for the
body in a weightless
environment.

Pelvic girdle
lighter.

Leg bones very similar
to arm bones. Patella
(knee bone) remains but
much smaller.

Foot bones remodified
to become hand bones,
suitable for gripping
in weightless conditions.

Adapting the body to cope with zero pressure
might seem as simple as adapting it to cope with
zero gravity, but the task would be more
complicated. Considerable changes would have to be
made in the body's outer covering, to permit all its
apertures to be tightly sealed. Tear ducts and sweat
glands would probably have to be dispensed with
altogether. Their functions would have to be
performed some other way. Keeping the eyeball
moist in a vacuum would be impossible, and the eye
would have to be modified to take account of this.
The skin of men adapted for the void would have to
be much tougher, in order to protect everything that
lies within it, but this would – ideally, at least –
have to be accomplished without any significant loss
in its elasticity.

In a sense, men engineered to cope temporarily
with the void would still have to be equipped with
the functional equivalent of the bulky pressure suits

which we see today's astronauts wearing when they
take their short walks in space or dance on the
surface of the Moon; they would simply have their
version of those suits biologically built in.

If men can be adapted to live in artificial
environments in space, another, more daring
possibility recommends itself for consideration: that
of adapting men to live on the surfaces of other
worlds. It seems that there is no other world within
the solar system where human life is possible. Even
Mars, once imagined to be a possible abode of life, is
hostile. Some kinds of micro-organisms might be
adapted to live there, but even that would be
difficult. Adapting men to draw oxygen from such a
thin atmosphere, or to stay warm in such low
temperatures, would be so difficult that it is almost
impossible to imagine an incentive great enough to
make human engineers want to try it. In the
fullness of time, however, there may be other worlds

than those of the solar system accessible to us. It takes a long time to travel across interstellar distances, but even a ship that takes many generations to complete such a journey could carry a human crew, and a human cargo.

Science fiction writers have been constantly optimistic about the possibility of finding worlds in other star systems so similar to Earth that men like ourselves simply step down from their starships and set up house there. But probably the men in the starships will not even look like us: they may have been redesigned for low gravity. In any event, they are likely to find that other worlds, even those with a similar orbit around a star like our Sun, with their own life based on carbon-chain molecules, will, nevertheless, pose severe problems of adaptation before men could live there. In such circumstances, the services of genetic engineers would be a vital necessity.

This should not require us to summon up images of an infinite array of grotesque freaks, with bizarre combinations of features borrowed from whichever animals we happen to find most loathsome. There are in Earth's life system all kinds of successful models on which organisms can be built. Erect bipeds thrive alongside quadrupeds, spiders, centipedes and worms. Wherever humans go they should be able to keep the basic aspects of their form; even on alien worlds they will probably be able to live as erect bipeds of a size and physique not too far removed from our own. The changes which the human engineers will be forced to make will be, for the most part, subtle ones. They might be mostly adaptations of biochemistry and temperature control, allowing us to use different atmospheres and to be comfortable in environments which feature a different climatic balance. The organic environment, in all its complexity, would pose the most difficult challenges for would-be colonists of an alien world, whether they seek to import only themselves, or an entire supportive ecosystem. The ability to metabolize alien foods would be the most vital one of all; such an adaptation might call for great ingenuity on the part of human engineers without the resultant adapted men looking significantly different from one or all of the physical types of man with which we are already familiar.

Even if the problem of interstellar distances did not rule out interstellar commuting, the problem of adapting to conditions on different habitable worlds surely would. Each world, if we are ever to possess more than one, will almost certainly have to have its own particular human species. If there are no intelligent aliens elsewhere in the galaxy, we will have to invent them; they will be our descendants.

MAN MODIFIED FOR WAR AND PEACE
The possibility that we might create new human species in order to expand into new territories seems more attractive when set against the more nightmarish extreme of the spectrum of

MAN MODIFIED FOR WAR
Engineered men designed for war would be little more than mass-produced, expendable fighting machines. Even their brains would have to be modified to ensure that they remained under control of those guiding their actions.

Head
The sense organs of the future warrior would be much reduced and shielded. He would communicate by means of implanted radio transmitters and receivers. He might be adapted to take nourishment intravenously rather than through the mouth, rendering teeth unnecessary.

Skin
The skin would be toughened and scaly, made out of leaden material for protection against hard radiation or chemicals.

Body
The skeleton could be streamlined and the gut simplified, and the major organs enclosed in their own independent shielding. The bones and muscles of his limbs would be as powerful as possible. He would probably have no genital apparatus at all.

possibilities: the modification of the human body for the purposes of war. There are plenty of models in the natural world to fire the imagination of the would-be military engineer. In those few instances where different versions of individuals exist within a species – as with ants and termites – nature itself has engineered specialized warriors. If men could emulate the electric eel or the spitting cobra, hand-to-hand combat would become a very different contest. There are all kinds of ingenious ways in which people can be killed, and just as many ways of enhancing the killing abilities of engineered men. As with any arms race, the ingenuity in adapting men for attack would be matched by an equal ingenuity in adapting them for defence. If we have soldiers who can secrete deadly poisons, then we must have soldiers who are immune to those poisons.

Anyone can play the game of designing the perfect fighting man: big, tough, strong and armed with all manner of bizarre biological weaponry. But in all probability there is little point. Modern weaponry has actually passed beyond the stage where the physical properties of soldiers are of much significance. In the face of nuclear weapons, it will not matter how well people are adapted to kill one another in personal combat. Even tanks and automatic rifles make any advantages which could be gained from engineering soldiers marginal. If there *are* to be major wars fought in the future, the one adaptation which would have significance is an increased resistance to the effects of hard radiation. Although it sounds simple enough, such an adaptation would be a very difficult one to accomplish. When exposed to gamma radiation, flesh is frail stuff indeed, and there is not much that could be done to decrease its frailty by any significant amount.

The logic of the situation therefore, suggests strongly that there would be little to be gained by applying techniques of human engineering to the creation of a race of soldiers. If only one could be confident that people preparing for war would pay serious attention to the logic of the situation, this is one set of possibilities that could safely be forgotten. Whether or not one can have such confidence, however, is a matter of opinion.

We may be confident that ethical reasoning will prevent some of the possible applications of genetic-engineering techniques to human beings, because if that confidence is misplaced there is not much point in thinking about the future at all. The question remains, however, as to where the ethical boundary is likely to be drawn. Adapting people for new environments will probably be permitted, largely on the grounds that humans would be attempting to move into those new environments anyway. Modifications in the name of improvement would probably also be permitted. But there is another motive that could arise for engineering new mankinds: the purely aesthetic motive of creating new possibilities for enjoyment. Here one is on much

134

An engineered flying man would have to weigh little more than a one-year-old baby, and all or part of his hands would be sacrificed to make wings. Even then he would be better at gliding than active, flapping flight, and very clumsy on the ground. The upper weight limit for active flight is about 12 kg. The heaviest and largest known flying animal was the Pteranodon, which weighed up to 18 kg and had a wingspan of 8 metres. It probably moved by gliding on upward air currents.

more ambiguous territory. It is difficult to make a reasoned guess as to the part which such motives might play in the future evolution of humanity.

It is worth noting, however, that there is one kind of adapted man which crops up with considerable regularity in imaginative fictions of all kinds, and that is man adapted for flight. The imagination of past generations gave wings to angels and fairies alike, and winged people are common in modern fantastic fiction. The fascination of the idea is such that in his great imaginary catalogue of all the races of man yet to come, Olaf Stapledon in *Last and First Men* imagined that the period when mankind takes to the air would be the happiest of all.

Given the power of this particular image it may not be too ambitious to suggest that human engineers may one day use their science to create a race of winged men. The task would not be easy, although the modifications involved might be

straightforward. A crucial limitation on the size of creatures that fly is set by the ratio of wingspan to total weight; even condors, the biggest and heaviest of birds, are much lighter than people. A secondary problem would involve the weight of the head. A flying man, in order to retain human intelligence, would presumably need a greater brain than is possessed by the average vulture, and this too would set an awkward problem in aerodynamics.

It might be hard to combine the manipulative function of arms and hands with their conversion to wings. If one assumes that winged men would retain their arms – so that, effectively, their wings would be a third pair of limbs – their bodies would have to be very spindly, and their brains might have to be dramatically compressed.

Whether the joys of flight really would compensate such a race for all that they would lose by such modifications is highly dubious. It is one thing to dream of being able to fly by supernatural means, and another to analyse the compromises which would have to be made before flying men could be brought into real existence. From our contemporary standpoint it is difficult to believe that there could ever be an ethically sufficient argument to justify such a project. When the day comes, however, that the plasticity of humankind is taken for granted – when there are many kinds of man and no one can imagine a time when there was only one kind – the ethical questions might seem very different in weight and substance. The exercise of godlike powers is bound to give us a different perspective on questions regarding the proper uses of such powers. What will eventually happen, in the fullness of time, will depend not on how *we* see these matters, but on how our grandchildren and their grandchildren will see them. They will themselves be of many kinds, and they may not be at all inhibited in the matter of multiplying their forms and capabilities *ad infinitum*.

135

Chapter 8

Control of the mind

We have seen that, given time, biotechnology is likely to give us the opportunity of manipulating the human body more or less as we wish. But will control over the body's biochemistry also give us control over the mind?

The fact that this question can now be asked reflects the radical change in our view of the relationship between the body and the mind that has taken place over the last 100 years. It used to be accepted almost universally that the mind was an entirely separate entity which merely happened to be lodged in the body but was, in principle, detachable from it. There were always difficulties with this notion, and even those who held it knew that mental phenomena could be affected by physical causes, such as psychotropic ('mind-changing') drugs. It is now widely taken for granted that the subjective realm of thoughts, feelings, images and ideas is firmly rooted in the electrical and biochemical behaviour of the brain.

If this is true, then a technology which could determine the pattern of electrical and biochemical events in our brain could also determine exactly what we see, think, feel, believe and do. If that were the case, there would no longer be any sense in saying that it was 'me' seeing, thinking, feeling, believing and acting. 'I' would then simply be the product of some outside agency, a kind of robot. 'I' would cease to be independent – would cease really to be a person at all, and would become purely a puppet dancing to someone else's tune. This is a fate which many might consider worse than death: the ultimate violation of the self, a destruction of freedom of thought, freedom of feeling, freedom of belief and freedom of the imagination. These prospects seem to have come steadily nearer since the day when Aldous Huxley's *Brave New World* (1932) offered a classic series of images to illustrate them.

It is difficult to predict whether the threat of total mind control will ever be realized, because we know so little about the physical basis of subjective phenomena such as thoughts, feelings, memories and ideas. We cannot point to a particular electrical pulse passing through the cells of the brain and say 'that is a thought', nor can we point to a particular group of cells and say 'this man's memory of his 21st

birthday is stored *there*'. There may be a sense in which thoughts, feelings and memories *are* physically located – they are certainly in the brain and perhaps even 'in' particular structures within the brain, but we cannot say precisely where they are, or what form they take.

We know much less about the workings of the brain than we do about the workings of any other part of the body; consequently, our knowledge is bound to increase more slowly. Most of our knowledge of physiology and biochemistry is based on experimental work done with animals. The biochemistry and functional organization of animal brains have much in common with human brains, but it is mainly the unique features of the human brain which interest us. If animals have minds, they do not have much in common with human minds, and what we can learn about the mind from the study of humans is limited by ethical considerations. Much of the information we have about the relationship between the brain and the higher functions of the mind comes from the study of nature's experiments – observation of mental impairment in people who have accidentally suffered brain damage – or from desperate attempts to relieve the misery of people suffering from extreme mental illness.

Although we still do not understand the details of the relationship of brain to mind, the structure and function of the brain have been studied extensively, and our knowledge of its mysterious mechanisms is increasing. As our knowledge increases, so do the possibilities of control. Electrical stimulation of various parts of the brain appears to have quite specific effects, such as sensations of pleasure or pain, causing repeated robot-like sequences of actions or calming aggression. The complexity of the brain's chemical transmitter systems is only now beginning to be unravelled, suggesting much greater possibilities of control by drugs.

There are reasons, therefore, to suspect that the power other people can have over our minds might increase dramatically, even if it never does reach the point of total control. We can imagine various methods being used, all of them extensions of methods of affecting the mind that already exist. It

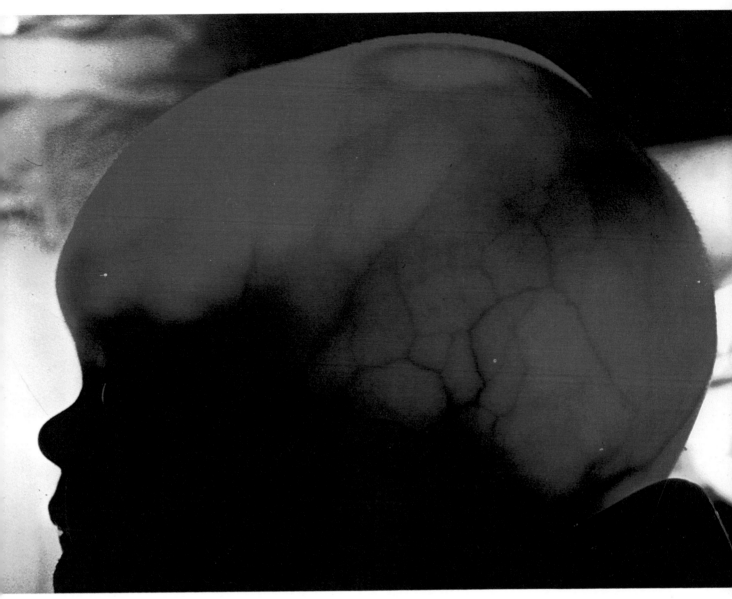

is easy to be led by such guesses into nightmarish realms.

We already know about hundreds of psychotropic drugs: tranquillizers, pep pills, hallucinogens, anti-depressants and euphorics. It is not hard to imagine that the future will produce drugs that can keep our feelings under complete control, so that we are always contented; nor is it hard to imagine that those in power would quite like to keep us that way.

We may wonder whether scientists might figure out ways to control us by electrical stimulation. Behaviourist psychology assumes that people, like animals, can be conditioned to behave automatically in a certain way by rewards and punishments. There are brainwashing techniques by which people can be force fed with whole sets of ideas and beliefs; and phenomena such as hypnosis suggest further ways, as yet little understood, by which one mind can come under the control of another. It seems only natural to worry about what really sophisticated brainwashers might do, armed with new drugs, electrodes and hypnotic techniques.

This child has hydrocephalus, a condition in which the skull contains too much cerebrospinal fluid, and sometimes becomes greatly enlarged. The brain is displaced and may be reduced to a very thin layer of brain cells lining the skull. In young babies with this condition, a light can be shone through the fluid-filled skull, as here – a phenomenon known as transilluminance. The condition often causes severe damage and mental retardation. Yet several cases have now been found in which such children have grown up into perfectly normal adults, although they have hardly any brain. This inexplicable discovery reveals the enormous extra capacity which seems to exist in the brain, since the cerebral cortex can apparently function normally even when reduced to a fraction of its usual size. Perhaps in the future we may learn how to use this extra capacity. The discovery also highlights the present limitations of our knowledge of how the brain works – limitations which mean that predicting future techniques of mind control is extremely difficult.

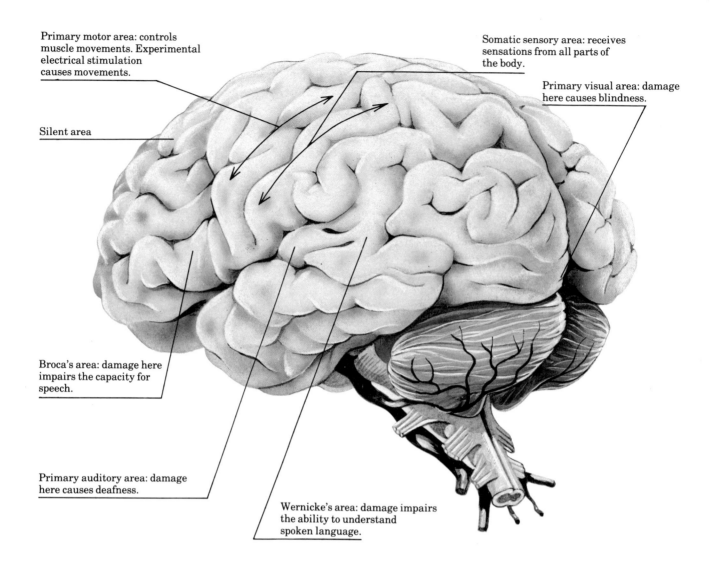

Primary motor area: controls muscle movements. Experimental electrical stimulation causes movements.

Silent area

Broca's area: damage here impairs the capacity for speech.

Primary auditory area: damage here causes deafness.

Somatic sensory area: receives sensations from all parts of the body.

Primary visual area: damage here causes blindness.

Wernicke's area: damage impairs the ability to understand spoken language.

The superior intelligence of human beings seems to reside in the cerebral cortex, which is much larger and more convoluted than in other animals. The cortex is a jelly-like mass surrounding the rest of the brain. We know very little about how the cortex 'thinks' though several of its more elementary functions have been located in specific areas.

CHEMICAL MIND CONTROL

Psychotropic drugs have been used since prehistoric times. Many plants produce, apparently as non-functional metabolic by-products, compounds capable of affecting brain chemistry in such a way as to alter conscious experience. Cannabis is a euphoric, giving rise to a floating sensation and a sense of well-being. Psilocybin, extracted from agaric mushrooms, distorts perception and causes hallucinations. Ethyl alcohol, which can be made by fermenting almost any plant material, is an intoxicant. Various derivatives of the opium poppy, including laudanum, morphine and heroin, reduce the general activity of the nervous system and may be used as anaesthetics or powerful euphorics. Such

natural products were used for millennia without anyone knowing how or why they worked.

The advent of organic chemistry made it possible to produce many new compounds, including new psychotropic drugs (though their psychotropic properties often remained undiscovered for some time, owing to the understandable reluctance of organic chemists to sample all their own wares). The first synthetic substance to come into common use was barbituritic acid, which began to be used as a hypnosedative (sleep-inducing drug) shortly after the turn of the century. By mid-century amphetamines were widely used as 'pep pills', having proved their potential in World War II by keeping American soldiers active in exhausting circumstances. The 1950s saw the rapid development of tranquillizers, both the powerful 'major tranquillizers' for treating severe psychological disorders, and the milder 'minor tranquillizers', such as Valium and Librium, which quickly passed into everyday use and are now the most popular psychotropic drugs prescribed by doctors. Another class of drugs which was first developed to treat the mentally ill, but expanded in use to take in large numbers of people, is the anti-depressants.

Many other psychotropic drugs have been discovered which have no apparent medical uses, but which have nevertheless spread far beyond the confines of experimental laboratories. The most famous of these has been the powerful hallucinogen lysergic acid diethylamide, or LSD. This has been widely used by people in search of exotic sensations, despite the fact that it is highly poisonous. The same is true of other substances, including PCP, or 'angel dust,' whose wholesale disruption of brain chemistry gives it a combination of euphoric and hallucinogenic effects. Some compounds which are in common use because of their other properties, such as the solvents in many kinds of glue, also distort perception and induce a peculiar kind of intoxication when inhaled.

We still do not know exactly how most of these drugs work. We can see their effects, but we do not know what biochemical processes are involved. This has not stopped the drugs being used widely. By 1980 more than 100 million prescriptions for minor tranquillizers were being issued annually in the United States alone, along with 50 million prescriptions for hypnosedatives and 20 million prescriptions for anti-depressants. Some 30 million people – nearly one-fifth of the population – were taking psychotropic medication on a more or less regular basis, tens of millions more on an occasional basis. When the level of illicit drug use is added to this, it becomes apparent that psychotropism is something which affects something like half the population in America. Anxiety about the situation has now begun to generate something of a backlash against the wilder excesses of psychotropic medicine.

Some psychotropic drugs appear to work by interfering with the chemicals which transmit electrical impulses across the synapses. For instance, anti-depressants inhibit the activity of the enzyme called monoamine oxidase (MAO). This enzyme is responsible for the metabolic breakdown of chemicals involved in the transmission of electrical impulses, mopping them up after their release. When the operation of MAO is inhibited, some systems of nerve cells become flooded with transmitter compounds, and the neurons 'fire' repeatedly. Monoamine transmitters also seem to be involved in some way with sleep, which is why MAO inhibitors are useful for keeping people awake.

As we fill the gaps in our understanding of the biochemistry of nerve cell transmission, some of the relatively crude psychotropic compounds we currently use could be replaced by much more complex compounds – probably proteins – which are more closely akin to the body's own brain enzymes. This will probably allow us to cut out some of the unpleasant side-effects associated with contemporary drugs. Furthermore, the large

number of transmitter substances already discovered suggests that there may be an equally large number of possibilities for acquiring new control over the mind. We still do not know exactly how the receiving neuron recognizes the transmitter chemicals released by the firing neuron. This is an important problem whose solution may, again, give us much greater control over the brain.

It seems that many psychotropic drugs may work by mimicking the activity of compounds that are already native to the body. In the case of the opiates, we now know that addiction is caused because the drugs substitute within the body for one of the naturally produced compounds called endorphins (endorphin is short for 'endogenous morphine'), which regulate the activity of the nervous system. As well as helping to control pain, endorphins may also play a role in pleasurable activities such as eating and sex. Endorphins are subject to control by a feedback loop – as concentrations of the substance build up to a threshold, production is cut back. When heroin or morphine is injected into the bloodstream regularly, it mimics the effect of endorphin, and the natural production of endorphin ceases altogether. If the external supply fails, the brain's own production of endorphin takes some time to be restored. Thus, heroin addicts who attempt to come off the drug face a painful period when the activity of the nervous system is uncontrolled and runs wild, generating extremely unpleasant sensations.

It is unlikely that the body produces its own hallucinogens, but it seems reasonable to look for an endogenous tranquillizer and perhaps for an endogenous amphetamine. Presumably there are biochemical mechanisms involved in the inducement of natural sleep, and it ought therefore to be possible to find a natural hypnosedative. These compounds might not be without their problems – even natural substances can have side-effects – but will very probably be safer than those currently in use. We are already trying to produce endorphin in quantity by means of genetically engineered bacteria, and this will be only the first of many brain compounds which we will produce in this way for experimental purposes and for use in clinical trials.

It is not clear whether the development of a natural psychopharmacopoeia would do much to help overcome problems of drug dependence. It is true that an abundant supply of genetically engineered endorphin might prove helpful in weaning addicts from heroin, but there would be nothing to stop them simply becoming addicted to endorphin instead. This might be better from the point of view of avoiding side-effects, but it would still be dependence. What might be more helpful would be a way of altering the feedback loop which controls the normal level of endorphin produced within the body, thus freeing addicts from dependence on any external supply. To regard this as a 'cure', however, would be to assume that the people who become heroin addicts are people whose own endorphin supply is naturally deficient and who therefore need some kind of adjustment. There is no evidence to suggest that this is really the case. Finding a method of adjusting the endorphin 'thermostat' might simply be discovering a way to allow people to become addicted to a natural product of their own bodies.

It could be argued, of course, that we are all 'endorphin junkies' already, and the main difference between ordinary people and heroin addicts is simply the narcotic level to which we are habituated. Most of us get by on our internal supply; heroin addicts have to go outside for a much bigger dose than their own brains can deliver. If the day comes when we can tamper with the feedback systems governing the internal supply of endorphins, then the distinction between ordinary people and junkies will become strangely blurred: 'taking a fix' might become part of everyone's repertoire of choices, and we might be able to apply to our doctors for routine adjustments to the base level of excitation with which we want to live.

A DRUGGED SOCIETY

Once we know more about the biochemistry of the brain, the possibility arises that we will be able to generate good or bad feelings directly by chemical manipulation – either by taking drugs or by injecting chemicals directly into the brain. We might develop drugs which would induce the sensations of fear, of ecstatic joy or even of orgasm. This kind of prediction has led writers of futuristic fiction to produce many images of a society where everyone is happy because they are permanently dosed with tranquillizers and euphorics. The society of *Brave New World* is based on the drug soma, with more powerful pills available for moments of crisis. This image is invariably presented as a horrific one, because the pill-induced happiness prevents people from reacting to the horrible realities of their society, and because it is a state not freely chosen but forced upon everybody by a dictator.

Our anxiety about the possibility of psychotropic drugs being used as a means of social control is heightened by the knowledge that they already are used in this way. Considerable controversy was caused in the late 1970s in America when Robert Maynard of the *Washington Post* publicized the extent to which schoolchildren in Omaha were being diagnosed as 'hyperactive' and given drugs to control them. The drugs were mainly amphetamines or a compound named Ritalin, which normally act as stimulants but which have an opposite, calming effect on troublesome and aggressive people. Maynard revealed that thousands of schoolchildren were taking these drugs on a daily basis, after being identified as hyperactive because they fidgeted a lot or behaved naughtily. It never became quite clear how many children in the whole United States were being given amphetamines or Ritalin for this reason, but it was probably in excess of half a million.

Amphetamines have also been given experimentally to unruly prisoners, and allegations that tranquillizing drugs are administered in prisons to control the inmates are not uncommon in Britain and America. Drugs are certainly used to tranquillize patients in mental institutions as a way of helping both patients and staff. To some extent, though, drugs are employed to control unruly and troublesome behaviour without any real reference to whether that behaviour arises from mental illness or not. Because such measures are so controversial this is done fairly discreetly at present, but it seems perfectly legitimate to wonder whether more oppressive rulers, should they come to power in the future, might become very much less discreet in their use of such methods of control.

One suggestion frequently made is that our water supplies might one day be doctored with psychotropic drugs in the same way as they are now doctored with fluoride. We would not be likely to vote for such a measure, but perhaps it could be done covertly, or even in the face of opposition. Present-day tranquillizers would be a pretty blunt instrument if used in this way, no different in essence from any other kind of brute force used by dictators in the past to maintain their rule. It is not beyond the bounds of possibility that discoveries in psychotropics may open up new opportunities for more refined methods of social control. It will be as well to be vigilant, and to become aware of any such dangers if and when they arise. However, the danger that future governments may use psychotropic drugs to win our enthusiastic support, even while they exploit us cruelly, is probably much exaggerated.

Even if we are not forced to take more psychotropic drugs, the possibility remains that we might choose to take them. If there is, in the future, a vast range of psychotropic drugs available, some of which induce good feelings – and it seems likely that there will be – then this might mean that we could buy our emotions from the chemist's shelf and move through the repertoire as we wish.

Such specifically acting drugs may never become available, because of the way in which psychotropic drugs work. The relationship between the biochemical state of various systems within the brain and the good emotions that we might want to cultivate is not so simple that we can simply add one chemical for pleasure and another for joy. Emotions generally involve *interaction* between perception of environmental circumstances and changes in internal chemistry. The effects of mind-changing drugs can therefore be various, depending on the situation in which they are administered.

Some evidence to support this view is to be found in studies of the effects of drugs that already exist. Not everyone who drinks experiences drunkenness in the same way, and being drunk may feel quite different on different occasions. There are also variations in the reports offered of what being high

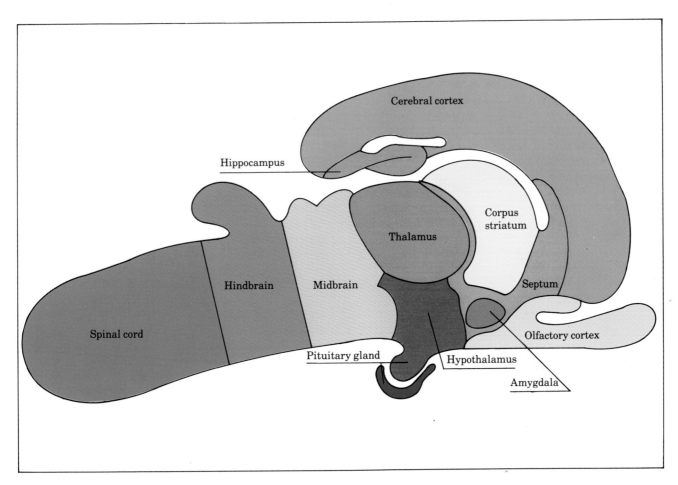

on cannabis feels like, and LSD appears to be very varied in the emotions which it induces – it can make people fearful as well as euphoric, and most users know the danger of 'bad trips'. People who use such drugs are often careful to make sure that they have recourse to them only in circumstances which will encourage good experiences rather than bad ones.

The extent to which people will make use of whatever psychotropic pharmacopoeia the future makes available will probably depend on how miserable their daily lives are likely to be without chemical support. If people live in circumstances that subject them to great stress, drive them toward despair or are intolerably boring, then they probably will take refuge in some kind of chemical insulation or stimulation, as people all over the world have been doing for centuries with alcohol, opium and *peyote*. The fact that more psychotropic drugs will be available will make it possible for them to exercise a wider choice, and to do so more safely, but the effect on the total demand for chemical relief will probably be marginal.

IMPROVING INTELLIGENCE
Better and more varied psychotropic drugs may not permit reliable control of specific emotional states. Is it possible, though, that psychotropic effects might be extended to other properties of the mind? Could there be new drugs that will help us to be

Our emotions, especially basic ones connected with fighting, food and sex, seem to have their seat in the more primitive back and middle parts of the brain, which appeared early in evolution. The brain and spinal cord are shown schematically here. The hypothalamus and pituitary gland regulate all the complicated biochemical systems of the body, including metabolism, digestion, sleeping and waking, growth, reproduction, appetite and blood vessel size. Both the hypothalamus and the septal area seem to be 'pleasure centres' when stimulated electrically, while stimulation of the hippocampus causes unpleasant sensations.

more intelligent or give us better memories? These are attractive ideas. Our fortunes in life depend so much on our educational achievements – what knowledge we have managed to absorb, what talent we have for solving problems – that everyone would leap at the chance to take a pill that was a biochemical shortcut to knowledge and intelligence.

Several substances have been used to stimulate the brains of rats and monkeys, and have apparently enabled them to learn tasks much more quickly. The substances include caffeine, amphetamine, nicotine, picrotoxin (a strychnine-like poison), and a convulsant called Metrazol. Chemicals produced naturally by the pituitary gland have also been tried with promising results. There may even be a connection between endorphins and learning capacity: several different groups of scientists have reported that very small doses of endorphins given under the skin have improved the learning abilities of rats, although we have no idea how this could happen, since the 'blood-brain barrier' should prevent them from entering the brain. These procedures are not safe enough to test on humans, and the difference between human and animal ways of learning may mean that this research is unlikely to produce a simple way of enhancing our learning capacity.

Although we still do not know much about how memories are stored in the brain, we do suspect strongly that RNA has something to do with it. There is some evidence that substances which enhance the synthesis of RNA, such as magnesium pemoline, do have an effect on the capacity of experimental animals to remember things. Some theorists, inspired by experiments on animals which suggest that memories can be transferred from one animal to another by injecting extracts from the brain, or even feeding them to each other, have

imagined that we might some day be able to inject ourselves with specific memories. This is unlikely, because whatever processes are involved in memory storage they are sure to be more complicated than this kind of thinking will allow.

It seems reasonable all the same to hope that in the future compounds might be discovered which either give a temporary boost to the retentive powers of the short-term memory, or which facilitate access to the 'deep memories' which are ordinarily beyond conscious recall. It is easy enough to think of uses for such drugs – to imagine students cramming for examinations doing so with the aid of temporary total recall, or to imagine witnesses to a crime being enabled to remember minute points of detail. It must be emphasized, though, that a good memory is not one that simply holds on to everything that is poured into it.

The real key to efficient memory use is not so much the ability to retain information as to select which information is worth retaining. The best memory, arguably, is the one which is most adept at the delicate art of forgetting; a sharp mind is one which ignores irrelevancies and cuts to the heart of a problem. Memory-enhancing drugs would certainly have their uses, particularly in halting the decline of old people's memories, but they could not assist people to discriminate between useful and useless information. If they help students who have to cram for exams, they will simply make exams less helpful in measuring the real intellectual abilities of students.

Can we improve those abilities with a drug for enhancing intelligence? It has been discovered that differences in IQ are highly correlated with differences in reaction time, and this suggests that intelligence may be partly a matter of the speed with which the brain absorbs and processes

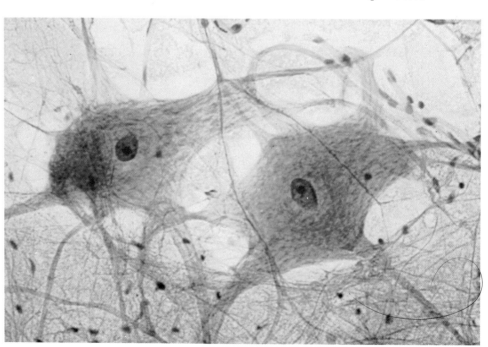

Two of the 15,000 million nerve cells or neurons which form the 'wiring' of the brain. Like ordinary cells neurons have a nucleus, a cell body and an outer membrane, but their shape is unique: each has thousands of branching extensions which connect with other neurons across tiny gaps called synapses.

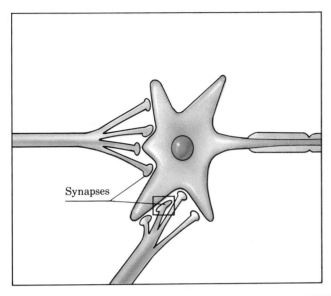

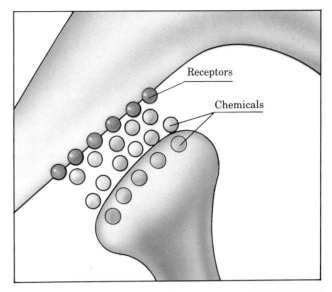

Synapse
Electrical signals in the brain
are transmitted from one
neuron to another across gaps
or synapses. Transmitter
chemicals are released by the
firing neurons which bind to
receptors on the receiving
neuron, thus passing on the
signal.

Endorphin
The brain produces many
types of its own opiate-like
substance known as endorphin
('endogenous morphine').
Endorphin is important in the
control of pain, and may play
many other roles. This model
of how endorphin might work
shows a firing neuron picking
up endorphin on special 'opiate
receptors'. The endorphin
reduces the amount of
transmitter chemical produced
by the neuron.

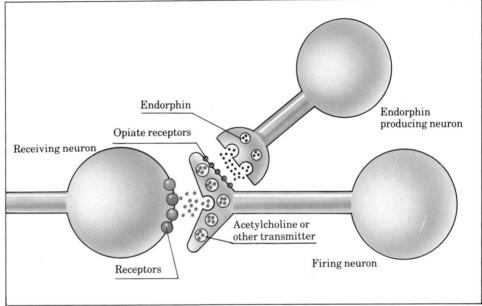

information. This speed might be increased by
drugs, but it seems unlikely that a real rise in
intelligence would result. The method of
information processing must be more important
than mere speed. The nature of the brain doing the
processing is also important. Intelligence may be
related to the number and nature of the connections
between the millions of neurons in the brain,
something which could not easily be influenced by
drugs. We already know that a stimulating
environment can help young children to develop
their intelligence: it may be possible to stimulate
the growth of the neuronal network in unborn
babies.

Several other methods of increasing intelligence
have been tried or proposed. A decompression
chamber, which creates a partial vacuum over a
pregnant woman's abdomen, was originally
invented to make childbirth easier, but there have
been claims that the children turn out unusually
intelligent. The treatment supposedly increases the
oxygen supply to the baby's brain in the last stages
of pregnancy, when the baby is growing very fast
but the placenta has stopped growing. Another
suggestion assumes that a larger brain could make
us more intelligent. All the cells which will go to
make up the adult nervous system are already
present in the foetus from the fifth month from
conception. If the cells of the cerebral cortex could be
persuaded to undergo one further doubling, this
would greatly increase the size of the brain – and
also of the head, so such engineered babies would
have to be born by Caesarian section.

It would probably be far easier to impede
memory and reduce intelligence by the use of drugs
than to improve them. Millions of children today
have their capacity for learning reduced by severe
undernourishment before or soon after birth, and
their incapacity cannot be completely cured by
treatment later. Drugs which might have the same
effect would have no practical uses except in an evil
dictatorship, where certain members of society were

143

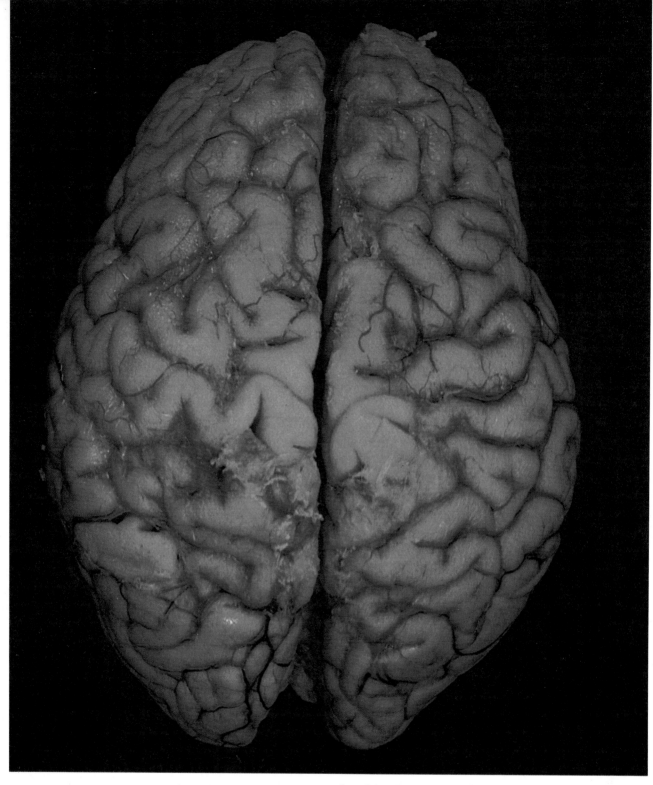

The left side of the brain controls the right side of the body, and vice versa. In cognitive tasks, however, the two halves of the brain perform very different functions. In most of us, the left hemisphere controls speech, language and mathematics, while the right hemisphere deals with visual and spatial tasks and expressing emotions. The left half is the 'dominant' or vital half: extensive damage to the right half can be suffered with very little effect, but minor damage to the language areas of the left half may rob someone of speech. A small percentage of people have some of their brain functions reversed – for instance, they have speech centres in their right half. This minority overlaps only partially with the minority who are left-handed. The fact that major functions are concentrated into just one half of the brain is another surprising example of nature's redundancy, again suggesting unused capacity which future man might exploit.

fitted for their subservient role by ensuring that they were stupid. Memory-obliterating drugs would also be highly dangerous substances. They would offer malicious individuals an ingenious way of harming others, and might appeal as a gentler form of self-elimination than suicide.

MENTAL ILLNESS

If we cannot hope to enhance our mental capabilities very much with a better understanding of biochemistry, can we expect to develop better treatments for mental illness? The answer must be a cautious 'yes'. Some kinds of mental abnormality are correlated with specific biochemical deficiencies

144

in the brain. Many manic-depressives can be stabilized with lithium carbonate.

Recently a breakthrough appeared to have been made in the treatment of schizophrenia by connecting it with a raised level of endorphins. A drug called Naloxone, which was developed to bring round victims of opiate overdose, appears to displace endorphin molecules from the brain's receptors and prevent them from working. Some promising results were obtained from treating schizophrenics with Naloxone, but in other cases no improvement was noted.

This does not mean that endorphins and schizophrenia are unconnected, but the connections between them are not yet clear. Like cancer, schizophrenia probably derives from a number of different causes. Many observers have pointed out similarities between the effects of hallucinogenic drugs, such as LSD and mescalin, and some kinds of mental illness, especially schizophrenia. It has been suggested that some mental illnesses are natural malfunctions in the biochemical systems which these drugs disrupt artificially. Little progress has been made in checking this hypothesis, since in spite of intensive research we know very little about the biochemistry of hallucinogens. It seems probable, though, that the biochemistry of some mental disorders will be better understood by the end of the century, and that this new understanding will permit more specific and effective treatment of many severely disturbed people.

Hallucinogenic drugs presumably operate in the biochemical systems that are implicated in the process of fantasizing and making images. We can imagine influencing our dreams through similar drugs, selecting a dream in the same way as we can select a videotape to play back on the TV. It seems unlikely, however, that interference could ever be precise enough to conjure up a particular visual image in our heads, or set us forth in a particular imaginary narrative.

What goes on in the mind can be profoundly affected by interference with the biochemistry of the brain. Perception can be distorted, moods altered, strange sensations generated. The future will add to this repertoire of effects, but it will probably not affect their essential coarseness and generality. What psychotropic drugs cannot do is to affect the programming of the brain in specific ways. They may scramble memories, they may even change personalities and scramble identities, but they do not do this in a careful and directed fashion.

There may well be drugs to affect memory, but they will not allow us to imbibe specific memories from a bottle. There may well be drugs to invoke feelings of exultation – of joy, or triumph, or sexual pleasure – but there is no danger of our ever coming to rely too heavily on such synthetic emotions, or preferring them to the real thing, because physiological reactions are actually less important than the context of experience. Mind-controlling drugs are extremely powerful weapons, and lethal in the wrong hands, but they cannot turn us into robots with our minds and brains completely controlled by other people.

ELECTRICAL STIMULATION OF THE BRAIN

We can affect the brain by transmitting electrical impulses into it from outside. This involves implanting electrodes into different parts of the brain through holes drilled in the skull, a task requiring a good deal of surgical skill. The brain itself feels no pain, and the electrodes can be left in place for weeks or months. The electrical impulses can be produced by remote control, for instance by radio signals picked up by a receiver on the outside of the scalp. Small receivers have also been made that can be inserted inside the skull, and even transmit signals from the brain back to the operator or to a computer.

The most spectacular discovery connected with electrostimulation was first made by James Olds, who found that there are regions deep within the brain where a slight shock administered by an implanted electrode apparently offers a powerful reward to an animal. If a rat is given the means to administer shocks to this area of its brain by pressing a lever it will do so repeatedly, never becoming satiated. Virtually all animals stimulating themselves in this way will break off periodically to eat, drink, sleep, rest and groom themselves, but once the animal's basic needs are taken care of it will return to incessant pressing of the lever.

People were quick to name the relevant regions of the brain 'pleasure areas', or 'pleasure centres'. There are also areas close to the pleasure areas where stimulation has the opposite effect, acting as a very powerful disincentive. Experiments of this kind have been carried out on a handful of human volunteers, mainly under the umbrella of research into epilepsy, and have shown that humans do have pain and pleasure centres, though their reactions to stimulation are much more ambigious than those of animals.

Robert Heath of Tulane University in the USA equipped several volunteers with self-stimulators. Their reports of their sensations varied quite widely. Some reported quasi-sexual excitement, others a feeling of intoxication. Some felt they were on the brink of remembering something. Stimulation of the septal area of the brain seemed to bring the most pleasure, while stimulation of the hippocampus caused feelings of nausea. Some people did press their buttons repeatedly, but Heath noted that they sometimes continued to do so after he had covertly switched off the electric current. (This implies that they may simply have been acting as they thought they were expected to act.) Heath found that electrical stimulation of the septal area was more likely to cause intensely pleasurable sensations if the patient were ill or upset.

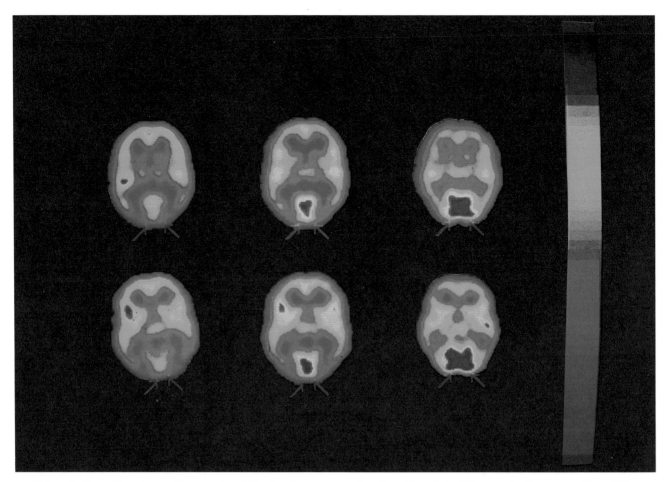

Stimulation of various other parts of the brain has been reported to reduce or increase aggression in both animals and humans. Heath gave self-stimulators to some very aggressive mentally ill people, and claimed that some used them to forestall attacks of violent feelings. José Delgado, who spent many years at Yale University investigating both chemical and electrical stimulation of the brain in animals, claimed that he could reliably reduce aggression in cats, monkeys, gibbons and chimpanzees by stimulating part of the brain called the caudate nucleus. The animals became docile and easy to catch, or stopped dominating other animals and sank to a lower place in the social hierarchy.

In his most famous experiment, Delgado went into a bull-ring with a bull that had been trained to charge human beings on sight. When it began its charge, he transmitted a signal to an electrode implanted in its brain. The bull stopped dead in its tracks and walked away. This sequence was repeated several times, until the bull no longer charged when Delgado walked into the ring. Delgado and others concluded that he had actually succeeded in switching off the bull's aggression, making it docile. Some observers, though, have argued that what the implanted electrode actually did was to interfere with the bull's motor control. They suggest that the bull eventually gave up because it was stunned rather than because it had ceased to be aggressive. Delgado also found that

when he stimulated the central grey matter of the brain, he could apparently switch on ferociously aggressive behaviour. He admitted, however, that the situation of the animal could make a great difference to its response: gibbons in the wild became more active and noisy, instead of more aggressive.

On the basis of Olds' findings some people have imagined that human beings fitted with self-stimulators connected to their pleasure areas would become hopeless 'electricity junkies', likely to die of self-neglect. Heath's experiments with human subjects lend very little support to this idea. Another speculation is that the implanted devices might be automatically triggered by physiological changes. No doubt the machinery for doing this would be complicated, but there is no reason in principle why implanted electrostimulators could not be activated by the release of adrenalin into the bloodstream. As the release of adrenalin is associated with getting angry, such a system would effectively deprive people of the ability to become angry. Unfortunately, adrenalin also performs a lot of other functions within the body as well as shifting the metabolism into a higher gear preparatory to fight or flight, and the system would have side-effects that could easily prove fatal.

It is improbable that any highly specific behavioural engineering could ever be accomplished by this kind of strategy. Thoughts and even feelings

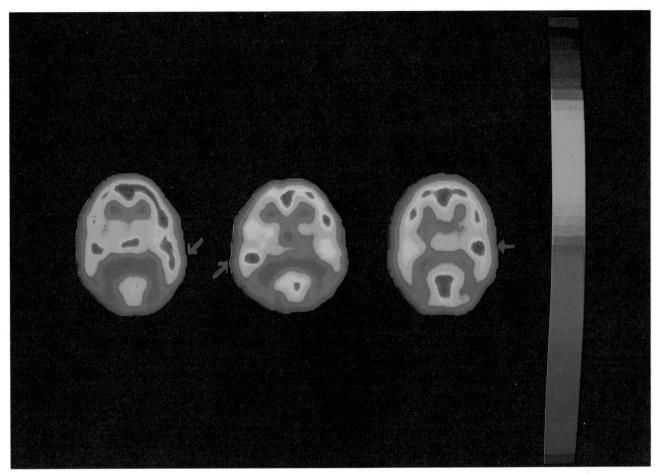

are not so distinct biochemically that a machine could identify a particular one, such as an intention to break the law, but it is conceivable that such a device could be made sensitive to a particular drug. By such means, therefore, a person might be made to react very strongly to an injection of heroin. Extrapolation from Delgado's experiments has suggested that a dictator could secure his rule by implanting electrodes in everyone's brain and making them incapable of aggressive action. It is doubtful whether the plan could be made to work; human minds are not as simple as those of animals appear to be. In addition, there would be the practical problem of persuading people to have the electrodes implanted in the first place.

If tranquillizers are a chemical blunt instrument, then electrostimulation is surely even blunter when it comes to specific effects on mental phenomena. Blunt instrument or not, though, we have attempted to use electric shocks to the brain in the treatment of mental disorder. Electro-convulsive therapy (ECT), although surrounded by controversy, is quite widely used in the treatment of depression. The treatment orginated as a result of work by Ladislas von Meduna, who argued (wrongly) that schizophrenia and epilepsy never occurred together and that schizophrenics might therefore be cured if they could be made to undergo pseudo-epileptic convulsions. He used drugs to induce such convulsions, but other workers used electricity. A

Brain scans made by PCT (positron computed tomography) show the rate of metabolism in different parts of the brain during different tasks. A radioactive chemical is injected, which binds to glucose in the blood. The glucose becomes most concentrated in the areas of the brain which are working hardest. The radiation is measured and analysed by a computer. In these scans, the colour scale shows increasing levels of metabolic activity, with red the highest.

(Above) Musical stimulation
Untrained listeners react to music more with the right intuitive hemisphere, while trained musicians tend to use the left, logical side of the brain. Two scans (left and centre) show right-handed subjects judging whether sequences of notes were the same or different. The person on the left had a subjective approach, while the subject in the centre had an analytical approach. The subject on the right is listening to pairs of musical chords and judging whether they are identical or different.

(Left) Visual stimulation
Two scans of three subjects are shown. Left: this subject has closed eyes and is wearing light-tight patches. Centre: this subject is looking at a bright light. Right: this subject is sitting in a park with his eyes open. The visual cortex, at the back of the brain, shows increasing activity as the scene being viewed becomes more complex.

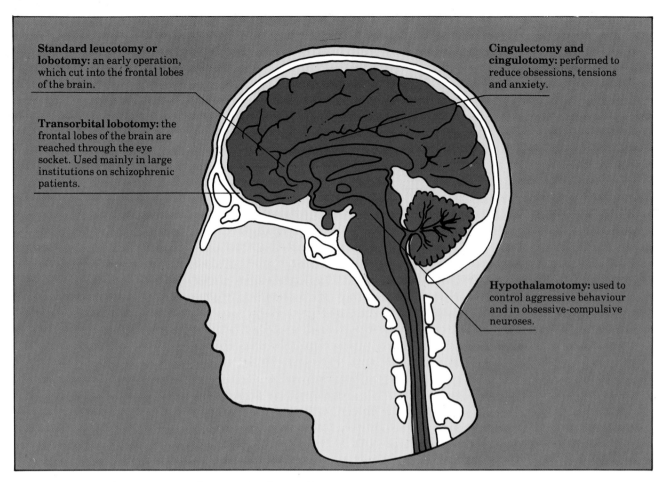

Standard leucotomy or lobotomy: an early operation, which cut into the frontal lobes of the brain.

Transorbital lobotomy: the frontal lobes of the brain are reached through the eye socket. Used mainly in large institutions on schizophrenic patients.

Cingulectomy and cingulotomy: performed to reduce obsessions, tensions and anxiety.

Hypothalamotomy: used to control aggressive behaviour and in obsessive-compulsive neuroses.

Psychosurgery – the attempt to influence the mind by cutting into the brain – has been performed for thousands of years. Since the 1880s it has developed into a more exact science, and has given good results in treating mental illness, though improvements in drug therapy have now largely replaced it. Cuts can be made with a sharp instrument, or lesions caused with chemicals, sucking out tissue, lasers, freezing, or radiation. Words ending in -otomy mean simply cutting; in -ectomy that part of the brain has been removed.

common side-effect of the early treatments was broken bones, but later users began to use ECT in association with muscle-relaxants or anaesthetics so that only the brain would be affected. Although it is no longer used as a treatment for schizophrenia, it seems that depression frequently can be dispelled by ECT. Many patients do claim to have been helped by the treatment, though some have said that there have been undesirable side-effects, including memory loss.

The research of Delgado and others may lead to a useful treatment for epilepsy. During a convulsion, the neurons fire in an excessive, uncontrolled way which, if it continues too long, can cause brain damage. Implanted electrodes might sense the approach of an epileptic seizure and feed this information into a micro-computer, which would trigger a counter-attack in the form of electrical or chemical stimulation, rather as a heart pacemaker reacts to an episode of malfunctioning in the heart.

We cannot rule out the possibility that it may one day be possible to evoke specific feelings by electrostimulation, but it is not easy to imagine that there will ever be practical uses for such methods. A self-stimulator which would relieve pain would, however, be a useful addition to medicine's armoury. Other more general states of the body might one day be controllable by electrostimulation. It might be possible to turn on sexual potency, sleep or wakefulness, hunger or loss of appetite. If wearing such a self-stimulating apparatus became acceptable, or even fashionable, control of the individual through misuse of the apparatus by others might become more likely. At present, though, it does not seem likely that electrostimulation will play any substantial role in the affairs of future man.

CONDITIONING
The fact that stimulation of the 'pleasure areas' has much less clear effects on humans than on rats is not surprising. The behaviour of rats can be largely explained in terms of automatic responses to environmental stimuli. Although some of these responses will be inborn (i.e. instinctive), many arise through learning, according to the pattern of 'conditioning' described by Pavlov and later behaviourist psychologists. One might expect, therefore, that rats' brains would provide an internal mechanism of reward and punishment

148

A hole has been drilled in this monkey's skull and a cannula inserted, so that brain fluids can be drawn off for analysis. The device can also be used to introduce drugs into the brain. The cannula can be left in place for several months to monitor the effects of different drugs on behaviour.

which facilitates the learning of new patterns of response. When behaviourist psychologists give rats food pellets or electric shocks to train them in new patterns of behaviour, they are merely duplicating externally something that goes on internally, as the rat learns to repeat behaviours that have advantageous results and avoid behaviours that have disadvantageous results.

How much human behaviour patterns depend on this kind of subconscious conditioning remains controversial. The behaviourist B. F. Skinner has argued strongly that we can explain a great deal of what happens in the human world by reference to presumed conditioning of responses, but there have been many attempts to show up the limitations of Skinner's arguments. It does seem that in humans conscious rational thought is a substitute for the kind of conditioning that shapes the behaviour of rats, and we would therefore expect the human 'pleasure areas' to be much less important in controlling what we do.

In spite of these counter-attacks, a behaviourist school of psychology has grown up which holds that much talk about the 'mind' is unnecessarily confused and confusing, and that behaviour can be understood largely in terms of stereotyped responses to stimuli. These psychologists claim to be able to condition people to behave in a certain way. Some of their techniques are successful: people who suffer from irrational fears (phobias) can often be

reconditioned by degrees until the stimulus no longer provokes the fear response. This method has helped people suffering from exaggerated fear of such things as cats, spiders, snakes and birds. People who wish to be 'cured' of behaviour such as alcoholism or homosexuality can take 'aversion therapy', whereby images associated with the desires to be suppressed are presented in association with electric shocks or nauseating drugs until the images are themselves sufficient to generate unpleasant sensations. This technique, too, has some success, but the effect tends to wear off if it is not periodically reinforced.

Conditioning is most successful when the person being conditioned is already committed to learning a new pattern of behaviour. In a non-compliant subject it is not easy to apply, and the effect rapidly wears off. It has been suggested that criminals of the future might be fitted with implanted electrodes to their pleasure and pain centres so that external controllers could reward them for good behaviour and punish them for bad. It might by this means be possible to superimpose a crude and simple pattern of conditioning upon the ordinarily more complicated behaviour of a person. This would be a morally dubious course of action even in the treatment of criminals – a case which is argued very strongly in Anthony Burgess's famous novel *A Clockwork Orange*. Implanted electrodes might, however, be of use in conditioning willing subjects.

149

The rewards usually used – sweets, praise, tokens – do not seem to be as effective in humans as food pellets are in rats. Heath has already used stimulation of the septal pleasure centre as the rewarding stimulus in apparently converting a man's sexual orientation from homosexual to heterosexual.

BRAINWASHING

Brainwashing is basically a matter of changing people's behaviour, often against their will, by forcing or encouraging them to accept a new concept of self. This usually necessitates the breaking down of the one which they already have. The Communists in Korea were easily able to strip their prisoners of all the emblems of their identity, because they could control what a prisoner could wear, what he could possess and with whom he came into contact. It was easy, too, for them to reduce prisoners to a state of total dependency, whereby provision of the necessities of life was dependent on their behaving in certain ways. Constant interrogations at irregular intervals and lack of sleep could be used to disorientate the prisoners, and thus prepare them for re-education. It proved possible in some cases to instil in the prisoners a very strong sense of guilt, apparently by mobilizing a kind of reservoir of guilt feelings which everyone has, and thus to make them eager for some kind of redemption, which was offered in the shape of the new ideology of Communism.

Despite the fact that they had all the advantages that force could give them, the Communists failed to break down many of their subjects, and even when they succeeded completely in implanting a new ideology, their success was temporary: once the prisoners were sent back to the West the implanted ideology began to decay. Without constant environmental support and reinforcement, rigid sets of ideas lose their rigidity, and people begin to think for themselves again. This is why people who do maintain rigid ideologies over a long period of time tend to live in isolated communities of like-minded believers.

The religious groups which are accused of brainwashing their converts obviously do not have the same advantages as the Korean Communists in the matter of breaking down the self-image of their 'victims'. What they can do, though, is to capitalize on situations where people are already vulnerable because they feel uncertain, dissatisfied and lost. These people can be invited to visit groups whose members apparently have everything that the vulnerable individual lacks: loving friends, a sense of purpose, moral convictions and secure beliefs. They are enticed rather than forced into a regime where they are always active, either hard at work or hard at play, and never left alone. They are given slogans as instruments of thought, and there is a similar exploitation of vague sensations of guilt and the hunger for redemption from that guilt.

The religious cults possess one advantage that the Korean Communists did not: they never do have to send their converts back to the greater world, but can keep them in protected enclaves where their commitment can be continually reinforced. If the brainwashing is to be cancelled out, therefore, by the process that has come to be known as 'deprogramming', they must first be removed from the coercive environment, perhaps even by force.

Closed communities of this kind are usually successful only in the short term. Eventually, internal stresses begin to tear them apart. In addition, the people who run such closed communities, and who actually determine the rigid ideology which pertains there, seem to suffer – perhaps understandably – from a growing megalomania which tends to confuse what may be initially selfless motives with the sheer exultation of exercising power. In Jonestown, Guyana, an isolated community of this kind eventually became subject to a reign of terror; after an unsuccessful attempt to conceal from a party of investigators the true state of affairs, there followed an appalling orgy of murder and mass suicide.

If the future is to see the development of better techniques of brainwashing, it will probably be through the provision of better methods of disorientation, involving psychotropic drugs. Such drugs would probably be helpful only in the first phase of the procedure, but with the aid of drugs that dull the mind, or drugs that induce amnesia, people might fairly quickly be rendered into a state where they would be ripe for re-education. Because of the way that contemporary psychotropic drugs work, it is far easier to imagine new drugs whose function is essentially destructive than ones which will permit delicate control.

The real problem with controlling ideologies is not implanting them but maintaining them, and it is harder to imagine ways in which future discoveries might assist in this. Writers such as Aldous Huxley have supposed that whole societies might be turned into closed ideological communities, where no one would ever be permitted to form a self-image or a set of ideas except for the approved one. In Huxley's *Brave New World* there is no need to *re*-educate anyone, because all children are indoctrinated from birth, and live until death in an environment which constantly reinforces the official doctrine by such methods as hypnopaedia (the constant repetition of information to sleeping subjects).

Hypnopaedia is now generally believed to be ineffective, but various techniques are supposed to exist by which ideas and commands can be planted covertly in someone's mind. These include subliminal communication and hypnotic suggestion. The first method involves transmitting messages through the senses in such a way that the conscious mind does not notice them – for instance, by flashing words on a cinema screen in between the pictures so

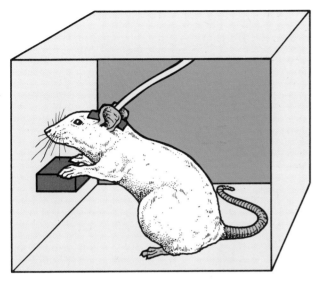

The 'pleasure areas' of the brain were discovered by James Olds, who implanted electrodes in the brains of rats. The rats could stimulate their own pleasure centres by pressing a bar. The record of one of his experiments shows that the rat pressed the bar continuously with 2000 presses per hour for 24 hours, without pausing to eat or drink. Each sweep of the curve represents 500 pressings of the bar. The rat slept most of the next day, then went back to its repeated self-stimulation.

48 hours		
Noon		4 pm
4 pm		8 pm
8 pm		Midnight
Midnight		4 am
4 am		8 am
8 am		Noon
Noon		4 pm
4 pm		8 pm
8 pm		Midnight
Midnight		4 am
4 am		8 am
8 am		Noon
Noon		4 pm

Electrodes have been implanted in the brains of many animals in experiments to study brain function. The apparatus shown here, held in place by steel clamps, has been superseded by newer devices which leave the animal free to move. Implanted electrodes can now be operated by remote control, using a receiver inserted inside the skull.

(Opposite page)
Experimental work on the brain is often done on rats since they develop very quickly. A cell taken from the visual part of a rat's cerebral cortex two days after birth **(top)** has only two branches. 16 days after birth a cell of the same type **(bottom)** has developed a complex network of branches connecting with other cells. Brain cells in the human visual cortex develop in the same way.

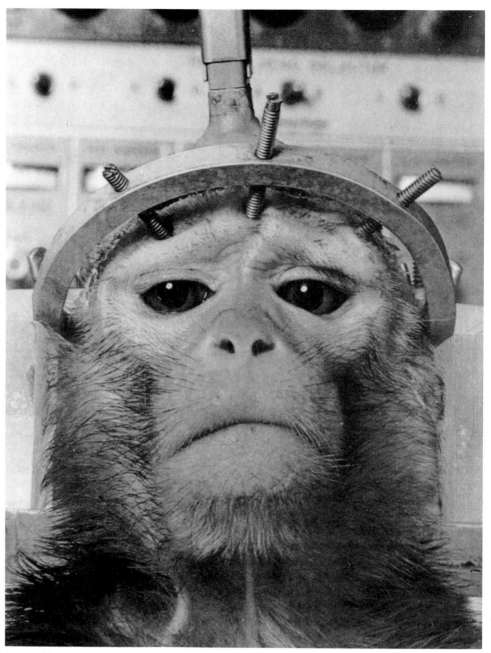

briefly that they cannot be read. It is said that these messages can still be picked up subconsciously. Experiments carried out by psychologists suggest that commands communicated in this way will not have any effect, but advertizers have maintained a continued interest in this kind of suggestion, and some recent research suggests that where people are actually making a decision, and hesitating over what to do, subliminal suggestion may help to tip the balance. If worded messages are incorporated into the muzak played in supermarkets, too quietly to be consciously heard, they *can* have an effect on some kinds of action. Shoppers will not respond to commands to buy certain products, but there apparently is some response to commands not to steal.

The power of hypnotic suggestion remains controversial. It certainly seems that hypnosis does

work, at least to some extent, with willing subjects, but it is not clear that anyone can be induced to do something by hypnosis that they are not already prepared to do. Nevertheless, the suggestibility of someone in a light or deep trance has many possible uses, such as recalling lost memories, increasing motivation or controlling pain. Hypnosis is already widely practised by the police and doctors, psychotherapists and others. Unfortunately, some of the things which witnesses to crimes 'remember' with the aid of hypnosis turn out to be false, so this is a rather treacherous tool.

Some of the techniques of persuasion which Huxley features in *Brave New World* are ones which have always worked: the provision of slogans as instruments of thought, and the ritual chanting of such slogans. George Orwell probably understood this better than anyone, and devoted much attention

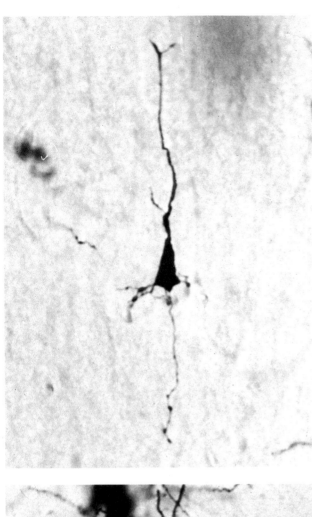

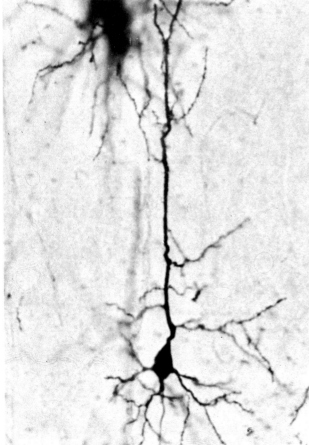

in *Nineteen Eighty-Four* to the control of language. The names which are given to things do influence the way we think about them, and various organizations attempt to make use of this fact. Examples are political movements that call themselves 'democratic' when they are exactly the opposite, or the vocabulary of war in which the enemy simply has 'losses' while soldiers on one's own side are 'killed'. Orwell was also sensible in weighing up the limitations of this kind of thought control. He saw clearly enough that at least some people would find opportunities for 'thought-crime', even though they might not be able to stand up to closer personal attention from the re-educators. He observed, too, the implications of the fact that there would have to be an elite who were not subject to the limitations which they placed upon the thought of others, and who would exhibit all the corruption proverbially associated with absolute power.

None of these methods stops the person who is being controlled from having ideas and generating commitments of his own. Even the most competent brainwashers – the religious sects which organize environments and experiences very carefully – cannot entirely block other inputs into the minds of their subjects. It is conceivable, all the same, that even without such refinements as hypnotic control and subliminal communication the children of some not-too-distant future really might be conditioned from birth into particular patterns of thought, feeling and belief by a constant bombardment of reinforcements. A closed ideological world of this kind might be self-reproducing once it existed, but *creating* such a world by historical process out of the one we live in now would be a very difficult proposition. As Orwell observes in *Nineteen Eighty-Four*, it could only happen if the great mass of the people accepted apathetically all the things that were done to them, without resistance and almost without question.

In our everyday lives we are routinely subjected to all kinds of attempts to influence what we will do. No doubt some of this influence works. We *are* to some extent the products of our early moral education; we *are* to some extent guided in our spending by the advertizing which surrounds us. We may often feel that we are 'under control', that our freedom of action is being eroded, or that we are helpless in the grip of powerful forces. Nevertheless, when we are influenced it is because we are content to be influenced. We allow our behaviour to be partly controlled and partly routinized, because there is a certain relief in not always having to make choices. It takes the strain off us to let other people occasionally take decisions for us, and to guide us in what we do. Some individuals surrender their prerogatives of choice to a much greater extent than others, but we all do it because it is a reasonable, and perhaps a necessary, thing to do.

In spite of this surrender, however – which creates the opportunities for those who are

We still do not understand the purpose of sleep, nor its mechanisms, though much research has been done on it. Here the EEG, eye movements and position are being monitored. Periods of deep sleep alternate with lighter sleep during which our eyes move rapidly and we often dream. These periods of REM (rapid eye movement) sleep occur more in the later part of the night. Greater knowledge of the brain's biochemistry should lead to better sedatives related to the body's own sleep-inducing compounds.

interested in influencing us to do their worst – there is still an essential freedom which remains quite untouched by the manipulative forces. It does always remain open to us to reject manipulation, to cast off the puppet-strings. This kind of control relies on a co-operation which we *can* withdraw – although those controlling us will always try to attach disincentives to that withdrawal.

MENTAL SUPERMEN

Some people believe that at least some minds already possess unusual abilities that are not apparent in everyday life: the ability to 'read' other minds; the ability to foresee the future; the ability to move or bend objects by mental power alone. The overwhelming probability is, however, that these are mere illusions. It is easy to understand how such ideas come to be plausible, given the way we experience our own mental life, but on further analysis the plausibility quickly fades away.

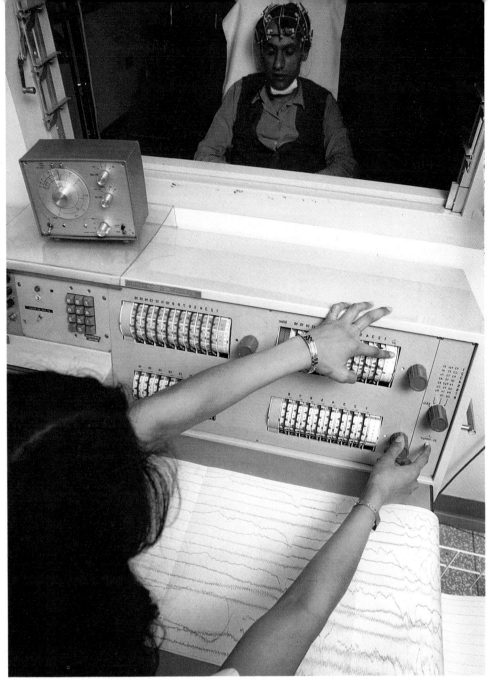

Our understanding of the brain has increased with the development of electroencephalograpy (EEG). Here the electrical activity of a subject breathing deeply or 'hyperventilating' is being recorded and printed out.

Because we experience our own thoughts rather as if they were words 'spoken' inside our heads, it is easy to imagine that someone else could eavesdrop upon them. Because we can will our hands to move, it seems possible in principle that we might be able to make objects outside our bodies move too, if only we could get the hang of it. Because we are always looking to the future, trying to calculate the outcomes of our actions and decisions so that we can choose them more wisely, the temptation to believe that we could miraculously extend the gift of foresight beyond rational calculation and speculation to actual precognition is almost overwhelming.

In fact, though, our thoughts are not sounds, and cannot be overheard. The reason that we can will our hands to move is that there are nerves connecting them to our brains, which can carry instructions. We are not conscious of these instructions travelling along the nerves, but this does not mean that the nerves are dispensible. Precognition is simply wishful thinking. Countless speculative writers have demonstrated that acceptance of the notion has paradoxical implications.

Biotechnology, fortunately or unfortunately, will not turn us into mental supermen. Nor will it make us their victims. This does not mean that the future will see no change at all in the competences which our minds possess. There *is* scope for improvement in the power which the mind can exercise over its own domain – the body. We sometimes forget or overlook how very little of the brain's work comes under the authority of the conscious mind. The brain regulates conditions within the body automatically. This applies to much of the working of the nerves, and almost all of the working of the hormones. We do know, though, that we can learn to take conscious control over some bodily systems that are not normally amenable to it.

155

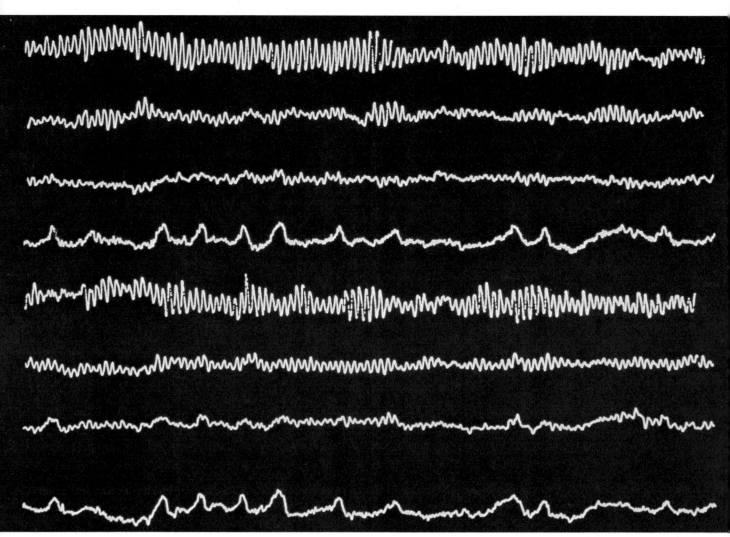

Biofeedback could help us influence our minds and emotions. Here, an EEG or electroencephalograph picks up the weak but continuous electrical activity of the brain. Traces are shown from eight electrodes placed in different positions on the scalp. The first and fifth traces, and parts of others, show alpha waves – low frequency waves associated with a relaxed or resting state. When fed with information about when alpha waves are being produced, either by seeing the EEG trace or by a signal such as a light or a tone, many people can learn to produce alpha waves a far higher percentage of the time than is normal.

When it first became possible to monitor something of what was happening in the brain, using electroencephalographs to map out basic 'rhythms' of electrical activity, it also became possible for people to learn a measure of control over those rhythms. Once they could see on a screen whether or not the so-called alpha-rhythm was present in the traces recorded by electrodes attached to the skull, at least some of them mastered the technique of producing it or cancelling it at will. The alpha-rhythm seems to be a basic 'resting state' which appears when people are relaxed – it tends to disappear once the attention is caught and they begin to respond to stimuli. Inducing it at will is reported by some to give a way of relaxing oneself, thus becoming calm and detached.

This kind of technique is known as 'biofeedback'. We learn mental skills by experience, and it is necessary to receive information about the results of our efforts in order to refine those efforts. Ordinarily we have no such way of obtaining information about what is going on within our bodies, but medical technology is now providing dozens of devices which allow people to monitor what is going on inside themselves, and this opens up new possibilities for extending the scope of self-control.

It may be possible to obtain a degree of conscious control over the production of the substances which control the activity of the brain – the endorphins and various other compounds which are only now being identified. Investigation of the 'placebo effect' has shown that people will very often exhibit the effects of drugs which they only think they have been given. To some extent this is mere suggestibility, but in some cases measurable physiological changes can be detected. This suggests that the capacity may be there for people to provide their own internal medication for some kinds of problems, if only they could get the knack. One day, it might not be necessary to take psychotropic drugs: it might be possible to reproduce their effects by sheer mental effort.

There may, therefore, be scope for us to become mental supermen of a particular kind. We will never learn to read minds or bend spoons by mind power, or look into the future, but we might learn to control the internal states of our bodies much more precisely. By this means, we might yet achieve control of fear, control of pain and control of our health, at least in some degree.

If this is so, and arguments presented elsewhere in this chapter are also reasonably good, then perhaps we should think of the future of mind control not in terms of other people's ability to exercise more power over our innermost selves, but rather in terms of our ability to exercise more self-control over our own well-being. That kind of improved mind control would lead us toward greater freedom rather than less, and toward competence rather than impotence.

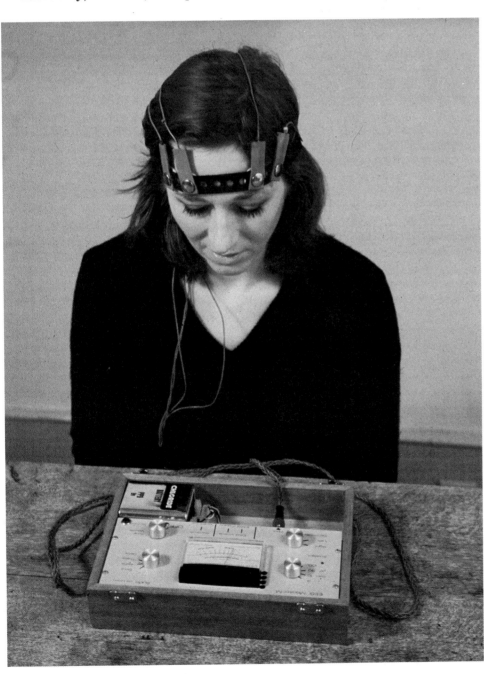

Biofeedback can help us to improve our health by our own willpower without any physical treatment. For instance, unconsciously tensed muscles can cause pain such as headache or backache and may be related to psychological problems. When the tiny electrical impulses in the muscles are made visible to the patient, as with the EMG (electromyograph) apparatus shown here, a great deal of control can be gained over minute components of the muscle, as small as a few cells.

Chapter 9

The extensions of man

By inventing technology, human beings became capable of greater feats of strength, speed and perception than any other species, despite the fact that other animals are often better equipped by nature than we are in one or more of these respects. There remain, however, some things that other creatures can still do better than we can. It is often the smallest animals which defy imitation, because they are possessed of a delicacy which our machines find difficult to match. It is only in recent times that we have begun to compete with silkworms and spiders in producing very delicate fibres, and even with the benefits of micro-miniaturization we cannot yet build electronic computers with the same kind of capacity as a brain.

With the aid of organic chemistry we are beginning to produce materials more closely akin to those made by living cells, but our synthetic fibres and our plastics still cannot match some natural products in all respects. The capacity of wool to absorb moisture and conserve heat still defies precise imitation, and the hardness of dental enamel has proved difficult to duplicate. Most of the structural materials used in living systems are proteins, and the long-chain molecules we have so far been able to build in the laboratory have nowhere near the same versatility.

The biotechnological revolution will alter this situation. So far we have discussed the power this will give us to use and alter living creatures, including human beings, but the power does not stop there. It will enable us to manufacture all the materials that nature has used throughout the billions of years that life has existed on Earth. Ultimately, we will be able to design and produce new materials which natural selection never managed to invent.

We may expect to see more and more organic materials incorporated into our machines, displacing to some extent the metals and plastics that we currently use. The displacement will not be total, because there are many tasks that metals and plastics are uniquely fitted for, but in time we will be able to build into our machines organic systems which are biochemically active in the same way as living systems. The machines themselves will become more and more like living entities, and we will enter into a much more intimate association with them.

We have already begun to integrate biological and mechanical systems in a primitive way, by hooking people up to artificial kidneys and developing the biosensors mentioned in Chapter Five. The era of complete integration of organic and inorganic technologies is still a long way off; but even a crude kind of integration would have important consequences. We may one day be able to extend man directly by linking his brain to other brains, to computers or to any of the new mechanical systems we shall have the ability to create.

ORGANIC TECHNOLOGY

The first applications of biotechnology to the manufacture of materials will undoubtedly be in the reproduction of substances already known in nature. The polysaccharide chitin, used by insects and fungi to supply the framework of their bodies, might have as much potential as wood (which is mostly made of other polysaccharides, cellulose and lignin). Ivory from elephants' tusks is at present a scarce and precious commodity, but biotechnology might be able to produce it in much more considerable blocks in the fairly near future. Genetic engineers have already cloned the gene for one of the four components of tooth enamel. Selective breeding has produced silkworms which are marvellously prolific in spinning the silk that they wrap around their cocoons, but biotechnology holds out the prospect of cutting out these living middlemen in much the same way as it promises to cut out living animals as suppliers of meat.

More complicated natural materials will undoubtedly be more difficult to manufacture, but if the incentive is there then the technical problems will ultimately be solved. Just as we may hope eventually to design 'quasi-eggs' that will develop into fillet steaks without bothering to produce whole cows, so we may hope eventually to produce cartilage by the block and skin (with or without fur) by the sheet.

Instead of being engineered to specialize in one particular function, future man could be equipped with a variety of interfaces so that he could 'plug in' different kinds of equipment.

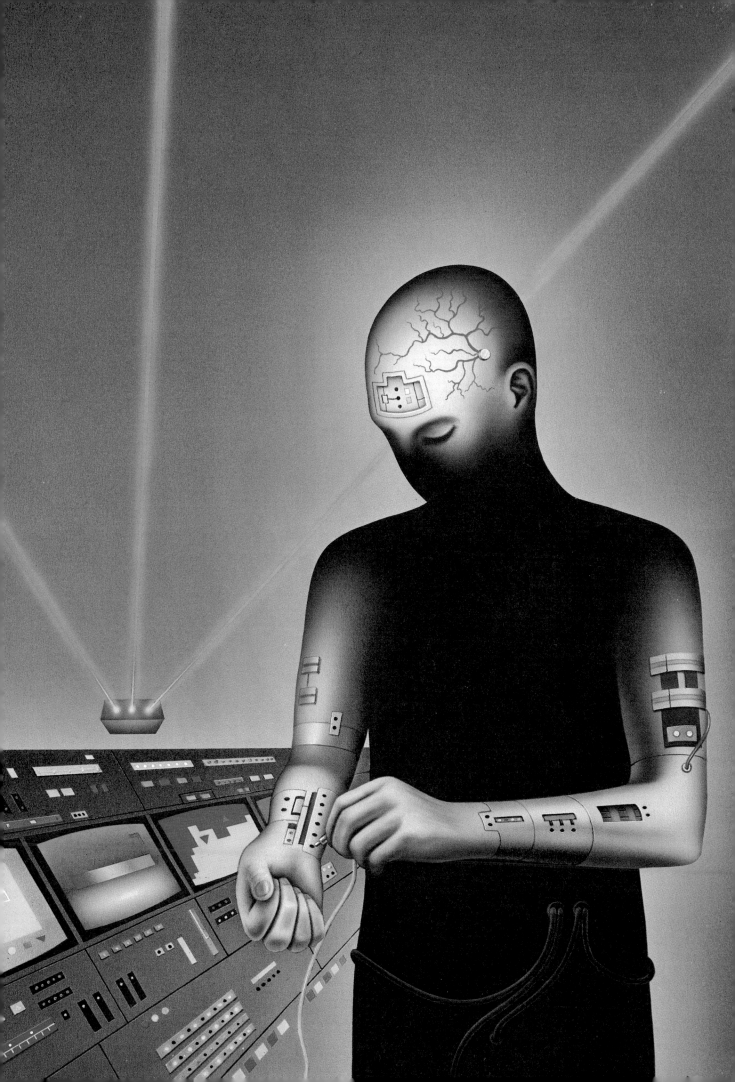

Some of the newest developments of present-day technology are devoted to capturing the light energy of the sun. Future organic technology may allow us to make better use of the sun's energy, for instance by artificial photosynthetic systems. **(Right)** A solar power satellite may soon be constructed in this way in a low earth orbit. A space shuttle is shown docking at an assembly bay, while another vehicle approaches with cargo. Satellites with large arrays of photoelectric cells could power space stations, or beam power in microwave form to receiving stations on Earth.

As time goes by, we can expect experimentation to produce a continual flow of new materials, including better synthetic replacements for wood, rubber, animal hides, wool, cotton and catgut. There will probably be a gradual replacement of the materials we know today by new ones more closely adapted to the purposes that they serve. It is not difficult to think of needs that might one day be answered in this way – most modern houses, for instance, develop all kinds of faults because cheap materials do not serve their various purposes very well.

In the long term, the possibilities of manufacturing more complicated objects are limitless. Eventually, there may well be a complete breakdown in the distinction between the living and the non-living: the boundary between the two will be blurred and filled in by systems which involve both the machinery of life and the machinery of metal, plastic and glass. We will use living organisms as machines, and will import biological systems into our machinery. By degrees, our modes of manufacture will alter until we can no longer distinguish the business of growing things from the business of making things.

One of the tasks at which our inorganic machines are much more efficient than nature's flesh machines is producing power. We used to speak of locomotives and internal combustion engines in terms of the number of 'horsepower' they could generate, to emphasize their superiority over nature. It would take many fireflies to generate as much light as an electric light bulb, and many electric eels to recharge a car battery. This does not mean, however, that we will have no use in the future for biological power sources or biological systems that generate particular kinds of energy, such as light or electric current. Once the systems can be divorced from the actual organisms, they could become useful.

We should remember that the prolific production of power in the contemporary world is based on the use of non-renewable resources such as coal, oil and uranium. Even in the short term, we may have to look to biotechnology to help us out with supplies of various kinds of fuel. In the long term, we should perhaps consider streamlining the way in which we harness the energy of the sun. At present we do this indirectly by burning carbonaceous compounds produced by plants. These chemical middlemen – coal, oil, alcohol and even wood – are, in principle, capable of elimination by a really sophisticated biotechnology. It is possible that in the far future we may be able to produce heat and make electricity direct from a quasi-living system.

Producing energy by means of organic technology would involve the artificial photosynthetic systems discussed in Chapter Three.

160

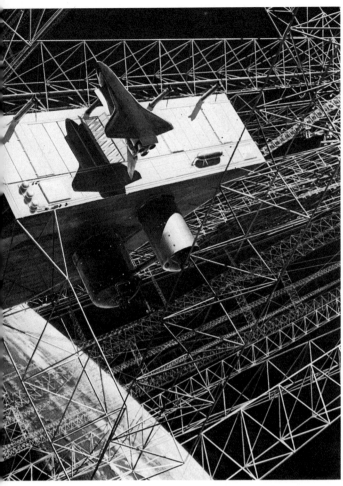

Scientists have already constructed a molecule in the laboratory which mimics the capture of light energy by natural photosynthetic compounds, although it resembles the photosynthetic molecules used by red and brown seaweeds more closely than it does the chlorophyll molecules of green plants. This is one small step on the way to constructing a whole biochemical apparatus that can not only capture light energy efficiently, but also deploy that energy in the manufacture of organic products or transform it into electrical energy. One day in the far future, there may be houses which are built (or perhaps grown) entirely out of organic materials, with roofs and walls decked with organic solar panels to absorb, store and apply the energy of solar radiation. The great architect Le Corbusier once described a house as a 'machine for living in'. One day, a house might become a living organism for living in.

MAN/MACHINE HYBRIDS

The integration of the biological systems of man's body with mechanical systems already has a name: cyborgization. (Cyborg is short for 'cybernetic organism'.) Medical science, in developing artificial limbs and artificial organs, has already created the first generation of cyborgs. The intensity of research promises that the second generation will benefit from a much more intimate association with their mechanical parts. Mention has already been made of the crucial importance of devising an 'organo-metallic synapse' – an interface allowing information to be transmitted from the nerves of the body to the electronic systems of a mechanical device such as an artificial arm or an artificial eye. In Chapter Five the innovation was discussed only in its straightforward medical implications, but it is clear that much wider possibilities are opened up by such devices. If human brains could be connected, *via* nerves and wires, to electronic and mechanical systems which they could then control directly, then machines would become extensions of people in a literal sense.

Cyborgization opens up possibilities in human engineering rather different from those associated with direct manipulation of the genes. Genetic engineering might permit many different kinds of people to be designed and made, but one individual can only have one set of genes. The body may be modifiable in minor ways, but for all intents and purposes a genetically engineered man has only one basic set of characteristics. If a man can be equipped to link up to machines, however, then he can effectively acquire a whole range of extended selves. He may become a basic functional control unit which can be fitted into machines of many different kinds. Men equipped for cyborgization would become extremely versatile. Their versatility is limited only by the number and complexity of the interfaces, and the ability of the brain to give out and take in information across those interfaces.

Some specific improvements to human capabilities might be achieved more easily by cyborgization than by transforming human egg cells. If we wanted to be able to equip people with new senses, we might well turn first to mechanical implants and artificial synaptic interfaces rather than try to build in new sensory equipment by manipulating the genes, or by modifying the bodies of adults. This would certainly be the preferable alternative where people wanted to use such equipment occasionally rather than permanently – for instance, if they only needed the improved senses when working in the dark or in deep water.

For example, a radio receiver that can be hooked up directly to the auditory nerves, and powered either by long-lasting batteries or by the body's own biological systems, may be feasible within a couple of generations. Such a device would, of course, be crucially different from present-day receivers which simply produce sounds close to the eardrum. This receiver would not have to decode its signals into sound waves at all, but would pass them on to the brain for direct decoding. This sounds rather pointless, until one recalls that such a receiver must have its counterpart transmitter, similarly powered, which is not picking up information from a microphone into which someone is speaking, but encoding signals fed into it directly from another brain.

When and if we do begin engineering people for

161

the purposes of war, or for the purpose of working in space, we will turn first to the possibilities offered by cyborgization and only later to the possibilities offered by genetic engineering. We will not, of course, be restricted to using one approach or the other exclusively, and will very probably use a combination of the two at least for a transitional period. The techniques are essentially complementary and may continue to be linked. In the very far future, when the distinction between flesh and machinery eventually breaks down altogether, it may no longer be necessary to consider them as separate approaches at all.

Whole human beings can already be linked up to machines in a fairly intimate fashion. Some sufferers from kidney disease have been equipped with plastic 'sockets' so that they can effectively plug themselves straight in to a kidney machine, though the gain in convenience is not great and the practice has never become widespread. Once we have working artificial synapses, we could establish sets of sockets at convenient points along a man's arms or legs, so that he could temporarily direct his conscious efforts from controlling his hands or feet to operating an electronic system of some kind.

Establishing interfaces which connected with the nerves in the limbs, rather than siting them closer to the brain, might place limitations on the amount of information that could be channelled through them; but even if we planted them in the brain, there might be acute problems involved in trying to train the brain to use them, since the conscious mind has very little control over the chemical behaviour of the brain's cells. The one big advantage that human engineers would have if they connected artificial synapses to the nerves already in a limb is that the mind already has the ability to transmit conscious commands through those nerves.

The images called to mind by this discussion will inevitably be bizarre if we think in terms of the kinds of plugs and sockets with which our machines of today are equipped, but we must remember that the materials used in our machines are likely to change as the biotechnological revolution progresses. It may allow us to equip our electronic machines with 'nervous systems' as delicate and precise as those found in the bodies of living organisms. As this becomes possible, so the interfaces that we might design for integrating human and mechanical systems might become equally clever. The problem of infection entering through breaches in the skin would have to be overcome, possibly by implanting part of the device beneath the skin and transmitting signals to or from

In the future more organic materials will be incorporated into our machines, and machines will become more like living systems. Eventually the distinction between 'making' and 'growing' something may become blurred. Even car bodies might be 'grown' in nutrient baths to the exact shape and size required.

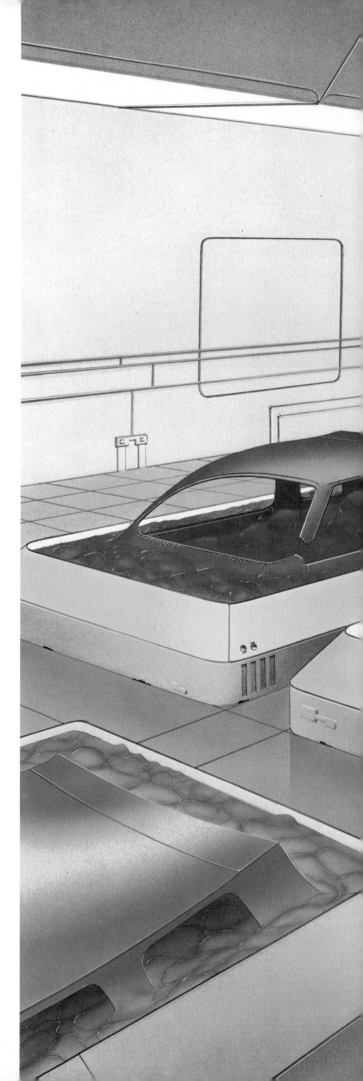

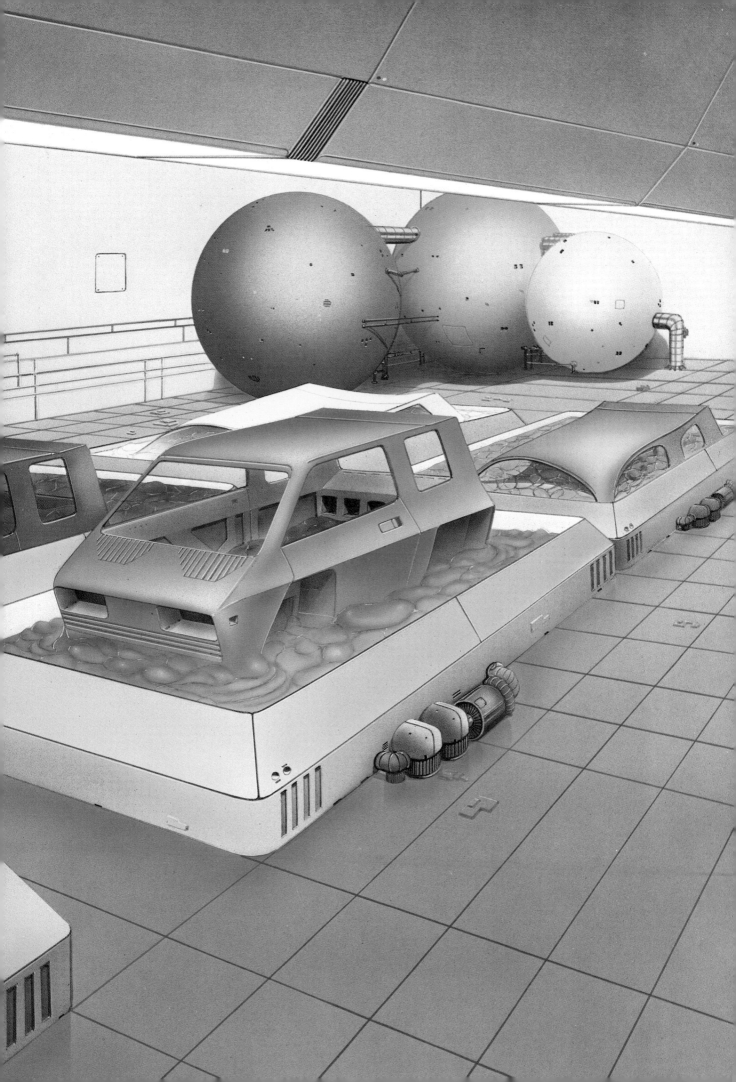

Although the wiring of the brain and a computer have many similarities, there is a crucial difference. The factors which cause a neuron to fire or not to fire at its axon are much more complex than the simple on/off switches of a computer. A neuron learns to fire or not to fire according to the firing patterns at its thousands of synapses. This 'learning' is controlled by a dominant synapse.

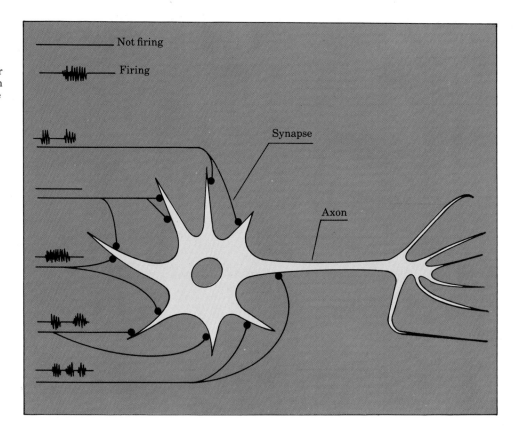

it rather than having permanent wiring through the skin. The adaptations which people might have to undergo in order to be fitted with such link-up capacity would undoubtedly be complicated, but the end result would not necessarily be obtrusive. There is no need to imagine people walking around with panels set into their forearms that resemble the backplate of a video cassette recorder.

This kind of cyborgization, in which whole bodies are equipped with points of intersection, might become a rather attractive prospect for other than strictly pragmatic reasons. One might imagine a society of the future where individuals are enthusiastic to undergo the operations that will allow them to plug themselves in to different kinds of machinery. There is, however, another kind of cyborgization which has a much more horrific aspect: the replacement of parts of the body by stronger mechanical parts. This is carried to its extreme in science fiction stories of human brains placed in mechanical bodies of various sorts, or maintained outside the body.

The first possibility would be technically very difficult, because of the complex systems needed to supply the brain with oxygenated blood and keep it sterile. Animal brains have, however, been removed from their bodies and continued electrical activity has been recorded for some time. If a human brain could be similarly maintained apart from the body, then with the use of artificial synapses, it might be able to receive information, to communicate, or to control complicated machinery.

BRAINS AND COMPUTERS

Our first ventures into purposeful cyborgization are likely to be modest ones, involving the hooking up of already functional nerves to a single channel of information transmission. Making entirely new connections between the brain and the world, so that it could receive information of a new kind, or move machinery other than that which substitutes for a lost limb, will probably not be done for some considerable time. One day, though, it will be done. If a man will soon be able to use his brain to issue commands directly to an artificial arm, then he might also use it to issue commands directly to an automated factory. If a man can use his brain to decipher information transmitted into it by an artificial eye, there is no reason in principle why he should not have transmitted into his brain information from an electronic computer.

In the last chapter arguments were put forward to suggest that there might not be as much scope as we suppose for improving the memory or enhancing problem-solving abilities by using drugs to boost the performance of the brain. Linking up the brain to other systems capable of memorization and calculation could conceivably be a better way to enhance the power of the mind. In a sense, it is inconvenient to have to carry around all our memories in our heads all the time, and we all know how difficult it is on occasions to remember things as and when we want to. There is a certain attractiveness in the idea of having a memory that we could plug in whenever necessary, which would

164

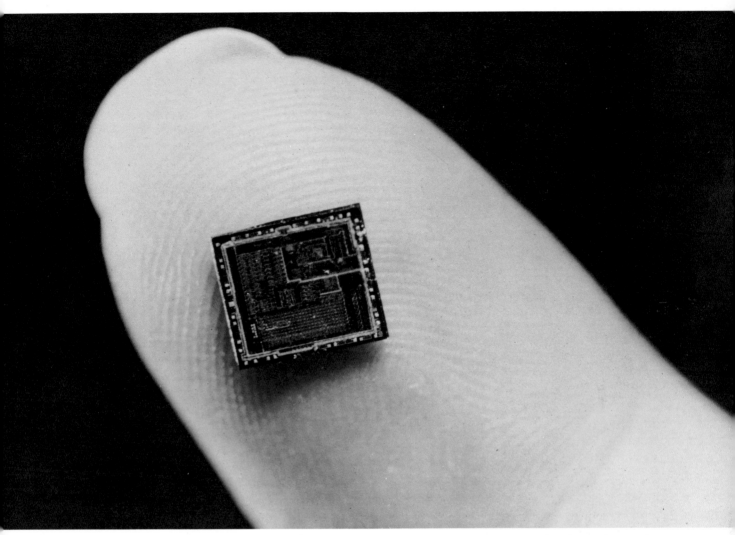

store large quantities of information in such a way that orderly recall could be conveniently triggered. Electronic memory chips are already small enough to allow us to imagine very considerable computer capacity being grafted on to the body without weighing it down.

Connecting the brain and the machine in such a way that the mind could *use* the extra capacity would be much more difficult than it sounds. The view that the brain's own storage capacity is drastically under-used is a familiar one, but it does seem to be true that the brain contains much more tissue than is necessary for the uses we make of it. This is strongly suggested by the now-numerous cases discovered in which hydrocephalic children, whose skulls are mostly filled by fluid instead of nervous tissue, can still function normally with only a thin 'rind' of brain. Some grow up into perfectly normal adults. It might be that they do have the same number of brain cells as ordinary people, though much more tightly packed. Whatever the explanation, it certainly seems that a lot more storage capacity could be crammed into the space we already have.

The implication is that we should not need to hook our brains up to mini-computers in order to get

The silicon chip – which has made the microcomputer revolution possible – is a piece of silicon about 6mm square, with a memory which is not erased when the power is switched off. It is covered with minute electrical connections joining together thousands of transistors. The chip is hermetically sealed inside a plastic case to prevent damage by dust.

access to extra storage capacity; it may already be there waiting to be used, or might be grown without too much effort. Instead of linking the brain to a computer simply to acquire a better memory, it might be done in order to make use of the talents computers have which human brains do not possess, such as for making very rapid numerical calculations or for the efficient processing of vast amounts of data.

Computers work in a way that is similar in some respects to the way the human brain works. They are made up of millions of switches, each capable of being either on or off. Each switch has many connections with other switches, and the number of potential pathways for information is almost infinite. In the brain, the neurons are the switches, each with thousands of branching connections with other neurons. In a computer, a string of combinations of 'on' and 'off' (or 0 and 1) can be used to symbolize a number or anything else we choose. A

Computers can perform tasks which are too dangerous for human beings, such as monitoring and adjusting conditions in a nuclear reactor. The control room, shown here, allows man to oversee the computer, but the possibility of computer error leads many people to view with alarm our increasing reliance on such control systems.

(Right)
Much stressful and repetitive factory work can now be done by robots. Factories controlled by computers, with a robot workforce, need have hardly any human employees at all. Here we see robots soldering in the Renault factory in Brussels.

computer programme tells the computer what meanings and values to assign to its symbols.

Human brains are at present much more intelligent than computers. However, such rapid strides are being made in the development of artificial intelligence, that we must consider the possibility that before we learn how to integrate human brains and mechanical systems, we might already have learned how to make electronic brains more capable than human ones. Computers can already simulate certain functions of the human brain, such as problem solving, comprehension and use of language, memory storage and retrieval, learning from experience and reasoning capacity.

There are some things, however, that computers so far cannot do. One is generalizing: for instance, in vision, the ability to take the salient features from an image and recognize them again in a different form or context. This ability is integral to the way human beings see, and essential in interpreting handwriting or recognizing a face. Recently there has been another approach to the building of intelligent machines. Instead of trying to programme a computer to act like a human brain, some researchers have analysed what makes a human brain *different* from a computer, and tried instead to build a machine as like a human brain as possible. One result was WISARD, a machine built to imitate the human optical system. WISARD *can* generalize: it can recognize someone's face even

though the person is making a grimace or wearing a false moustache, and a prototype was very successful at recognizing handwritten characters.

Like present-day computers, WISARD is based on silicon chips, each equivalent in storage capacity to a mini-computer. Each chip represents one neuron – a recognition of the fact that the firing of a neuron is vastly more complex than the simple on/off of the electronic switches in a computer's memory. A neuron may receive simultaneous signals across synapses from thousands of other neurons, some telling it to fire, some telling it not to fire. Not all the signals are given equal value, and sometimes there is a 'master synapse', which overrides all the others.

WISARD'S silicon neurons are connected together in networks similar to those of the human brain. WISARD is not programmed, as a computer is, but simply connected to a source of information – in this case visual images. Versions are now commercially available to provide pattern recognition in robot and other applications. It may be from this kind of machine, rather than from computers, that the artificial intelligence closest to man's will emerge. Creating an electronic brain similar to man's might not have much practical application, but we might learn a great deal in the process about the relationship of brain to mind and the way the human brain works.

There is some controversy over the issue of

Computers originated in an attempt to find a quicker way of performing mathematical calculations. Before they were invented, the job was done by a human being known as a 'computer', armed with a calculator capable only of addition and subtraction (like many microcomputers). Each element of the 'computer's' job is represented in the structure of a present-day microcomputer. The numerical language of the computer – made up entirely of Os and 1s – can be used to symbolize not only numbers but also letters and words.

(**Opposite page**)
Robots and automated machinery can be made much more useful by giving them a mechanical equivalent of human feedback systems. In such a system, information is received, a decision is made to act (or not to act), the action is carried out, and more information is received about the results of the action. Shown here is a feedback system by which a human or a machine could judge whether a room was too dark and turn a light on.

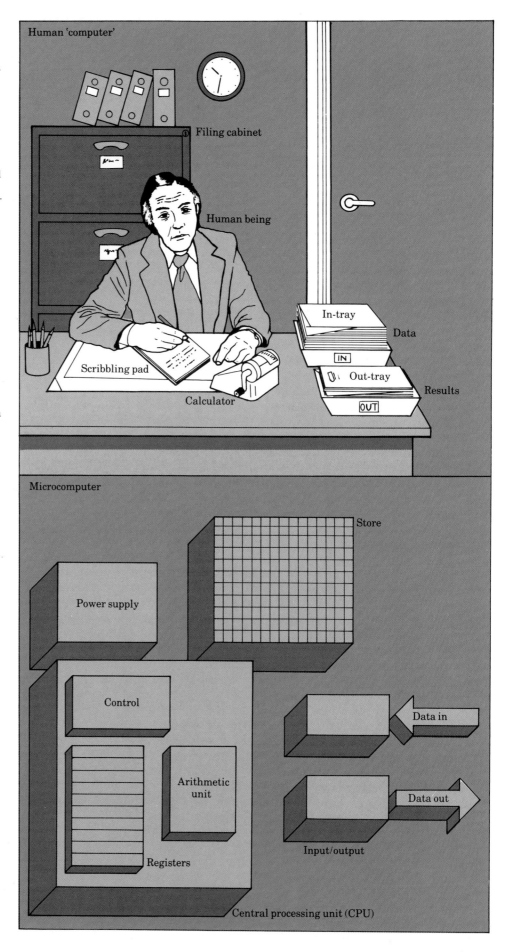

Human 'computer'

Filing cabinet

Human being

In-tray

Data

Scribbling pad

Out-tray

Results

Calculator

Microcomputer

Store

Power supply

Control

Data in

Arithmetic unit

Data out

Registers

Input/output

Central processing unit (CPU)

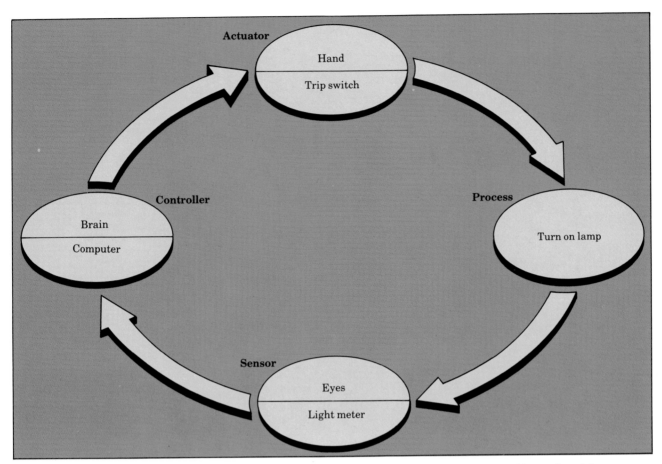

whether computers or electronic brains can ever possess the properties of our minds which we consider to be characteristically human. Can we create a machine which is self-aware or one which feels emotions, or one capable of free will? It requires something of an imaginative leap to be prepared to answer 'yes' to these questions, and many people find themselves unable to make that leap. Logically, though, there seems to be no reason why artificial intelligence should not develop to the point where it can match or outstrip human intelligence.

SUPER-INTELLIGENT MACHINES

Human beings evolved from unintelligent ancestors. Our intelligent brains have been put together over millions of years by the trial and error process of natural selection. The whole essence of the biotechnological revolution is that men are learning to take control of the systems generated by natural selection, to duplicate and improve upon its achievements. If natural selection could produce the human mind, then human ingenuity, given appropriate techniques, can produce artificial minds. There is very little room for doubt that in the future artificial intelligences will be able to put their creators in the shade in many different ways.

If this is so, then some of the kinds of cyborgization which will become possible will also become unnecessary. There is no point in linking human brains to automated factories if automated factories could behave as intelligently without any such intrusion. If motor cars and spaceships can have their own built-in artificial intelligence, they will not even need drivers or pilots, let alone resident human brains.

There might, of course, be disadvantages to having functional machinery of various kinds controlled by artificial intelligences as capable as human minds. The whole point of factories and motor vehicles is that they will perform tasks for which we need them. If they become individuals in their own right, capable of making their own decisions and choices, they might (reasonably) wonder why they should devote their lives to doing things for human beings. Once an automated factory has its own highly sophisticated guiding intelligence, it might conceivably decide that it doesn't want to be an automated factory, but would prefer to be a free spirit pursuing its own ends.

It might be a mistake to assume that it is practical – let alone moral – to create artificial intelligences purely for use as slaves. Karel Capek's play *R.U.R.*, which introduced the word 'robot' into several languages, suggests that when men can make machines as sophisticated as themselves in order to provide for all their needs, the machines will rightly conclude that there is no point in having humans around at all, because they are obviously redundant.

Given this kind of possibility, it may be that, as we become capable of making much cleverer machines, our relationship with those machines will have to be radically transformed. Just as future science may enable us to manipulate living organisms as though they were mere technological artifacts, so it may enable some technological artifacts to achieve a status which we are now prepared to concede only to a very few living organisms. We will have to begin to think of certain mechanical entities as individuals which not only have their own identity but their own private thoughts, ambitions and careers. If such entities are constructed out of the kinds of materials which we have become accustomed to calling 'organic' rather than out of metal and glass, we could well have difficulty in thinking of them as machines at all. They will effectively *be* living organisms – sentient products of an alternative creation. They will be *aliens* in the sense that science fiction writers use the term, except that they will not be extra-terrestials.

It is probable that we will learn enough within the next few generations to be able to create artificial intelligences which manifest most or all of the properties of human minds. It is also probable, though, that we will not go in for the wholesale manufacture of such entities; and if we are to have machines serving particular purposes for us, we will not make them capable of having purposes of their own. This may still leave scope for the kind of human/machine link-ups discussed in this chapter. It could well be that we will find it prudent to maintain our virtual monopoly on sentience and

intelligence except for the purposes of scientific experiment and inquiry.

Whether or not the particular man/machine hybrids discussed here are ever constructed, there is no doubt that they represent a kind of technological enterprise that we will be increasingly able to undertake. The potential is clearly there for a dramatic increase in the intimacy with which future generations of people can relate to machines. Machines in the future may well be able to become extensions of man in a much more literal sense than they ever have in the past. Working systems directed to particular tasks will one day be constructed that are part flesh and part machine, and the two will blend together where they interface.

With advances in technology, the self-replicating robot will soon become a reality. This will lead to more efficient factories and increases in productivity. At present robots are unintelligent machines made to perform one particular function, but machines as intelligent as man will probably be made one day. If they were to become self-replicating, they might well regard mankind as redundant.

Chapter 10

Scenarios for the future of mankind

Many people find it difficult to consider the prospects of a revolution in biological science optimistically. We are preparing to tamper extensively with the fundamental processes of life, and this is seen as trespassing on ground that ought to remain sacred. Use of the term 'genetic engineering' can cause a ripple of panic. It is often feared that such technology will permit the evolution of new and insidious possibilities of mass destruction in a world which is already well supplied with such means. These fears certainly have some justification.

We should not, however, think of the perfecting of techniques of biological engineering as something that will happen of its own accord, whether we want it to or not. Nor should we suppose that, as the techniques of biological engineering become more effective, they will force upon our society a pattern of responses that will carry us inexorably to our destiny, whether that destiny be a happy or disastrous one. The world is not bound to get better as a result of new discoveries in science and technology, nor is it bound to get worse; there will simply be new opportunities for making it better or worse. There are many ways in which new techniques in biotechnology will prove useful, and many ways in which they will help solve social problems, but they also have many potential uses which might work to the advantage of some and the detriment of others. It is also necessary to consider seriously whether unintended consequences of the development of biotechnology might be harmful enough to counterbalance or outweigh intended good consequences.

Most of the scenarios considered below are unpleasant ones, but this should not be taken to imply that biotechnology is more likely to make the world worse than it is to make it better. These accounts are recognitions of things that might go wrong if we are not careful. Only a full awareness of the things that *could* go wrong will prepare us for the task of trying to make sure that nothing does.

ARE WE IN CONTROL?
In the last 50 years we have seen the rapid proliferation of arguments that our tampering with nature has already brought us close to disaster. Throughout most of human history, the tools that

man used were not capable of dramatic overnight transformations of the environment. Human activity did result in some such changes, turning fertile lands in North Africa and the Middle East into deserts by allowing livestock to graze too liberally, and creating the American 'dust bowl' by exhausting the soil with over-intensive cultivation. On the whole, though, natural ecological systems have been resilient enough to accommodate primitive technologies. Nowadays, it is different. The more powerful machines of today allow us to modify our environment much more quickly and completely.

The natural environment – the ecosphere – is a very complicated set of systems. Living species are dependent on one another, and on the circumstances of their inorganic environment, in ways which are not all obvious to superficial inspection. A change in the fortunes of one species can easily trigger a chain reaction which may affect many other species, and even the inorganic environment. For example, cutting down forest trees may not only drive into extinction many of the animals and plants living in the forest. It may also create a desert, because the clouds from which the local rain falls are created by evaporation of the water held and circulated by the trees.

Paul Ehrlich has popularized the notion of 'ecocatastrophe', suggesting that the effects of human conduct have already seriously endangered the Earth's complex ecosystem, and that one day it will break down completely. He argues that the main dangers are unchecked population growth, profligate use of resources, destruction of plants and animal species and pollution of the environment by the by-products of our industries. Some of the consumption of non-reusable resources is due to the hungry majority in the world trying to scrape a living; but most of the consumption takes place in the rich nations, when many valuable resources are turned into luxury products which people are then persuaded by advertizing to consume. Not only do the manufacturing processes pollute the environment, but many of the products themselves do so too. For instance, cars emit poisonous fumes containing both carbon monoxide, which can destroy the haemoglobin in our blood and thus kill quickly

in an enclosed space, and lead, which is highly toxic and can cause long-term brain damage.

We now regularly discard into the environment many kinds of chemicals which do not usually exist there in high concentrations. For instance, coal contains some sulphur which is released as sulphur dioxide when we burn the coal. This combines with water in the atmosphere to cause 'acid rain', which kills trees and sterilizes streams and lakes hundreds or thousands of miles away. Many kinds of pollutants which factories pump into rivers may need only to poison a few kinds of algae in order to ruin the chances of survival of molluscs, fish and birds which feed there. We have also let loose many powerful poisons which were devised in an attempt to control the environment, such as DDT and other chlorinated hydrocarbons used as insecticides. Dioxin, a powerful toxic chemical which causes birth defects, has been used in war and released accidentally. Radioactive wastes from nuclear power

When forests and woods are cut down, the landscape may be devastated by erosion. The soil, no longer protected from wind and rain, is quickly washed away.

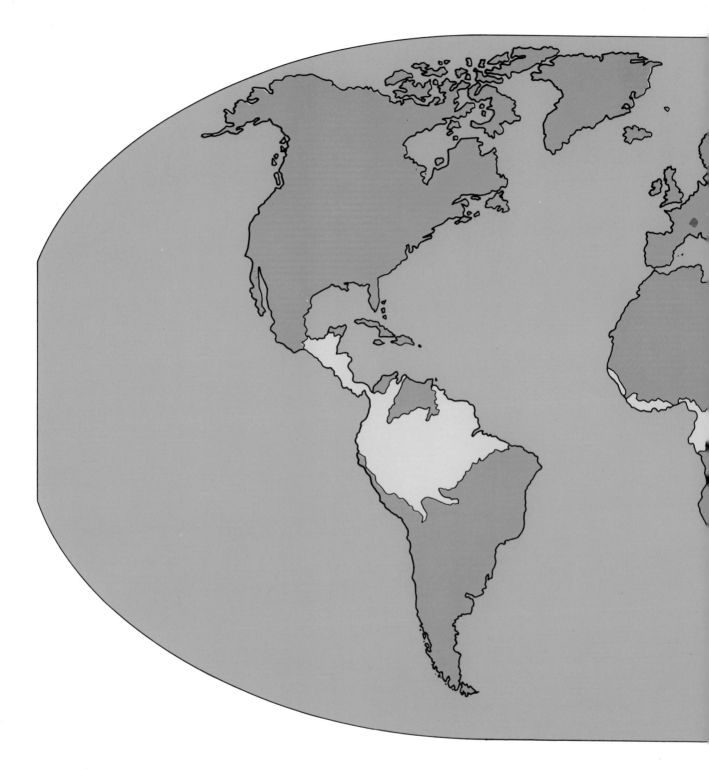

stations, which could cause cancer and genetic mutations, are discharged into the sea, dumped on the sea bed or buried in the earth.

Even the composition of the atmosphere is being affected by human activity. The ozone layer, which absorbs some of the harder radiation emitted by the sun and thus protects the Earth's surface from its effects, might be impoverished by a chemical used in aerosol spray cans. We have already referred to the possibility that the carbon dioxide added to the atmosphere when we burn fossil fuels may eventually trigger a 'greenhouse effect' whereby the

atmosphere would trap more of the sun's energy and gradually warm up. The climatic effects proceeding from such a warming could be ecologically devastating. At the same time, we are cutting down the trees which extract carbon dioxide from the air and replace it with the oxygen which we need for breathing.

The extinction of species as the forests and wildernesses are cleared is dangerous in another way. Apart from unbalancing complex ecosystems, whose stability is rooted in their diversity, it also robs us of a source of genetic variants in the plants

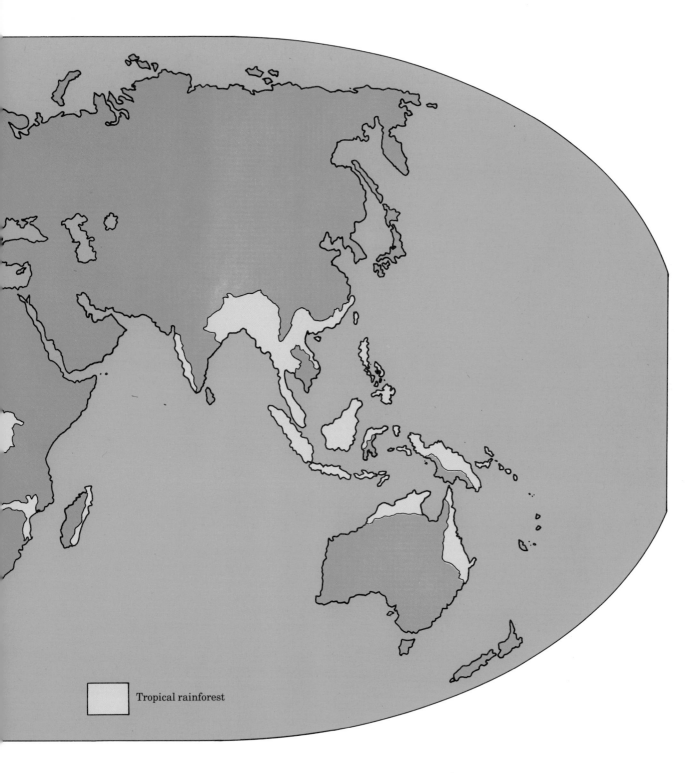

Tropical rainforest

and animals we exploit. Our super-productive modern hybrid crops are often very vulnerable to disease, and the admixture of new genes is needed to combat the changing genes of the disease-causing organisms that affect them. A wild strain of maize, resistant to four of the plant's seven main diseases, was recently discovered in Mexico when it was on the verge of extinction. Only 2,000 plants were left.

A nuclear war would constitute the ultimate ecocatastrophe. The direct results of radioactive fallout from even a fairly limited nuclear war would be devastating, and nuclear explosions on the

The extent of tropical rain · forest is decreasing annually at an alarming rate. Each year an area the size of Switzerland is destroyed. Rainforest makes productive use of some of the poorest soil in the world: the giant trees spread out their roots on the surface, receiving nourishment from debris on the forest floor. Once the forest is cut down so that crops can be grown or cattle raised, the soil is soon exhausted and a priceless resource has been lost for ever.

This gull was killed by DDT, one of the many poisons used as insecticides which have been found to be dangerous to animals and man. There is no mechanism in nature for breaking down DDT, so it accumulates in tissues throughout the food chain. The irresponsible use of insecticides will probably not be curbed unless bioengineers can create better methods of biological pest control, such as pest-resistant crop plants or insect predators to attack the pests.

Earth's surface would probably blast enough dust into the atmosphere to blot out the sun and thus rob the ecosphere of its source of energy. Rumours about computer failures, leading one or other of the superpowers to believe that it is being attacked by the other, encourage us to suspect that even if ambition, recklessness or population pressures do not cause a final war, we might be led to launch our engines of total destruction by mistake.

If the way we exercise the power which we already possess over the environment is so irresponsible – or so ham-fisted – that we are perilously close to destroying that environment, then would it not be very dangerous to exercise still greater power? Can we really be trusted with the discoveries we are making? Biotechnology will certainly give us new opportunities for disaster, some of which will be considered below. It will also, however, give us new ways of improving our world, and of rectifying some of the mistakes we have already made. Our new power of interference with nature will be much more sweeping than ever before. This should mean that it will become easier, not harder, to avoid a major ecocatastrophe.

PLAGUE AND WAR
Most of us associate bacteria with dangerous

The ultimate ecocatastrophe would be a nuclear war. The nuclear bomb dropped on Hiroshima in August 1945 killed 80,000 people immediately, and by 1980 200,000 had died from its effects. The total power of today's nuclear arsenals is estimated at one million times this size – enough to explode one such bomb every second for a fortnight. After even a limited nuclear exchange, the 'nuclear winter', with the sun blotted out by clouds of debris, would cut off most forms of life from their energy source. There is little that bioengineering can do in relation to such a catastrophe.

infections, and many therefore fear that transforming and engineering them could create new diseases worse than those from which we already suffer. The bacterium most commonly used in plasmid engineering, *Escherichia coli*, is one that *can* make us sick. It lives in many natural environments, including the human gut, and if it multiplies too rapidly there it induces stomach upsets and diarrhoea. Genetic engineers usually work with 'attenuated strains' of the bacterium – ones that can survive only in specially controlled laboratory conditions – and the plasmids that they try to insert have no bearing on the infective capabilities of the organism. The hit-or-miss nature of transformation techniques does, however, mean that there is a possibility of an unexpected accident.

Another factor generating anxiety is the experimental work geared to increasing rates of transformation. Many researchers are trying to use viruses as vectors to carry DNA into the cells they hope to transform. They are thus involved in the creation of new viruses, and these new viruses are sometimes being developed specifically to invade and transform animal cells. New infectious bacteria could probably be dealt with fairly easily by antibiotics, but new infectious viruses, if any were to be created in the laboratory and then let loose,

might be much more dangerous. It is obviously necessary for genetic engineers who are using viruses to be very careful indeed. We know that they *are* very careful, but we also know that people and precautionary systems are fallible.

The fear that a new disease-causing virus could be created accidentally can probably be discounted. As techniques in genetic engineering become more advanced and more ambitious, their specific effects will become more controllable. Moreover, it is the advancement of these techniques which offers us our best hope of winning the battle against the naturally occurring virus diseases which are at present so troublesome. The more detailed our knowledge of viruses becomes – as it must become if we are to make progress in understanding how the replication and expression of genes is controlled – the better we will be able to control their activity.

Perhaps the strongest reason to be anxious about the possibility of genetic engineers producing new plagues is the knowledge that some genetic engineers somewhere are probably trying to do exactly that. Medical problems provide only one of the main motivating forces for this kind of research, and it is such projects which are talked about openly. Research in biological warfare is mostly secret, but there is no doubt that it goes on.

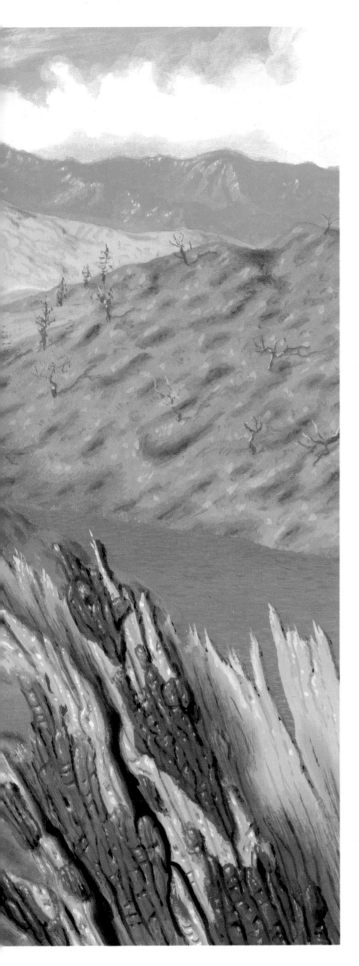

Chemical warfare has been banned under the Geneva Convention since the 1920s, and the ban seems to have worked fairly well in preventing chemical weapons being used on the battlefield, despite contemporary allegations that Iraq has used fungus-derived poisons, usually called 'yellow rain', in its war against Iran. However, the ban has never stopped research into chemical weapons, because many countries have felt it necessary to stockpile such things just in case someone else breaks the Convention. Thus, the richer nations probably all have their secret supplies of nerve gases and other deadly chemicals. It will surely be the same with biological weapons. The governments which can afford to sponsor such research will want their stockpiles of cholera, anthrax or new disease-causing organisms just in case anyone ever tries to use such weapons against them.

The line between chemical and biological warfare is blurred. A poison is something that disrupts the biochemistry of a living system, so the most effective poisons are often organic compounds. Many are biological in origin, being used for attack or defence by animals and plants. Some of the most virulent toxins are produced by bacteria, such as the botulinus toxin which causes botulism. It is only to be expected that genetic engineers will be instructed by their military masters to make bacteria which will be particularly effective in producing such toxins. As techniques become more advanced, biotechnologists will be required to produce new viruses whose usefulness will be in killing people quickly and spreading rapidly.

If there ever is an accidental release of a new bacterium or virus which causes an epidemic, it is far more likely that it will come from a laboratory specializing in military research than from a commercial or medical laboratory. In 1969 there was a newspaper report that the virus for Venezuelan equine encephalitis had escaped from biological warfare laboratories in Utah, USA, and was established in the local wild animal population. It may be even more likely that if new engineered viruses do get out and kill people on a large scale, their release will be deliberate rather than accidental.

The unfortunate thing about this kind of hazard is that it is not one which can be contained by any kind of safety regulation, or even by a total ban on research. The ban would be ineffective, and research would go on in secret. In the same way as a universal ban on nuclear weapons would increase tremendously the advantage that would accrue to anyone who *did* possess them, so a ban on biological

The possibility that engineered micro-organisms might escape from the laboratory or fermenter and cause havoc in the biosphere is a very real one. Bacteria might be engineered to digest cellulose, so that they could be grown on plant material in industrial processes. If they got out, grass, trees, crops and the whole associated food chain would be devastated.

weapons would make their possession that much more attractive to the unscrupulous.

It is difficult to imagine how a 'plague war' would actually be fought, and so it is not easy to weigh up the actual utility of biological weapons. The nation waging such a war would probably have relatively little difficulty in launching its attack and creating centres of infection in enemy territory, but it would then have to build its own defences against the spread of the epidemic to its own population. The readiest targets of biological weapons would be children and old people, and millions of people outside the enemy nation would also be endangered. A nation attacked in such a fashion would presumably respond as quickly and effectively as it could in the attempt to preserve its own military forces, though we must also bear in mind that it would be very difficult to detect the hand behind a plague attack. Rather than wiping out large numbers of another nation by a killing disease, the attacking nation might prefer to use an insidious disease which merely debilitated people, and made them more amenable to its plans.

Whether we like the idea or not, the only way to guard against such possibilities as these is to devote more effort and attention to biotechnological research, not less. The only way to make sure that no catastrophe of this kind happens is to make sure that if ever there is an attack mounted with biological weapons there is a defence which can meet and neutralize it. The possibility of new plagues can be countered best by developing methods of nullifying *all* plagues, and the only possible source of such methods is the new biotechnology.

The force of this argument is unlikely to make anyone less anxious about the future, but it is nonetheless undeniable. The ability to make biological weapons already exists, and cannot be wiped out. There is no alternative but to make every effort to build appropriate defences. Of course, the chain of developments will go on – there will be more sophisticated weapons requiring more sophisticated defences, and the same research will feed both. This has been the case throughout the history of technology, but there is no way of getting out of the cycle.

TYRANNY

One of the main anxieties about the possible uses of future technology is that it may enable those in power to control the lives of ordinary people more efficiently and more minutely. To what extent will the development of biotechnology encourage or facilitate oppression? What kind of future police states become imaginable in the light of earlier chapters?

Technology is certainly not necessary to the establishment of fearful tyranny – great tyrants of the past have sustained reigns of terror with

180

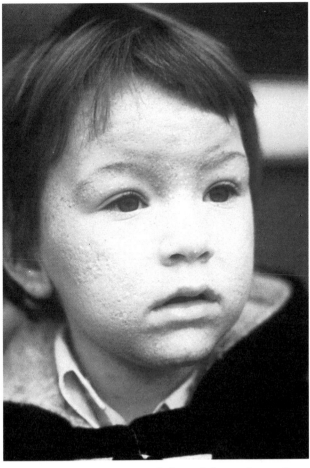

nothing more sophisticated than clubs and swords. Advanced technology, though, could conceivably increase the efficiency of tyrants to the point where they could never be deposed – perhaps even to the point where no one would wish to depose them.

Would-be tyrants have always been able to threaten us with death, but in recent times more subtle and more sinister possibilities have emerged: strategies by which would-be tyrants might one day be able to obtain our wholehearted consent to being tyrannized. Even under the worst tyrannies of past times, people retained a special kind of freedom. Their actions, and even what they said aloud, might be tightly controlled, but in their thoughts they were unreachable and uncontrollable. In the future, that might not be so. As our knowledge of developmental biology and the biology of the brain increases, there is a possibility that our rulers will inherit the power to make us think and feel the way they want us to think and feel.

As was argued in Chapter Eight, the idea that freedom of the will might be completely wiped out is less plausible than our anxieties make it seem. Nevertheless, even if we dismiss the idea that minds can be controlled biochemically with enough precision to create perfect slaves, there are other ways in which a small power elite could use biological engineering to make their subjects more pliable. The best opportunities for close social control are probably offered by cyborgization. The

(**Opposite**) This wasted landscape in Vietnam was caused by aerial spraying of a defoliant called Agent Orange containing the potent poison dioxin. Dioxin has caused cancer and genetic defects both in the victims on the ground and in those who performed the spraying. Genetic engineering will almost certainly be used to produce more efficient biological and chemical weapons, to cause disease in trees, crops and human beings.
(**Above**) Dioxin has been released into the atmosphere in several industrial accidents, such as the explosion at a factory in Seveso, Italy, in 1976. (**Right**) Workers in protective suits and masks remove contaminated earth. (**Left**) This girl from Seveso has chloracne, a painful proliferation of skin cells caused by exposure to dioxin. Many people fear that biotechnology, especially if used for manufacturing chemical weapons, will lead to more such accidents.

clever future tyrant will probably take the trouble to equip his subjects with tiny mechanical devices – perhaps located beneath the skull – that will allow their location always to be known, and their conversations to be monitored. Similar devices might also be used to administer shocks of pain in response to signals from a remote source.

This is a good deal simpler and cruder than producing tailor-made slaves by biological and behavioural engineering, and it is probably more practical. Of course, the would-be tyrant would have the problem of imposing such devices upon people, but he would be able to do it one step at a time, beginning with delinquents and criminals and slowly extending the net. By the time a substantial fraction of the population had been converted, it should be possible to use their support to enforce conversion upon the rest. There are rulers in the world at present who have sufficient political power to undertake such a programme if only the necessary technology were cheaply available.

Once such a system of tyrannical control were established, the way would then be opened for more sweeping uses of biological engineering. When political domination had been completed by these means, it would become feasible to begin using techniques to modify developing embryos without fear of too much opposition. Even if the minds of the oppressed could not be controlled closely enough to make perfect slaves, there is much that might be done to a body to fit it for a subservient role. In earlier chapters we have mentioned the possibility of making bodies fitter, tougher and longer-lived, but a small tyrannical elite might deliberately create an underclass of feeble and short-lived people who could do the hard work without having the physical resources to rebel. We need not doubt that there are people in the world who would be prepared to impose this kind of rule on their fellows. In the future, those who have the opportunity may try to reserve the benefits of technology for themselves, and may in fact use the technology to make sure that others cannot share in its rewards.

The only defence we will have in future against the possibility of such a tyranny will be exactly the same as the only defence we have had in the past: the determination not to let tyranny take hold and, if it ever does, the determination to root it out. It hardly needs to be pointed out that this has not always worked in the past, at least on a local scale. There may, therefore, be grounds for supposing that it will not always work in the future either. With the gradual advancement of technological means of suppressing rebellion, the danger of a permanent destruction of freedom obviously does exist. Perhaps we can find hope only in the awareness that the oppressed always outnumber the oppressors, and that oppressors are frequently divided among themselves. These factors have always left open the possibility of social change through violent conflict, and perhaps they always will.

182

All technology tends to add to the power that is available to tyrants. Biotechnology will be no exception to this rule, but there is no reason to think that it poses a special menace in this regard. If the benefits of the technology we have so far amassed are great enough to outweigh the increased scope for tyranny which it has created, then the same will probably be true of future technology.

HUMAN ENGINEERING
Some would argue that biotechnology, especially human engineering, is likely to be injurious to the quality of life, and that many aspects of it are morally unacceptable. Others fear that if we think of designing our children as we design objects, we will in effect be surrendering our humanity and becoming mere machines. In a way, this fear is more powerful than the fear that other people might forcibly mechanize us. It is the fear that by doing what we think is right, carefully and with forethought, we might actually be making a horrible mistake.

Although some useful things might be done by transforming cells in mature individuals, or controlling growth and metabolism in adult bodies, most of the opportunities which will open up to us will involve operating upon individuals at a much earlier stage in their development. In order to be efficient human engineers, our descendants will have to begin work on egg cells and continue to control matters as those eggs develop through all the stages of embryonic change. This can only be done if development from conception to birth takes place in an artificial womb. Competent human engineering will require ectogenesis: development outside the body.

The removal of foetal development into the laboratory would eliminate the role of the mother entirely until after birth, and if the genes in the egg cell are to be manipulated then the hereditary relevance of both parents is reduced. Even if children produced in this way are returned to their parents after birth, so that the mother can suckle the infant and bring it up, the connection between mother and child has been crucially broken. A society which practises a good deal of human engineering – with whatever ends in view – is certain to be one in which the intimate core of what we think of as normal family life is considerably disturbed, although ectogenesis would not necessarily be incompatible with forming relationships. Children born from artificial wombs might still be reared by the two human beings who contributed the egg and the sperm which provided the raw material for engineering, or they might be 'adopted' by the parents genetically unrelated to them.

J. B. S. Haldane (whose essay, 'Daedalus; or Science and the Future', written in 1923, provided the imaginative seed of Huxley's *Brave New World*) was the first man to take seriously the idea of future

Fertilized human embryos can now be frozen without destroying them. In Melbourne, Australia, they are stored as shown in liquid nitrogen at −196°C. A healthy baby girl, developed from an embryo which had been frozen for two months, was recently born there. The technique makes in vitro fertilization far more efficient, as only one operation to remove eggs is needed, and the embryo can be reimplanted at precisely the right point in the woman's cycle. Other uses of freezing, such as storing embryos before one of a couple is sterilized, are likely to become common and to lead to many more 'spare' embryos.

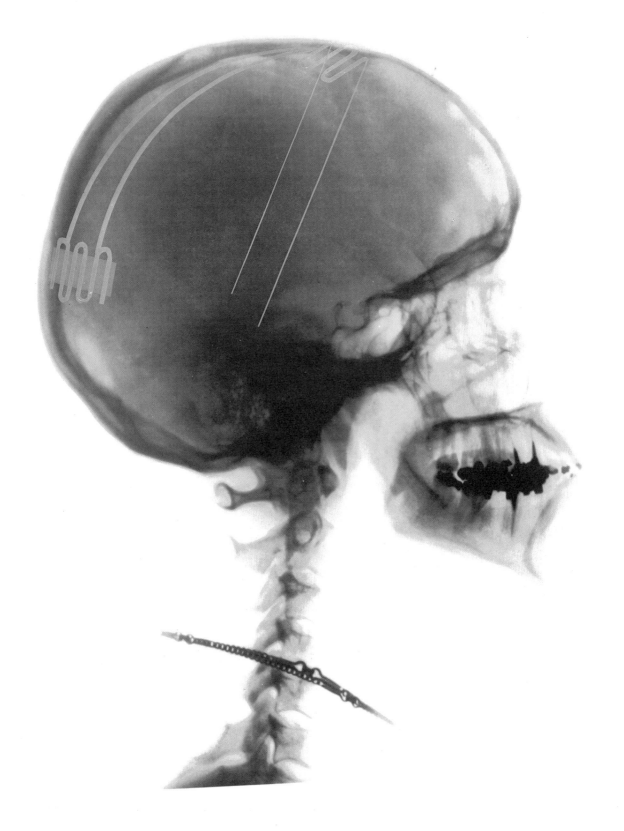

Future tyrants might have a device implanted in the brain of each of their subjects which would allow the authorities to listen to people's conversations and track their location. Electrodes going deep into the brain could stimulate the pain or pleasure centres or other parts of the brain when a signal was received. Implanted electrodes controlled by the patient have already been used in the treatment of mental illness such as phobias.

societies where ectogenesis would be common practice. He argued that any 'biological invention' was bound to seem initially a perversion, but that just as the biological inventions of the past (from milking cows to contraception) had been gradually accepted into our notions of morally proper behaviour, so too would the biological inventions of the future. This will probably be the case with ectogenesis. Babies will one day be nurtured in artificial wombs, and we will learn to accept this as a good and necessary thing. Our descendants will not be reconciled to this without difficulty, but eventually they will find it hard to believe that the old-fashioned way ever had its champions.

Even though moral standards may change to accommodate some of the opportunities of biotechnology, there are important issues of moral philosophy at stake in human engineering which will probably continue to be debated fiercely. We recognize that all human individuals are entitled to moral consideration, but in the past we had relatively little difficulty in identifying the point in time when that entitlement begins. Some cultures with institutionalized infanticide have been prepared to withdraw the protection of moral consideration from some infants, but in most societies babies are reckoned to acquire their human rights at birth. Until recently the possibility of interfering with the development of embryos hardly arose, and the question of their possible moral entitlements lay dormant. Now that question has become real and urgent. Doctors can interfere with the process of reproduction all along the line, and we have been forced to reconsider the question of when a human individual actually comes into being.

There is no 'true' answer to the question simply waiting to be discovered. It is a choice that we must make. Some argue that moral entitlement should commence at the moment of fertilization, others at the moment when the embryo implants in the womb, and yet others when the foetus becomes potentially capable of independent life (some time in the sixth month of its development). It is probable that the only way to keep disquiet to a minimum will be to accept the earliest point in time, and to accept with it the full burden of moral responsibility affecting the decisions we make about what we may justifiably do to developing embryos.

Research is already being done, however, in which 'spare' fertilized embryos – obtained when helping childless women to become pregnant – are grown in the laboratory for up to two weeks, beyond the age at which they would implant in the womb. It is inevitable, too, that very many fertilized embryos and developing foetuses would have to be sacrificed in refining techniques of human engineering. This seems unacceptable today, yet liberal abortion laws in many countries imply that the destruction of an embryo or foetus can be morally sanctioned if that is what the mother wants. It is highly likely that in the future societies where human engineering is practised, people will still be arguing about what should and should not be done.

This is only one of the many difficult ethical and social problems which will be caused by the biotechnological revolution. For instance, we are already seeing practical applications of our new power over the mechanisms of reproduction. Many babies have been born from 'donated' sperm, because a husband is infertile; often the child's true heredity is hidden from relatives and friends, and also from the child himself. Babies have now also been born from 'donated' eggs, thus acquiring two mothers – one genetic, and one who carries and bears the child.

This trend is due to the fervent desire of some barren couples to have children, even if half the child's genetic heritage is unknown. In a sense this is highlighted only because most of us still prefer that the children we raise should be genetically related to us. Our preference may change as society comes to accept genetic engineering, both as a way of curing defects, and also possibly as a way of choosing what kind of child to have. If, as seems likely, the world's increasing population makes political control of fertility necessary, it might become much more acceptable to ensure that a child had the desired characteristics.

The very existence of the family as a unit of procreation, and therefore as a social unit, is under threat from the population problem and possible solutions to it. If a global disaster does not drastically cut the number of human beings on the planet, then either famine will do the job or society will have to accept severe restrictions on who can have children and when. Fertility might have to be universally controlled. A form of eugenics could easily then be introduced, whereby sperms and eggs for fertilization could be tested and evaluated, and perhaps, in time, improved by genetic engineering.

A BETTER WORLD?
There are, as we have seen, many ways in which we can imaginatively construct worlds with sophisticated biotechnology that look worse than our present one. It is also possible to point out several ways in which biotechnology could help to make the world a better place than it is now.

Biotechnology can probably never banish disease entirely from human affairs, but in time it can promise to make the danger of serious illness and irreparable injury minimal. There is even the possibility that it will help us extend the human lifespan very considerably. A world which could hold disease and death at bay more efficiently than our own would surely be better, however far short of the ideal it might be.

Food technology will become more ingenious as we become more efficient biological engineers. In time, this may guarantee supplies of nourishing and palatable food adequate to support a world population much greater than the one we have today. Even if food production cannot keep pace with population growth, a better understanding of the fundamental processes of life will probably provide us with more efficient means of control over our own fertility. If we have the moral and political will to *use* the tools of biotechnology, then we will have the means to decide how fully the world should be populated, and to provide adequate sustenance for everyone. In time, we may even be able to do it

185

without exploiting other species.

Our other needs, too, might be more easily met with the aid of biotechnology. As well as food and water, we need fuel, shelter and raw materials. In previous chapters we have discussed ways in which biotechnology might help to supply all of these needs. Biological machines can help in mining, in energy supply – and even in building more efficient houses.

The ability to answer needs is in itself no guarantee that needs will be met. It has always been the case that some people have had a superabundance of the things they need, while others have had none at all, and have died as a result. The mere existence in the world of new biological technologies will not necessarily mean that they will be applied to the benefit of large numbers of people. There are, however, some grounds for doubting the cynical argument that biotechnology will simply help to make the rich better off without doing much for the poor. There are some important differences between biotechnology and the technology we are used to, which may make it more promising as an agent of social improvement.

Current research into biotechnology is very expensive, and the rewards so far produced have been dearly bought. Techniques of biological engineering will remain costly for some time yet, because they will be difficult to develop, difficult to use and very delicate. The products of biotechnology, though, will not necessarily remain expensive. Living systems are self-reproducing, and once they are initially put together there is no need for a production line that will continue to absorb expenditure indefinitely: artificial biological systems can be made to reproduce themselves by their own efforts.

It will undoubtedly be difficult to create new kinds of plant that will be more useful as food than the ones we already grow. It will be even more difficult to make 'quasi-eggs' that will grow in tissue culture to produce specific animal products such as meat and wool. We will have to allocate considerable resources to support the research and development of such innovations. Once such things do exist, though, the cost of keeping them in existence and multiplying them will dwindle very rapidly. After a period when only the richest nations will be able to sponsor biotechnology, there will be a period when its bounty is produced so cheaply that it will become easy for the poor nations to share its rewards.

Short-term applications of new biotechnology may involve an intensification of the kind of methods used in factory farming, and will undoubtedly enhance our power to convert land to our own purposes. In the long term, however, things may look rather different, as we pass through that phase of biotechnological usage into a more advanced one. In time, biotechnology may give us the means to reduce the intensity of our exploitation

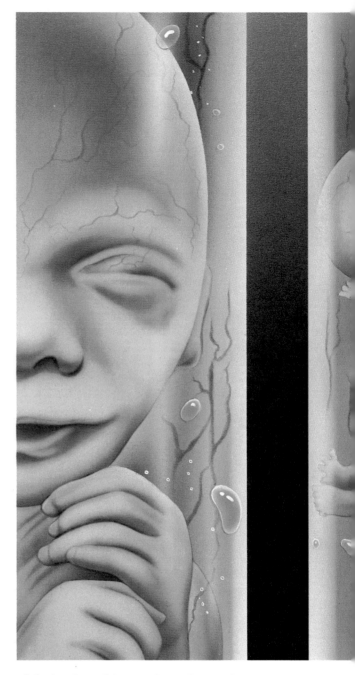

of the land, and free us from the need to control and pervert the development of living animals in order to obtain our favourite foods. Without a highly efficient biotechnology, we never will escape the need to exploit other species in order to supply our own needs, and all attempts at conservation must founder in the face of our over-riding responsibility to look after human interests first.

Biotechnology will develop, over the next few decades and the next few centuries, into an awesomely powerful force of social change. In refining it and applying it, we must think very carefully about the consequences of what we are doing. We must also think very carefully about the consequences of *not* doing things. It is not sensible to refuse opportunities to do good simply because the tools and techniques we would need might also be

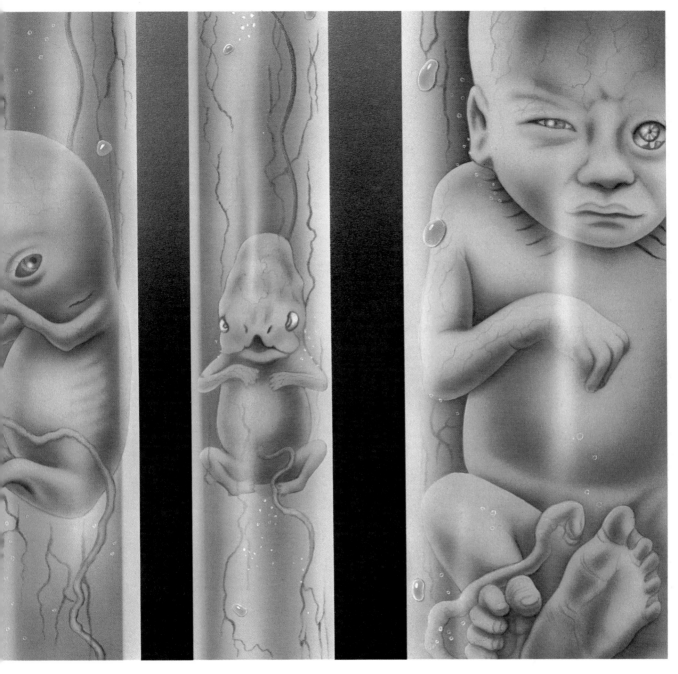

used to do harm. It is not sensible to regret the increase of man's dominion over nature, because it is to the increase of that dominion that we owe everything we possess and everything we value. The possession of great power requires us to exercise great responsibility, and to shrink from that responsibility is a kind of failure. It might, indeed, prove to be the case that our power over nature will eventually be used to destroy the world, but we already have enough power to annihilate ourselves, and if we did not have it in the past, we also did not have the power to defend ourselves against other annihilating forces. Our best hope for the future is that we can learn to turn our new powers to our advantage, building better defences against the forces of destruction, whether they be within or without.

In perfecting the techniques of genetic engineering on human egg cells, many deformed or dead embryos might be produced. They would be kept carefully to record the results of each experiment.

Acknowledgements

The author, editor and publishers would like to thank
Valerie Lewis Chandler for doing the index; Salim Patel
and Rose Taylor of the Science Photo Library; Professor
Gordon Leedale of Biophoto Associates; and Professor
Igor Aleksander, Matthew Beardmore-Gray, Hanya
Chlala, Elizabeth Drury, Dr Steve Dunnett, Glynis
Edwards, Emma Fisher, Dr R. D. Martin, Dr Jonathan
Miller, and Dr John G. Parnavelas.

Artwork

The following artists are thanked for their work, which
was specially commissioned: Cynthia Clark (courtesy of
The Sunday Times), Ian Craig, David Eaton, Peter
Goodfellow, Peter Gudynas, Hussein Hussein, Aziz
Khan, Terry Oakes, Jeff Ridge.

Artwork based on the following sources: pp 20, 22, 87,
143, *Human Biology*, British Museum (Natural
History)/ Cambridge University Press; p 23, *The
Sunday Times* 8 January 1984; p 27, *New Scientist* 26
August 1983; p 35, Genentech Inc.; p 45, *Nature at
Work*, British Museum (Natural History)/Cambridge
University Press 1978; p 50, *New Scientist* 29
September 1983; p 62, Trotter et al. (1959) in E. D.
Kilbourne, *Influenza Viruses and Influenza*; p 65,
Scientific American February 1983; pp 66-7, 70-1, *Origin
of Species*, British Museum (Natural
History)/Cambridge University Press 1981; pp 77, 79,
The Sunday Times 19 October 1980; p 83, *The Sunday
Times* March 1984; p 100, I. Davies, *Aging*, Edward
Arnold 1983; p 122, *Scientific American* August 1968;
p 141, *Scientific American* offprint, *The Brain*,
W. Freeman 1979; p 143, *Scientific American* March
1977; p 148, *The Humanist* July/August 1977; p 164,
The WISARD Adaptive Image Classifier, Brunel
University's Electrical Engineering Department; p 168,
E. H. Parr, *Beginner's Guide to Microprocessors*,
Butterworth 1982; p 169, Peter Marsh, *The Robot Age*,
Sphere 1982.

Other illustrations

The publishers would like to thank the following
organizations and individuals for their kind permission
in supplying the photographs used in this book:

Anderson/Simon/Science Photo Library 59; Biophoto
Associates 18 below, 19 below, 48, 52, 73 above left and
right, 82, 142; Boeing Aerospace/Science Photo library
160/161; Dr Tony Brain/Science Photo Library 37, 38,
39; British Union For The Abolition Of Vivisection 152;
Dr Jeremy Burgess/Science Photo Library 43 above and
below; Jane Burton/Bruce Coleman Ltd. 118 below;
Hanya Chlala 30, 95 above and below; Dr. R. P. Clark
and M. Goff/Science Photo Library 116; Dr.
C. Chumbley/Science Photo Library 144; Alan Compost/
Bruce Coleman Ltd 173; Daily Telegraph Colour Library
86, 154 left and right; Dr R. Dourmashkin/Science
Photo Library 61 above; *The Economist* 130, 165;
Farmers' Weekly 55; Jeff Foot/Bruce Coleman Ltd.
14/15, 101; Gower Scientific Photos 14 left, 24, 25, 32
above and below, 33 above and below, 74 above, 75
below, 137; Eric Grave/Science Photo Library 28 above,
centre and below, 29 above and below; Sally and
Richard Greenhill 9 left; Brian Gunn 149; Professor
David Hall/Science Photo Library 46/47; Robert
Harding Picture Library 8, 9, 90; Udo Hirsch/
Bruce Coleman Ltd. 176; Carol Hughes/Bruce Coleman
Ltd. 97 left; ICI Agricultural Division 40, 41; Stephen
J. Krasemann/Bruce Coleman Ltd. 188 above; Clive
Landon 93; David Leah/Science Photo Library 80 above
right; Leonard Lee Rue III/Bruce Coleman Ltd, 119,
Lowell Georgia/Science Photo Library 65; Jerry Mason/
Science Photo Library 155; *Nature* 26, 53; Charlie Ott/
Bruce Coleman Ltd. 97 right; Oxford Scientific Films
(G. I. Bernard) 88, (Waina Cheng) 89 above, (J. A. L.
Cooke) 89 below; Dr. G. Parnavelas 153 above and
below; Phelps/Mazziotta/Science Photo Library 146, 147;
Planet Earth Pictures: Seaphot 115 above; Popperfoto
p 63, from 'Powers of Ten' by Philip Morrison and
Phylis Morrison and The Office of Charles and Ray
Eames. Copyright © 1982 by Scientific American
Books 18 above, 21. All rights reserved; Prato/Bruce
Coleman Ltd. 44; Hans Reinhard/Bruce Coleman Ltd.
54, 115 below; Rex Features Ltd. 72 above, 84, 85, 166,
167, 177, 180, 181 left and right; Science Photo Library
19 above, 51, 61 below, 73 below, 81, 156; Science
Source/Science Photo Library 80 above left and below
right; Anthea Sieveking/Vision International 157; Barry
Sproson 182; The Sunday Times, London/Ian Yeomans
77; Kim Taylor/Bruce Coleman Ltd. 114; Trans Time
Inc. 107; Alexander Tsiaras/Colorific 60; John Watney
Photo Library 68, 69 above and below, 72 below, 75
centre, 112.

Index